DYNAMITE ENTERTAINMENT PRESENTS

# SHERLOCK
# HOLMES ™
## VOL. 3
### MORIARTY LIVES

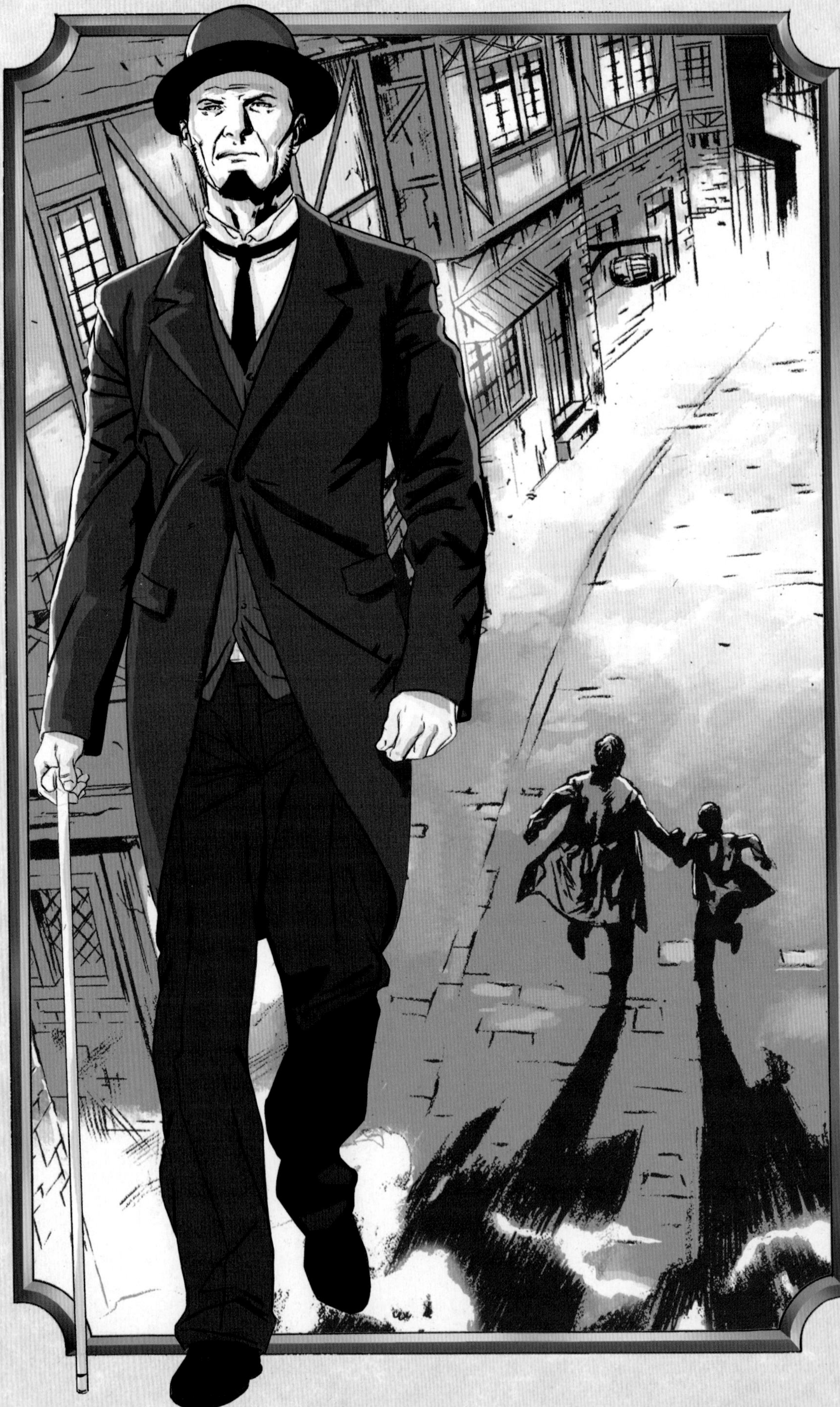

Written by:

# DAVID LISS

Illustrated by:

# DANIEL INDRO (issues 1-3)
# OLAVO COSTA (issue 3)
# CARLOS FURUZONO (issues 4-5)

Colored by:

# JOSAN GONZALEZ

Lettered by:

# JOSHUA COZINE

Cover by:

# FRANCESCO FRANCAVILLA

Dedicated to:

# SIR ARTHUR CONAN DOYLE

This volume collects issues one through five of the
Dynamite Entertainment series, Sherlock Holmes: Moriarty Lives.

Collection design by JOSH JOHNSON

Sherlock Holmes logo design by JASON ULLMEYER

Nick Barrucci, CEO / Publisher
Juan Collado, President / COO

Joe Rybandt, Senior Editor
Rachel Pinnelas, Associate Editor

Jason Ullmeyer, Design Director
Geoff Harkins, Graphic Designer
Chris Caniano, Digital Associate
Rachel Kilbury, Digital Assistant

Brandon Dante Primavera, Director of IT/Operations
Rich Young, Director of Business Development

Keith Davidsen, Marketing Manager
Kevin Pearl, Sales Associate

 Online at WWW.DYNAMITE.COM
Twitter @dynamitecomics
Facebook /Dynamitecomics
Instagram /Dynamitecomics
YouTube /Dynamitecomics
Tumblr dynamitecomics.tumblr.com

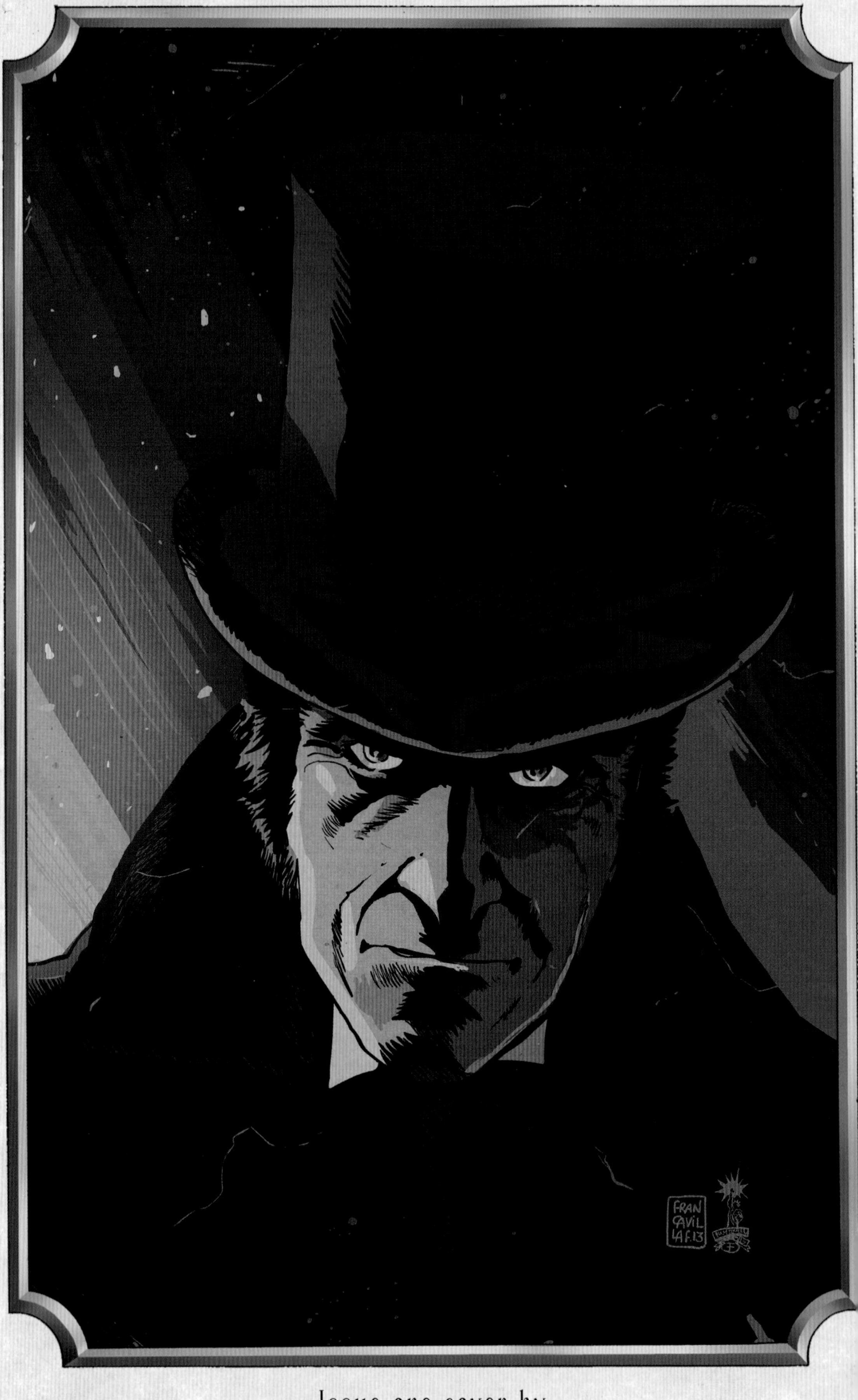

Issue one cover by

Francesco Francavilla

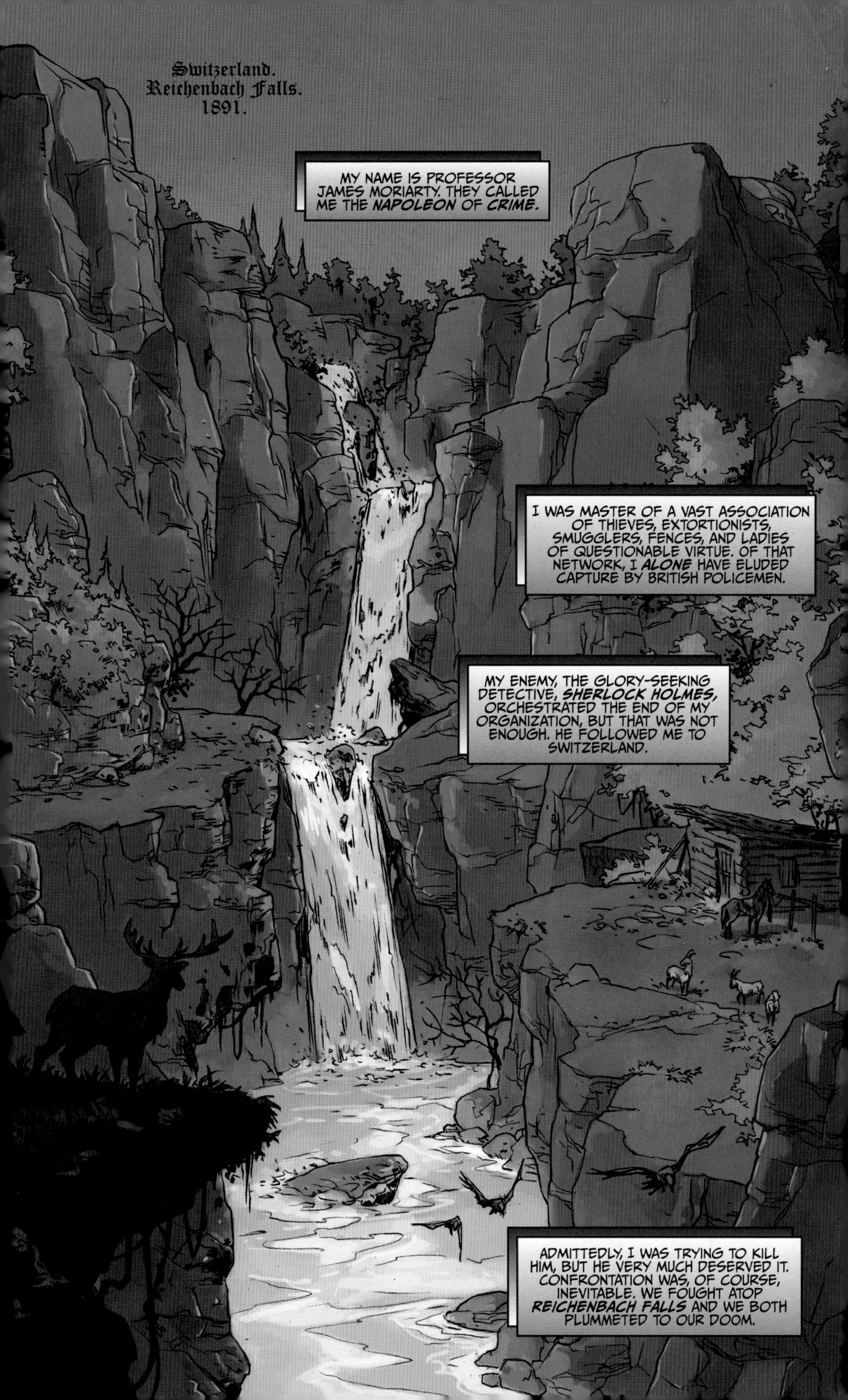
Switzerland. Reichenbach Falls. 1891.
MY NAME IS PROFESSOR JAMES MORIARTY. THEY CALLED ME THE NAPOLEON OF CRIME.
I WAS MASTER OF A VAST ASSOCIATION OF THIEVES, EXTORTIONISTS, SMUGGLERS, FENCES, AND LADIES OF QUESTIONABLE VIRTUE. OF THAT NETWORK, I ALONE HAVE ELUDED CAPTURE BY BRITISH POLICEMEN.
MY ENEMY, THE GLORY-SEEKING DETECTIVE, SHERLOCK HOLMES, ORCHESTRATED THE END OF MY ORGANIZATION, BUT THAT WAS NOT ENOUGH. HE FOLLOWED ME TO SWITZERLAND.
ADMITTEDLY, I WAS TRYING TO KILL HIM, BUT HE VERY MUCH DESERVED IT. CONFRONTATION WAS, OF COURSE, INEVITABLE. WE FOUGHT ATOP REICHENBACH FALLS AND WE BOTH PLUMMETED TO OUR DOOM.

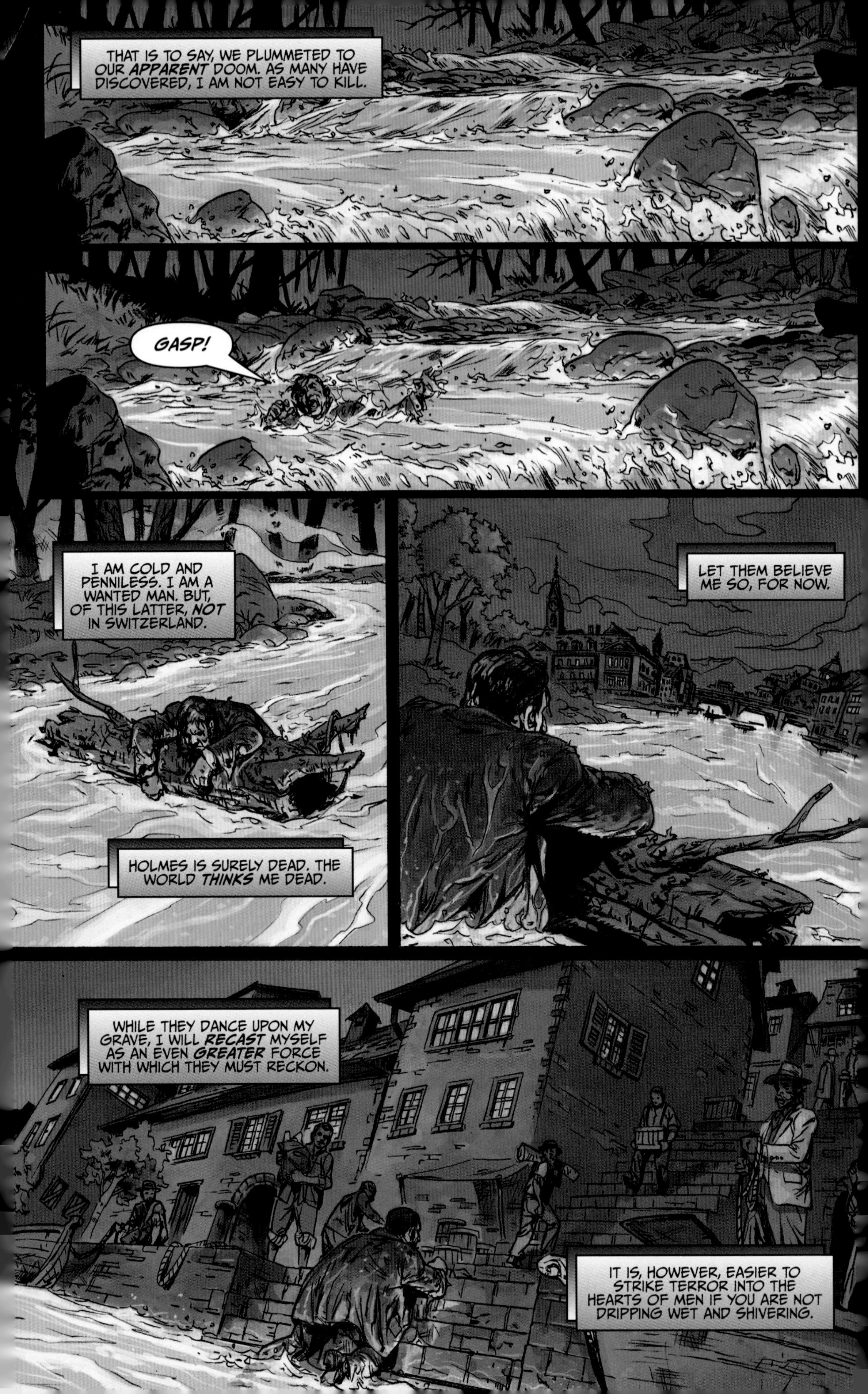
THAT IS TO SAY, WE PLUMMETED TO OUR APPARENT DOOM. AS MANY HAVE DISCOVERED, I AM NOT EASY TO KILL.
GASP!
I AM COLD AND PENNILESS. I AM A WANTED MAN. BUT, OF THIS LATTER, NOT IN SWITZERLAND.
HOLMES IS SURELY DEAD. THE WORLD THINKS ME DEAD.
LET THEM BELIEVE ME SO, FOR NOW.
WHILE THEY DANCE UPON MY GRAVE, I WILL RECAST MYSELF AS AN EVEN GREATER FORCE WITH WHICH THEY MUST RECKON.
IT IS, HOWEVER, EASIER TO STRIKE TERROR INTO THE HEARTS OF MEN IF YOU ARE NOT DRIPPING WET AND SHIVERING.

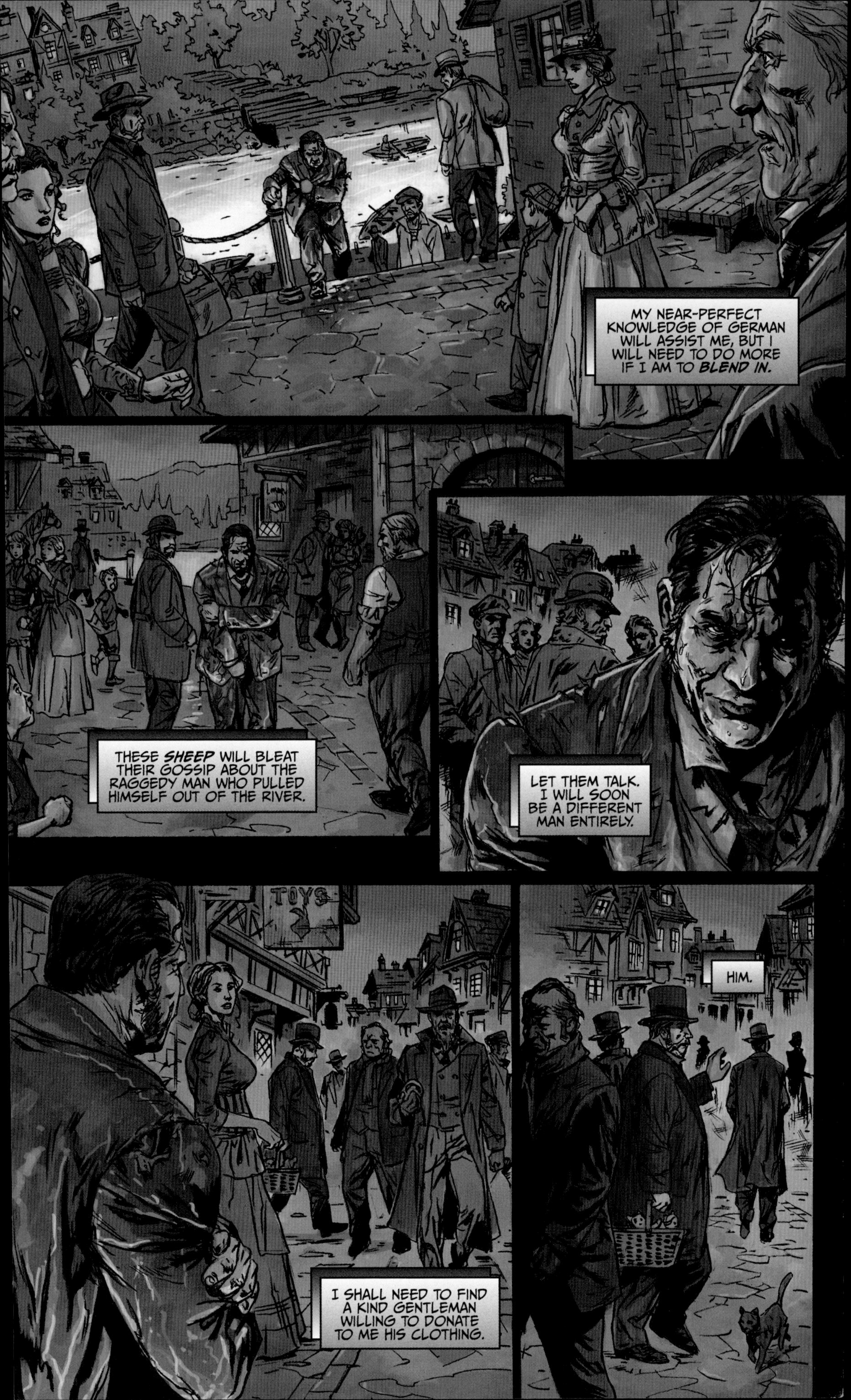
MY NEAR-PERFECT KNOWLEDGE OF GERMAN WILL ASSIST ME, BUT I WILL NEED TO DO MORE IF I AM TO ***BLEND IN.***
THESE ***SHEEP*** WILL BLEAT THEIR GOSSIP ABOUT THE RAGGEDY MAN WHO PULLED HIMSELF OUT OF THE RIVER.
LET THEM TALK. I WILL SOON BE A DIFFERENT MAN ENTIRELY.
TOYS
I SHALL NEED TO FIND A KIND GENTLEMAN WILLING TO DONATE TO ME HIS CLOTHING.
HIM.

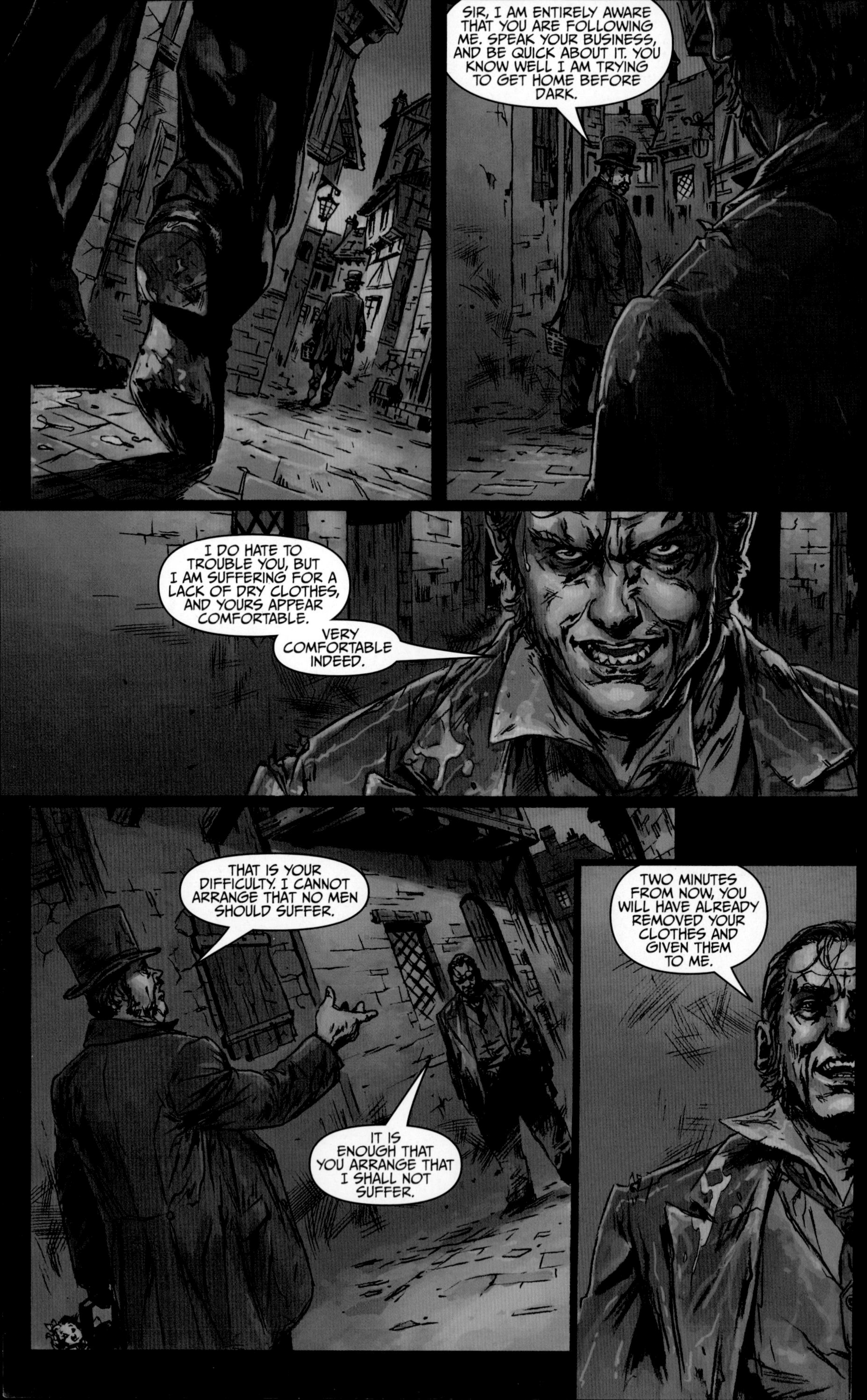
SIR, I AM ENTIRELY AWARE THAT YOU ARE FOLLOWING ME. SPEAK YOUR BUSINESS, AND BE QUICK ABOUT IT. YOU KNOW WELL I AM TRYING TO GET HOME BEFORE DARK.
I DO HATE TO TROUBLE YOU, BUT I AM SUFFERING FOR A LACK OF DRY CLOTHES, AND YOURS APPEAR COMFORTABLE.
VERY COMFORTABLE INDEED.
THAT IS YOUR DIFFICULTY. I CANNOT ARRANGE THAT NO MEN SHOULD SUFFER.
IT IS ENOUGH THAT YOU ARRANGE THAT I SHALL NOT SUFFER.
TWO MINUTES FROM NOW, YOU WILL HAVE ALREADY REMOVED YOUR CLOTHES AND GIVEN THEM TO ME.

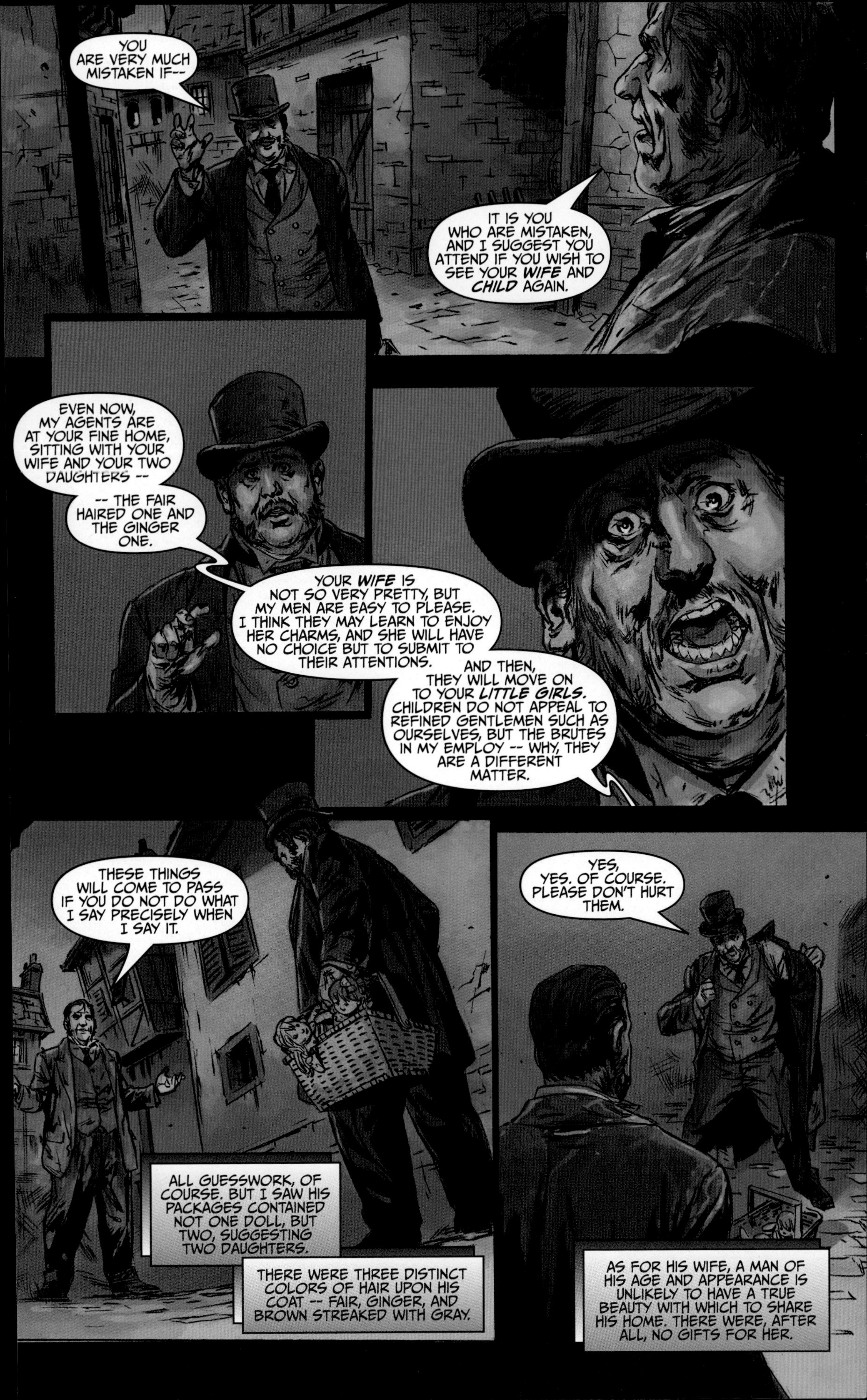
YOU ARE VERY MUCH MISTAKEN IF--
IT IS YOU WHO ARE MISTAKEN, AND I SUGGEST YOU ATTEND IF YOU WISH TO SEE YOUR WIFE AND CHILD AGAIN.
EVEN NOW, MY AGENTS ARE AT YOUR FINE HOME, SITTING WITH YOUR WIFE AND YOUR TWO DAUGHTERS --
-- THE FAIR HAIRED ONE AND THE GINGER ONE.
YOUR WIFE IS NOT SO VERY PRETTY, BUT MY MEN ARE EASY TO PLEASE. I THINK THEY MAY LEARN TO ENJOY HER CHARMS, AND SHE WILL HAVE NO CHOICE BUT TO SUBMIT TO THEIR ATTENTIONS.
AND THEN, THEY WILL MOVE ON TO YOUR LITTLE GIRLS. CHILDREN DO NOT APPEAL TO REFINED GENTLEMEN SUCH AS OURSELVES, BUT THE BRUTES IN MY EMPLOY -- WHY, THEY ARE A DIFFERENT MATTER.
THESE THINGS WILL COME TO PASS IF YOU DO NOT DO WHAT I SAY PRECISELY WHEN I SAY IT.
ALL GUESSWORK, OF COURSE. BUT I SAW HIS PACKAGES CONTAINED NOT ONE DOLL, BUT TWO, SUGGESTING TWO DAUGHTERS.
THERE WERE THREE DISTINCT COLORS OF HAIR UPON HIS COAT -- FAIR, GINGER, AND BROWN STREAKED WITH GRAY.
YES, YES. OF COURSE. PLEASE DON'T HURT THEM.
AS FOR HIS WIFE, A MAN OF HIS AGE AND APPEARANCE IS UNLIKELY TO HAVE A TRUE BEAUTY WITH WHICH TO SHARE HIS HOME. THERE WERE, AFTER ALL, NO GIFTS FOR HER.

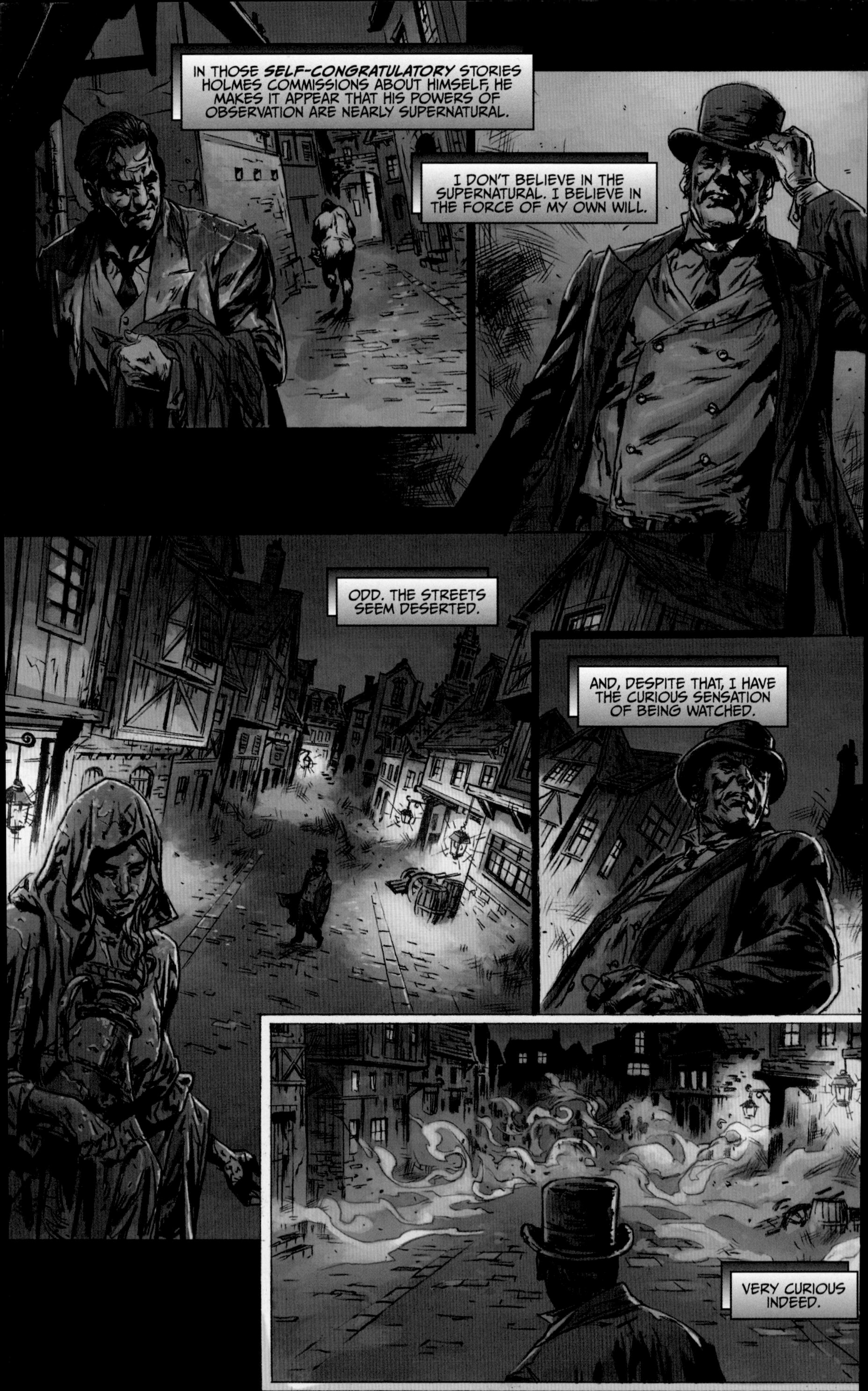
IN THOSE SELF-CONGRATULATORY STORIES HOLMES COMMISSIONS ABOUT HIMSELF, HE MAKES IT APPEAR THAT HIS POWERS OF OBSERVATION ARE NEARLY SUPERNATURAL.
I DON'T BELIEVE IN THE SUPERNATURAL. I BELIEVE IN THE FORCE OF MY OWN WILL.
ODD. THE STREETS SEEM DESERTED.
AND, DESPITE THAT, I HAVE THE CURIOUS SENSATION OF BEING WATCHED.
VERY CURIOUS INDEED.

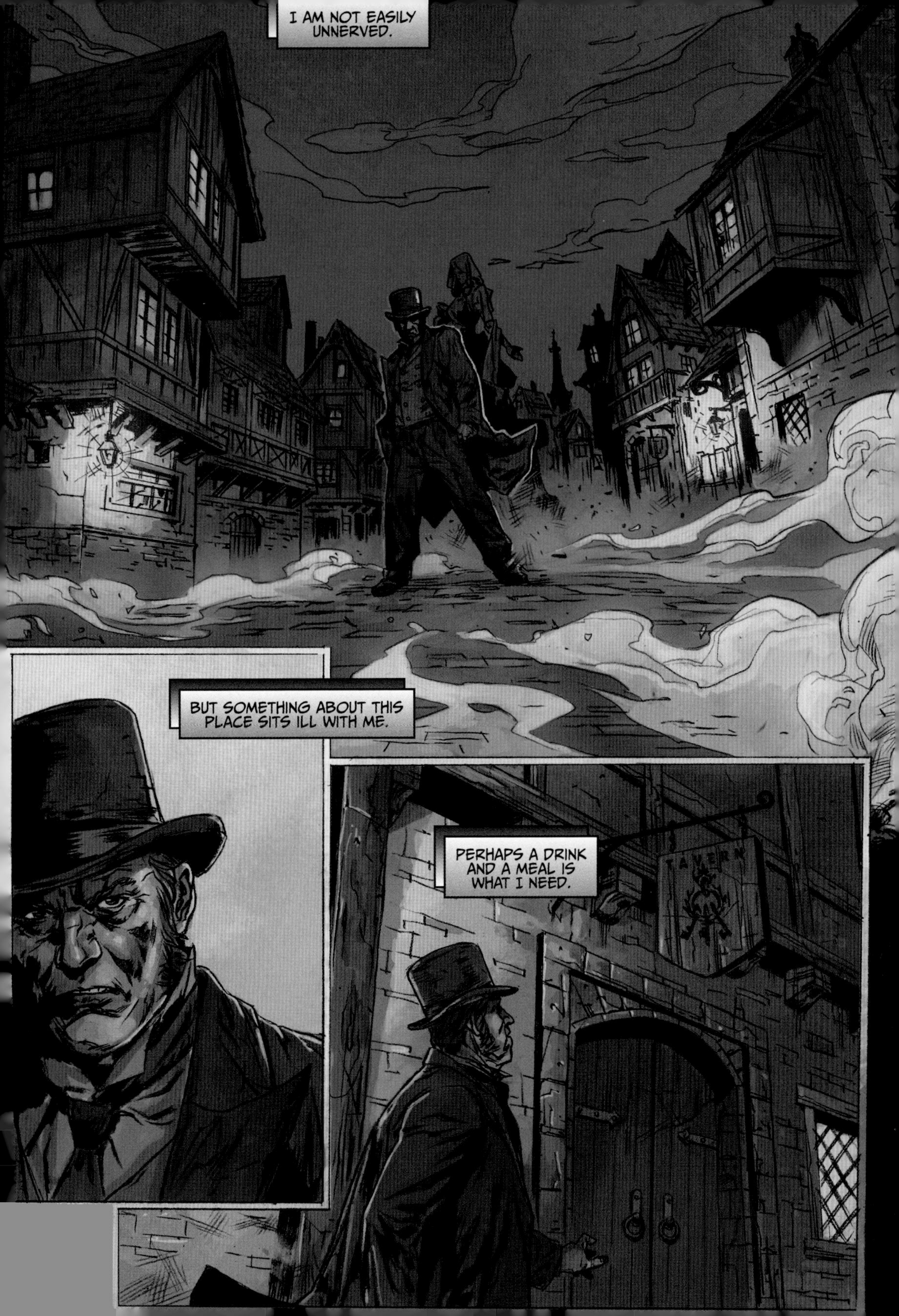
I AM NOT EASILY UNNERVED.
BUT SOMETHING ABOUT THIS PLACE SITS ILL WITH ME.
PERHAPS A DRINK AND A MEAL IS WHAT I NEED.

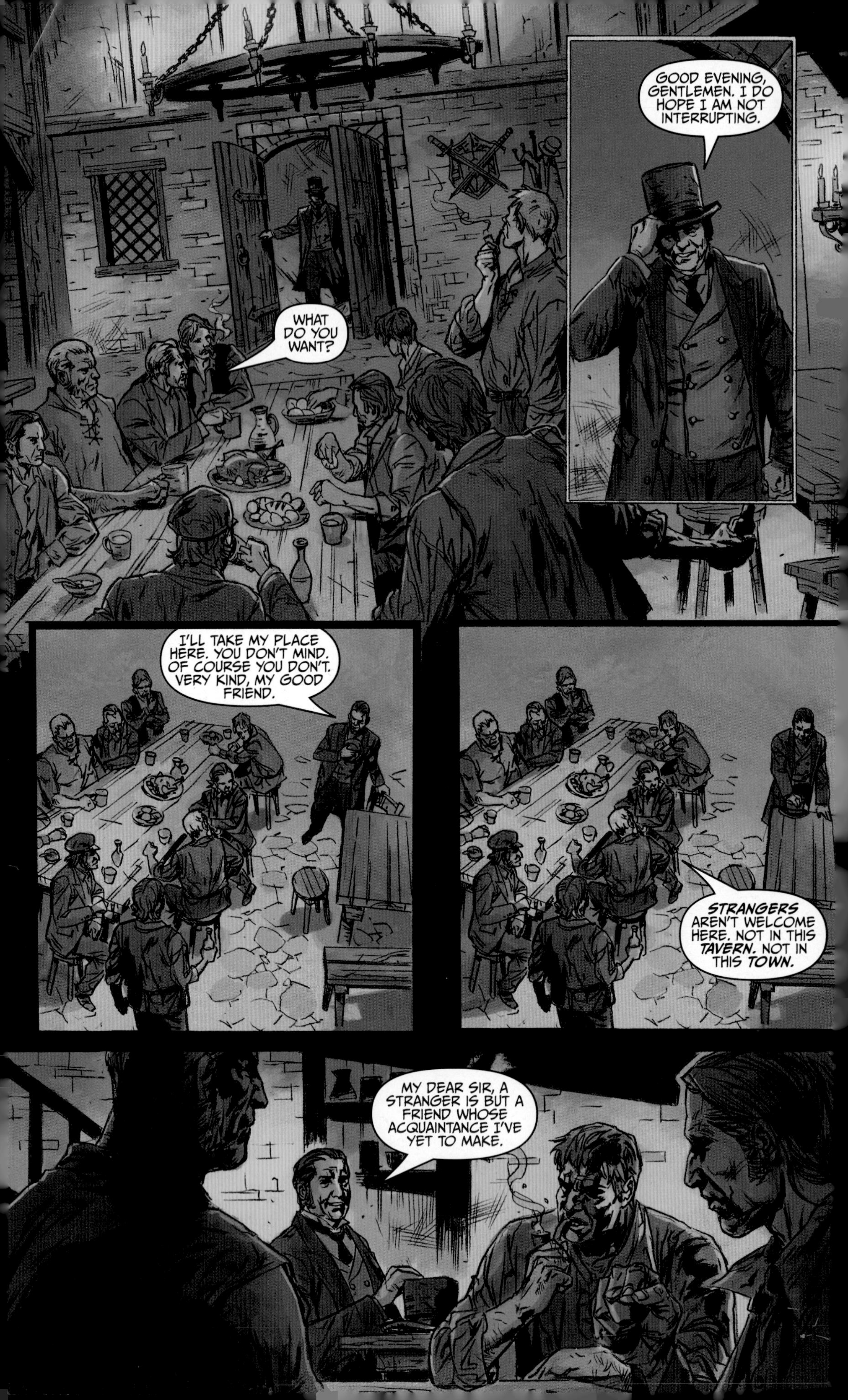
WHAT DO YOU WANT?
GOOD EVENING, GENTLEMEN. I DO HOPE I AM NOT INTERRUPTING.
I'LL TAKE MY PLACE HERE. YOU DON'T MIND. OF COURSE YOU DON'T. VERY KIND, MY GOOD FRIEND.
STRANGERS AREN'T WELCOME HERE. NOT IN THIS TAVERN. NOT IN THIS TOWN.
MY DEAR SIR, A STRANGER IS BUT A FRIEND WHOSE ACQUAINTANCE I'VE YET TO MAKE.

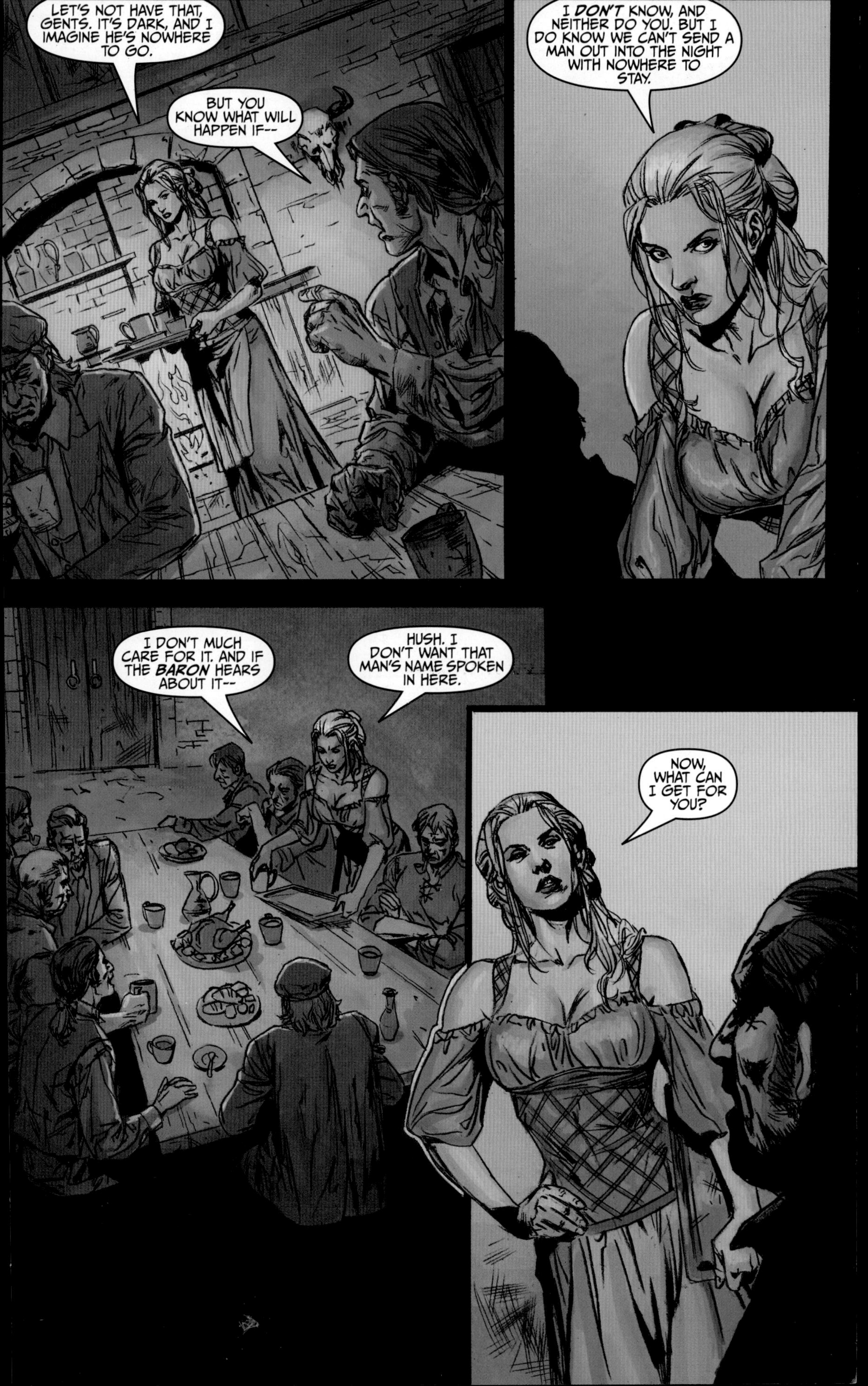
LET'S NOT HAVE THAT, GENTS. IT'S DARK, AND I IMAGINE HE'S NOWHERE TO GO.
BUT YOU KNOW WHAT WILL HAPPEN IF--
I *DON'T* KNOW, AND NEITHER DO YOU. BUT I DO KNOW WE CAN'T SEND A MAN OUT INTO THE NIGHT WITH NOWHERE TO STAY.
I DON'T MUCH CARE FOR IT. AND IF THE *BARON* HEARS ABOUT IT--
HUSH. I DON'T WANT THAT MAN'S NAME SPOKEN IN HERE.
NOW, WHAT CAN I GET FOR YOU?

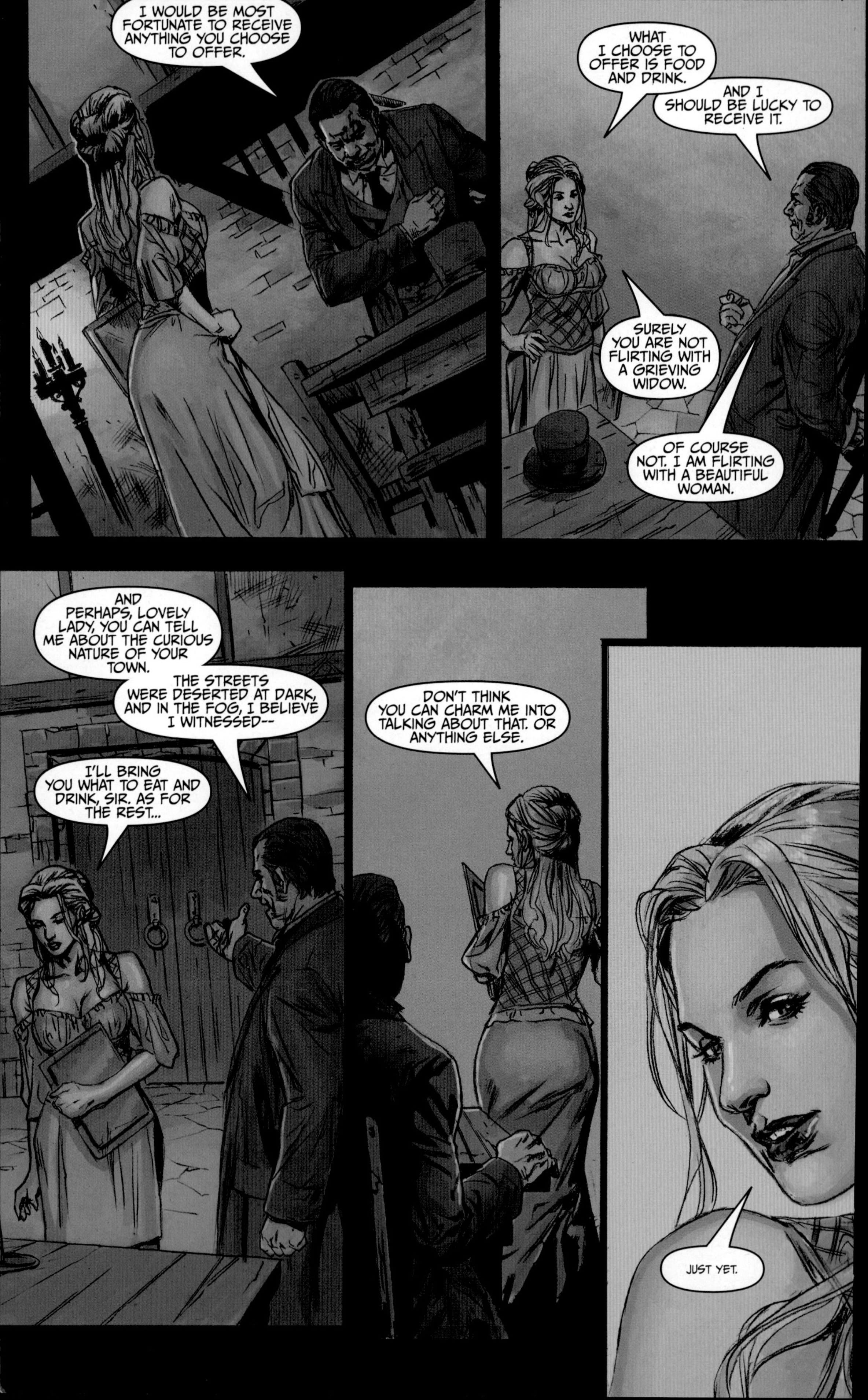
I WOULD BE MOST FORTUNATE TO RECEIVE ANYTHING YOU CHOOSE TO OFFER.
WHAT I CHOOSE TO OFFER IS FOOD AND DRINK.
AND I SHOULD BE LUCKY TO RECEIVE IT.
SURELY YOU ARE NOT FLIRTING WITH A GRIEVING WIDOW.
OF COURSE NOT. I AM FLIRTING WITH A BEAUTIFUL WOMAN.
AND PERHAPS, LOVELY LADY, YOU CAN TELL ME ABOUT THE CURIOUS NATURE OF YOUR TOWN.
THE STREETS WERE DESERTED AT DARK, AND IN THE FOG, I BELIEVE I WITNESSED--
I'LL BRING YOU WHAT TO EAT AND DRINK, SIR. AS FOR THE REST...
DON'T THINK YOU CAN CHARM ME INTO TALKING ABOUT THAT. OR ANYTHING ELSE.
JUST YET.

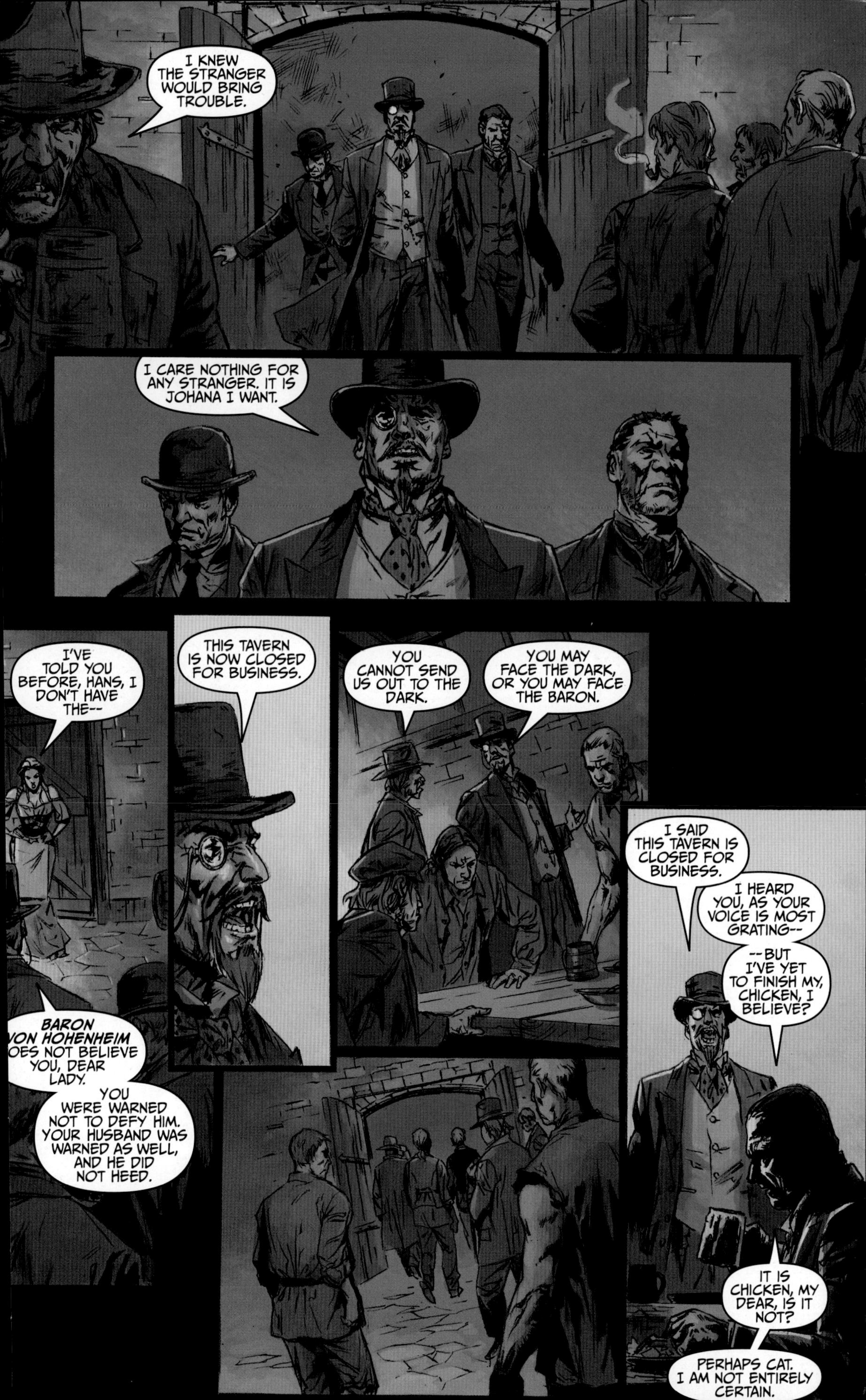
I KNEW THE STRANGER WOULD BRING TROUBLE.
I CARE NOTHING FOR ANY STRANGER. IT IS JOHANA I WANT.
I'VE TOLD YOU BEFORE, HANS, I DON'T HAVE THE--
THIS TAVERN IS NOW CLOSED FOR BUSINESS.
YOU CANNOT SEND US OUT TO THE DARK.
YOU MAY FACE THE DARK, OR YOU MAY FACE THE BARON.
BARON VON HOHENHEIM OES NOT BELIEVE YOU, DEAR LADY.
YOU WERE WARNED NOT TO DEFY HIM. YOUR HUSBAND WAS WARNED AS WELL, AND HE DID NOT HEED.
I SAID THIS TAVERN IS CLOSED FOR BUSINESS.
I HEARD YOU, AS YOUR VOICE IS MOST GRATING--
--BUT I'VE YET TO FINISH MY, CHICKEN, I BELIEVE?
IT IS CHICKEN, MY DEAR, IS IT NOT?
PERHAPS CAT. I AM NOT ENTIRELY CERTAIN.

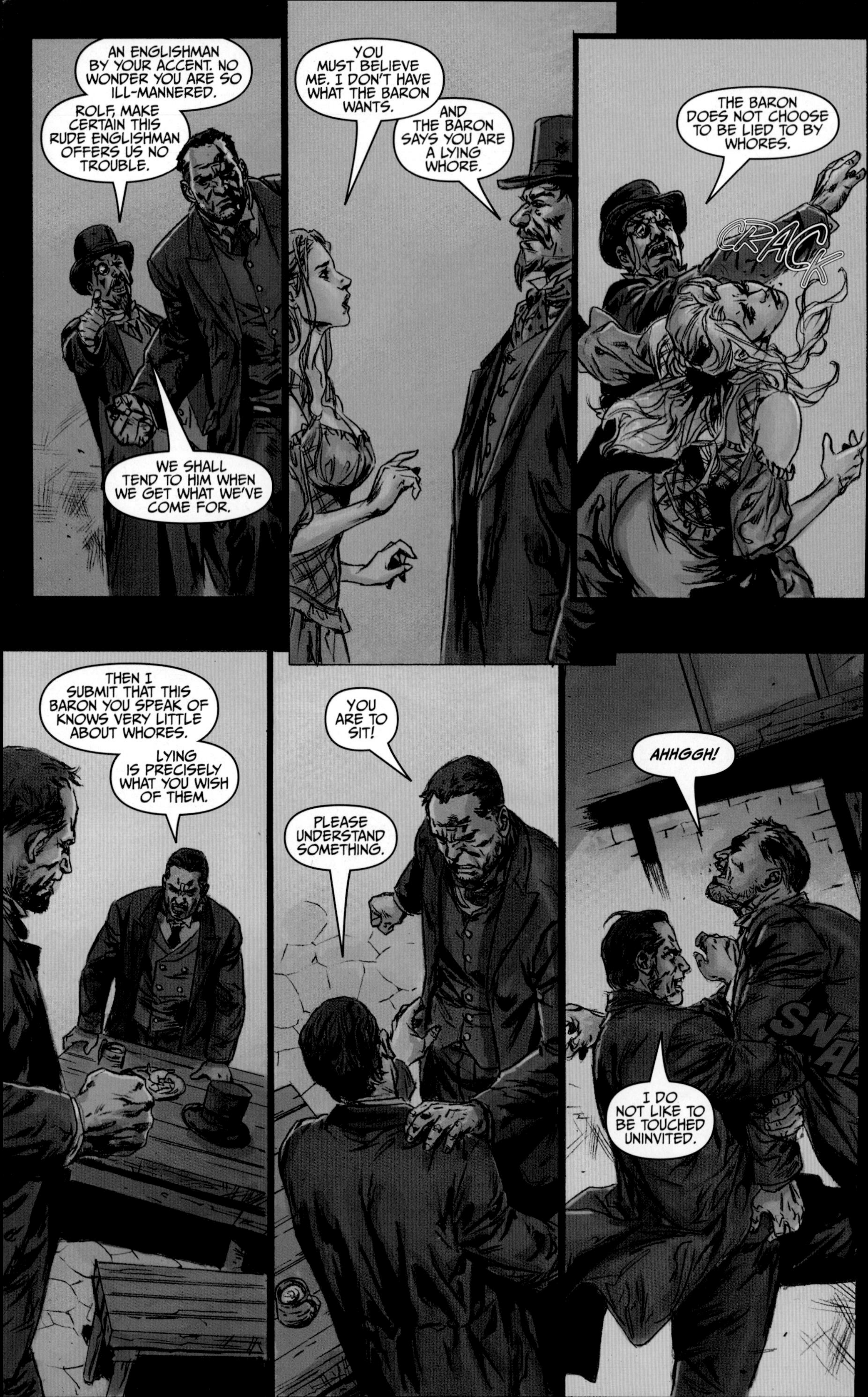

AN ENGLISHMAN BY YOUR ACCENT. NO WONDER YOU ARE SO ILL-MANNERED.
ROLF, MAKE CERTAIN THIS RUDE ENGLISHMAN OFFERS US NO TROUBLE.
WE SHALL TEND TO HIM WHEN WE GET WHAT WE'VE COME FOR.
YOU MUST BELIEVE ME. I DON'T HAVE WHAT THE BARON WANTS.
AND THE BARON SAYS YOU ARE A LYING WHORE.
THE BARON DOES NOT CHOOSE TO BE LIED TO BY WHORES.
CRACK
THEN I SUBMIT THAT THIS BARON YOU SPEAK OF KNOWS VERY LITTLE ABOUT WHORES.
LYING IS PRECISELY WHAT YOU WISH OF THEM.
YOU ARE TO SIT!
PLEASE UNDERSTAND SOMETHING.
AHHGGH!
I DO NOT LIKE TO BE TOUCHED UNINVITED.

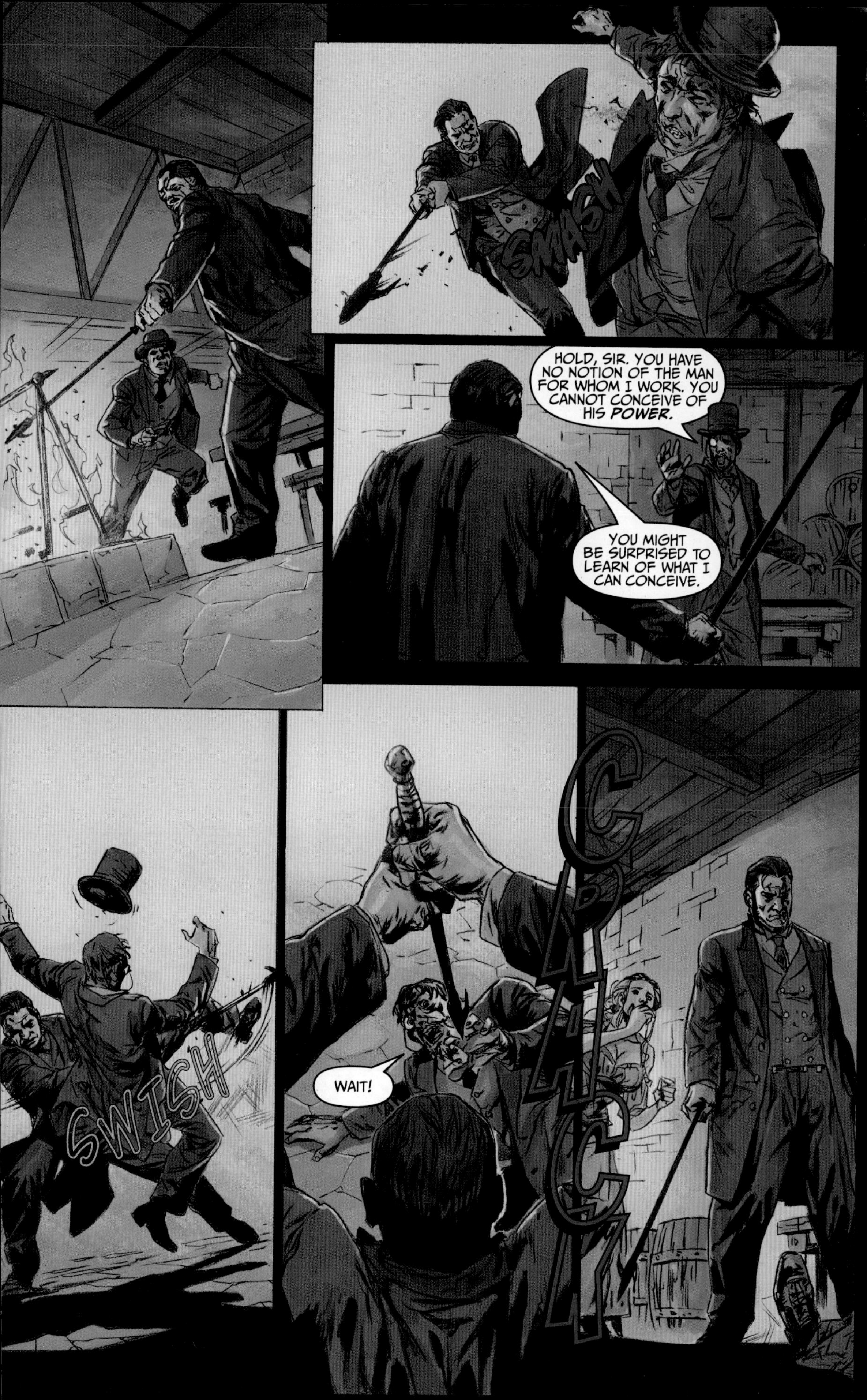
SMASH
HOLD, SIR. YOU HAVE NO NOTION OF THE MAN FOR WHOM I WORK. YOU CANNOT CONCEIVE OF HIS *POWER.*
YOU MIGHT BE SURPRISED TO LEARN OF WHAT I CAN CONCEIVE.
SWISH
WAIT!
CSHAKACHCK

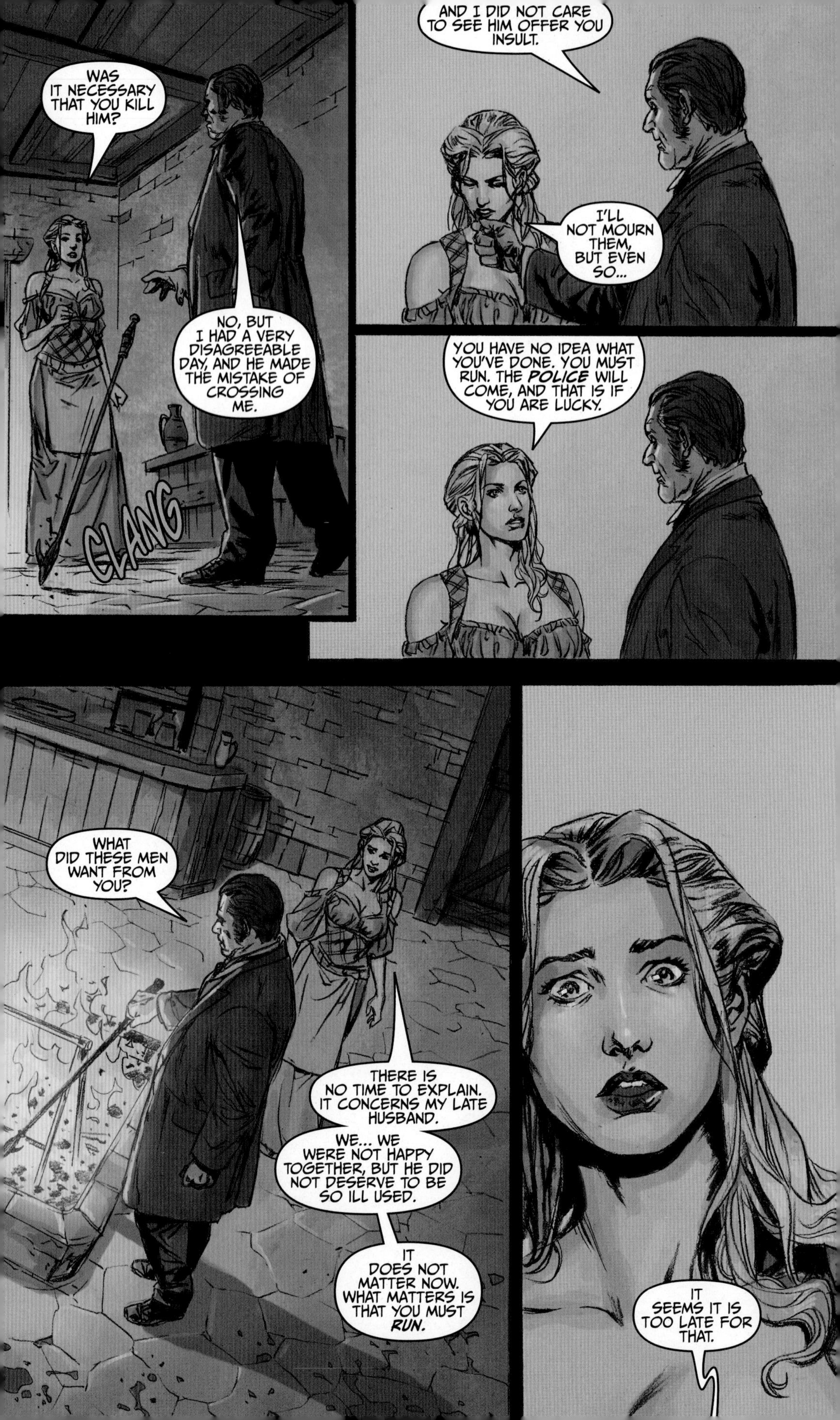
WAS IT NECESSARY THAT YOU KILL HIM?
NO, BUT I HAD A VERY DISAGREEABLE DAY, AND HE MADE THE MISTAKE OF CROSSING ME.
CLANG
AND I DID NOT CARE TO SEE HIM OFFER YOU INSULT.
I'LL NOT MOURN THEM, BUT EVEN SO...
YOU HAVE NO IDEA WHAT YOU'VE DONE. YOU MUST RUN. THE *POLICE* WILL COME, AND THAT IS IF YOU ARE LUCKY.
WHAT DID THESE MEN WANT FROM YOU?
THERE IS NO TIME TO EXPLAIN. IT CONCERNS MY LATE HUSBAND.
WE... WE WERE NOT HAPPY TOGETHER, BUT HE DID NOT DESERVE TO BE SO ILL USED.
IT DOES NOT MATTER NOW. WHAT MATTERS IS THAT YOU MUST *RUN.*
IT SEEMS IT IS TOO LATE FOR THAT.

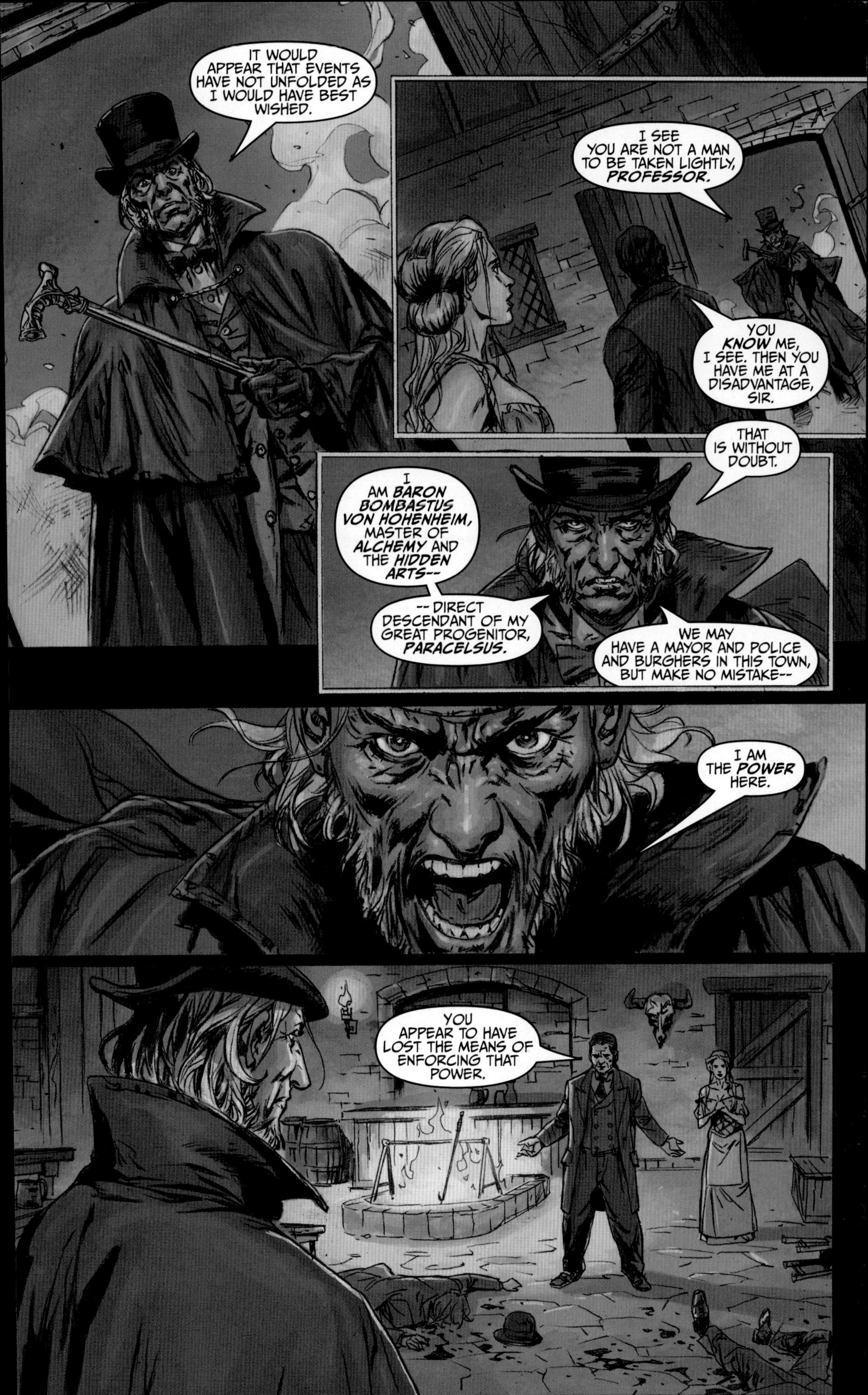
IT WOULD APPEAR THAT EVENTS HAVE NOT UNFOLDED AS I WOULD HAVE BEST WISHED.
I SEE YOU ARE NOT A MAN TO BE TAKEN LIGHTLY, PROFESSOR.
YOU KNOW ME, I SEE. THEN YOU HAVE ME AT A DISADVANTAGE, SIR.
THAT IS WITHOUT DOUBT.
I AM BARON BOMBASTUS VON HOHENHEIM, MASTER OF ALCHEMY AND THE HIDDEN ARTS--
--DIRECT DESCENDANT OF MY GREAT PROGENITOR, PARACELSUS.
WE MAY HAVE A MAYOR AND POLICE AND BURGHERS IN THIS TOWN, BUT MAKE NO MISTAKE--
I AM THE POWER HERE.
YOU APPEAR TO HAVE LOST THE MEANS OF ENFORCING THAT POWER.

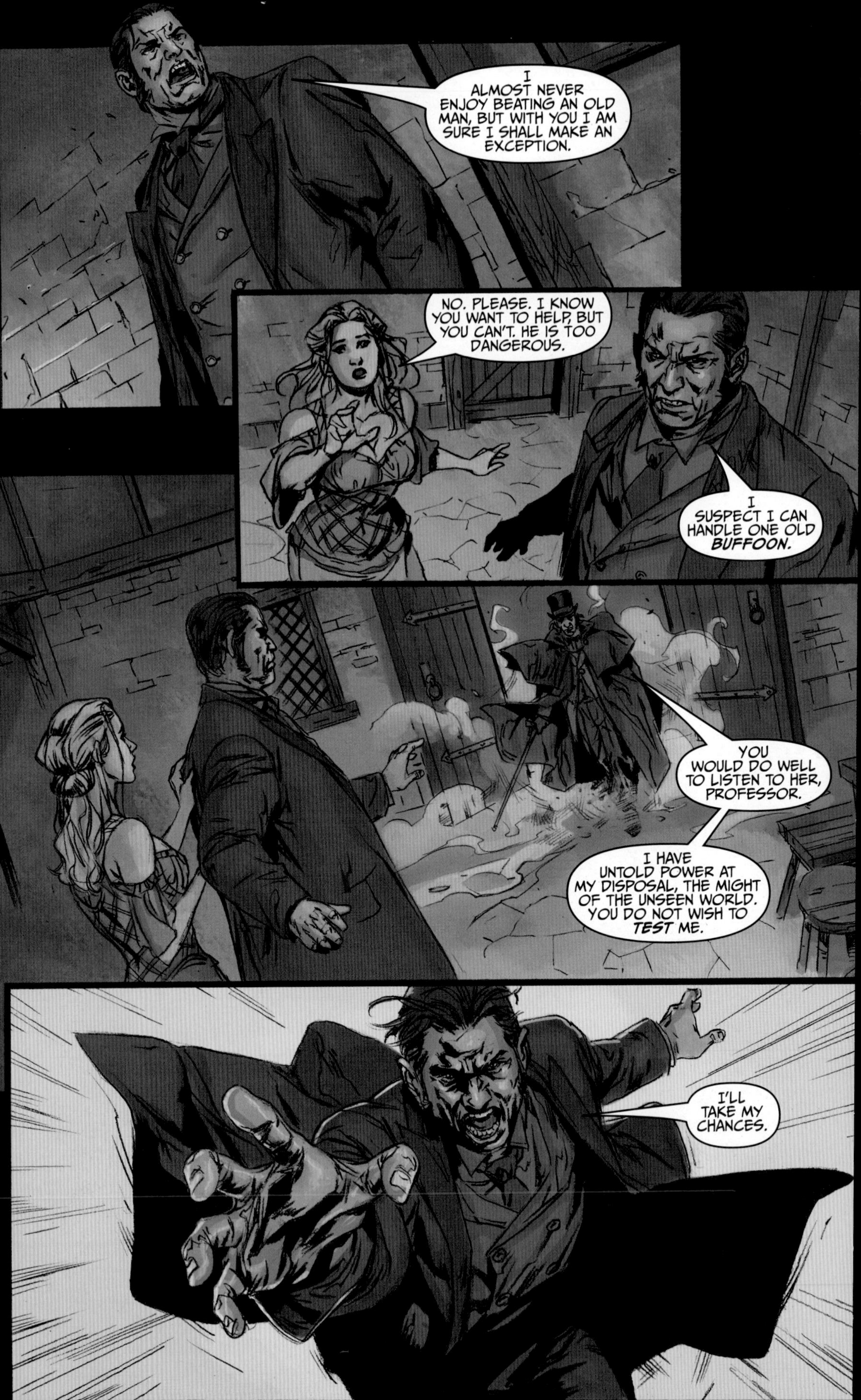
I ALMOST NEVER ENJOY BEATING AN OLD MAN, BUT WITH YOU I AM SURE I SHALL MAKE AN EXCEPTION.
NO. PLEASE. I KNOW YOU WANT TO HELP, BUT YOU CAN'T. HE IS TOO DANGEROUS.
I SUSPECT I CAN HANDLE ONE OLD *BUFFOON.*
YOU WOULD DO WELL TO LISTEN TO HER, PROFESSOR.
I HAVE UNTOLD POWER AT MY DISPOSAL, THE MIGHT OF THE UNSEEN WORLD. YOU DO NOT WISH TO *TEST* ME.
I'LL TAKE MY CHANCES.

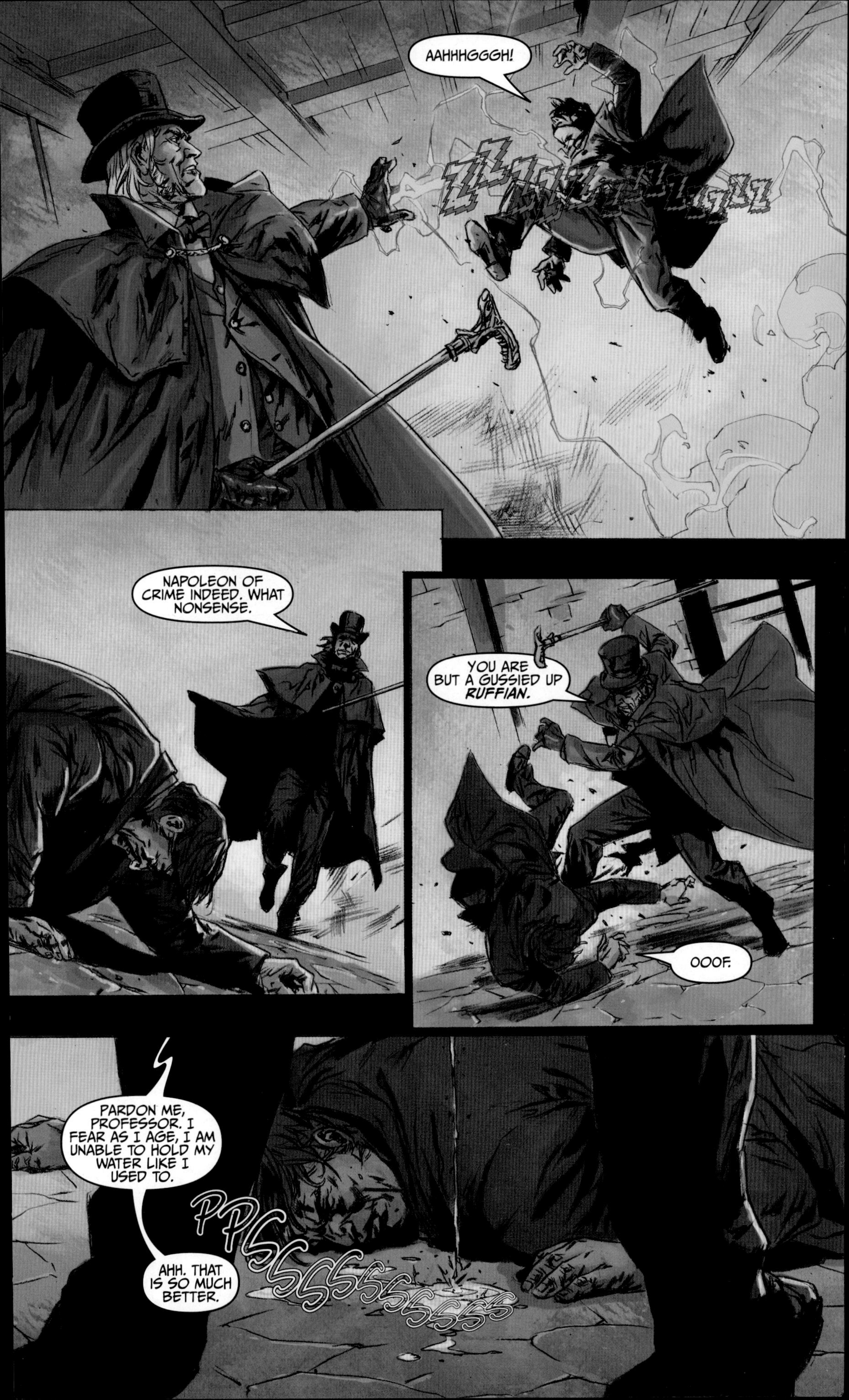
AAHHHGGGH!
ZZZZZZZZZZZZZZZZZ
NAPOLEON OF CRIME INDEED. WHAT NONSENSE.
YOU ARE BUT A GUSSIED UP *RUFFIAN.*
OOOF.
PARDON ME, PROFESSOR. I FEAR AS I AGE, I AM UNABLE TO HOLD MY WATER LIKE I USED TO.
PPSSSSSSSSSSSSS
AHH. THAT IS SO MUCH BETTER.

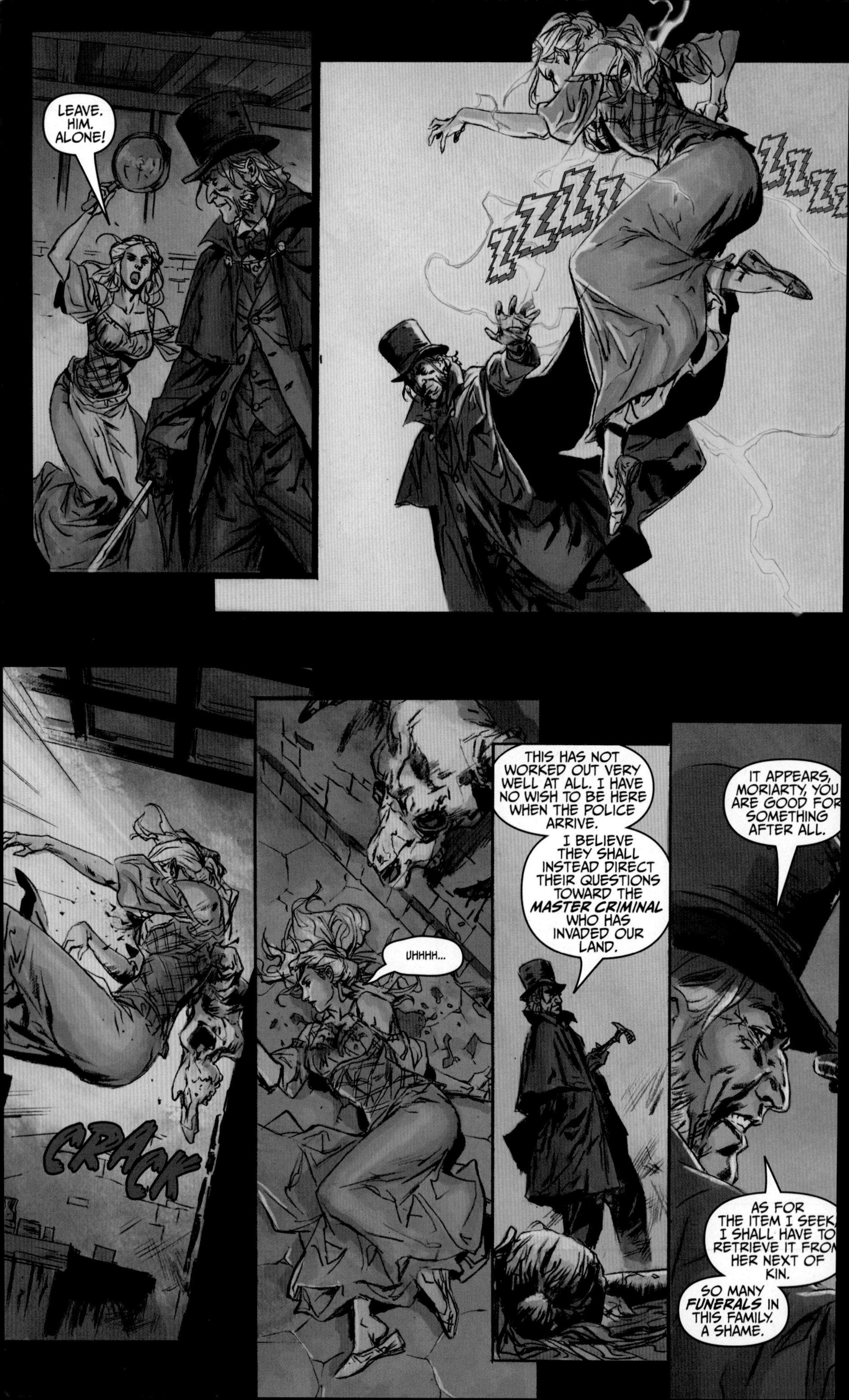
LEAVE. HIM. ALONE!
ZZZZZ
ZZZZ
CRACK
UHHHH...
THIS HAS NOT WORKED OUT VERY WELL AT ALL. I HAVE NO WISH TO BE HERE WHEN THE POLICE ARRIVE.
I BELIEVE THEY SHALL INSTEAD DIRECT THEIR QUESTIONS TOWARD THE MASTER CRIMINAL WHO HAS INVADED OUR LAND.
IT APPEARS, MORIARTY, YOU ARE GOOD FOR SOMETHING AFTER ALL.
AS FOR THE ITEM I SEEK, I SHALL HAVE TO RETRIEVE IT FROM HER NEXT OF KIN.
SO MANY FUNERALS IN THIS FAMILY. A SHAME.

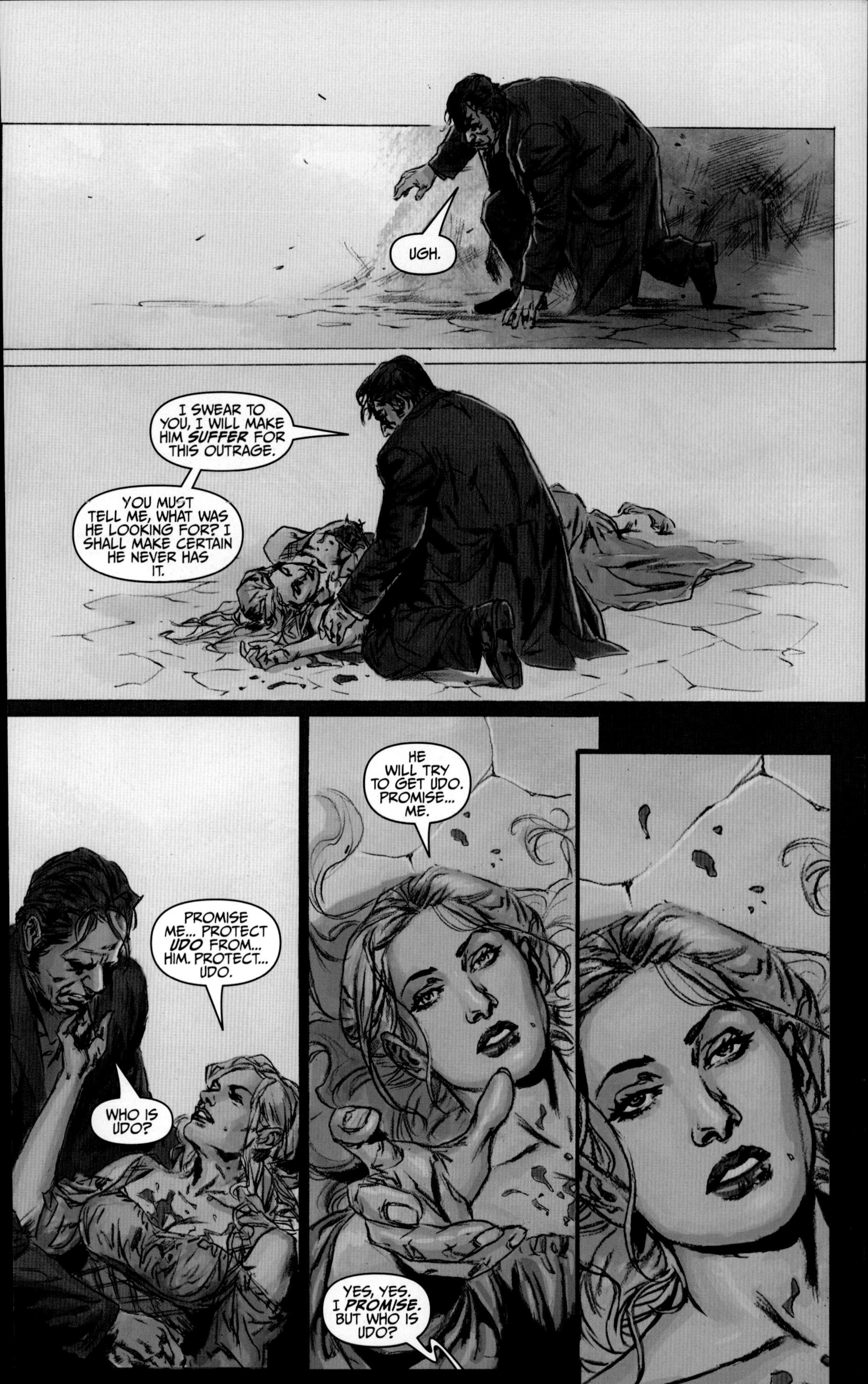
UGH.
I SWEAR TO YOU, I WILL MAKE HIM SUFFER FOR THIS OUTRAGE.
YOU MUST TELL ME, WHAT WAS HE LOOKING FOR? I SHALL MAKE CERTAIN HE NEVER HAS IT.
PROMISE ME... PROTECT UDO FROM... HIM. PROTECT... UDO.
WHO IS UDO?
HE WILL TRY TO GET UDO. PROMISE... ME.
YES, YES. I PROMISE. BUT WHO IS UDO?

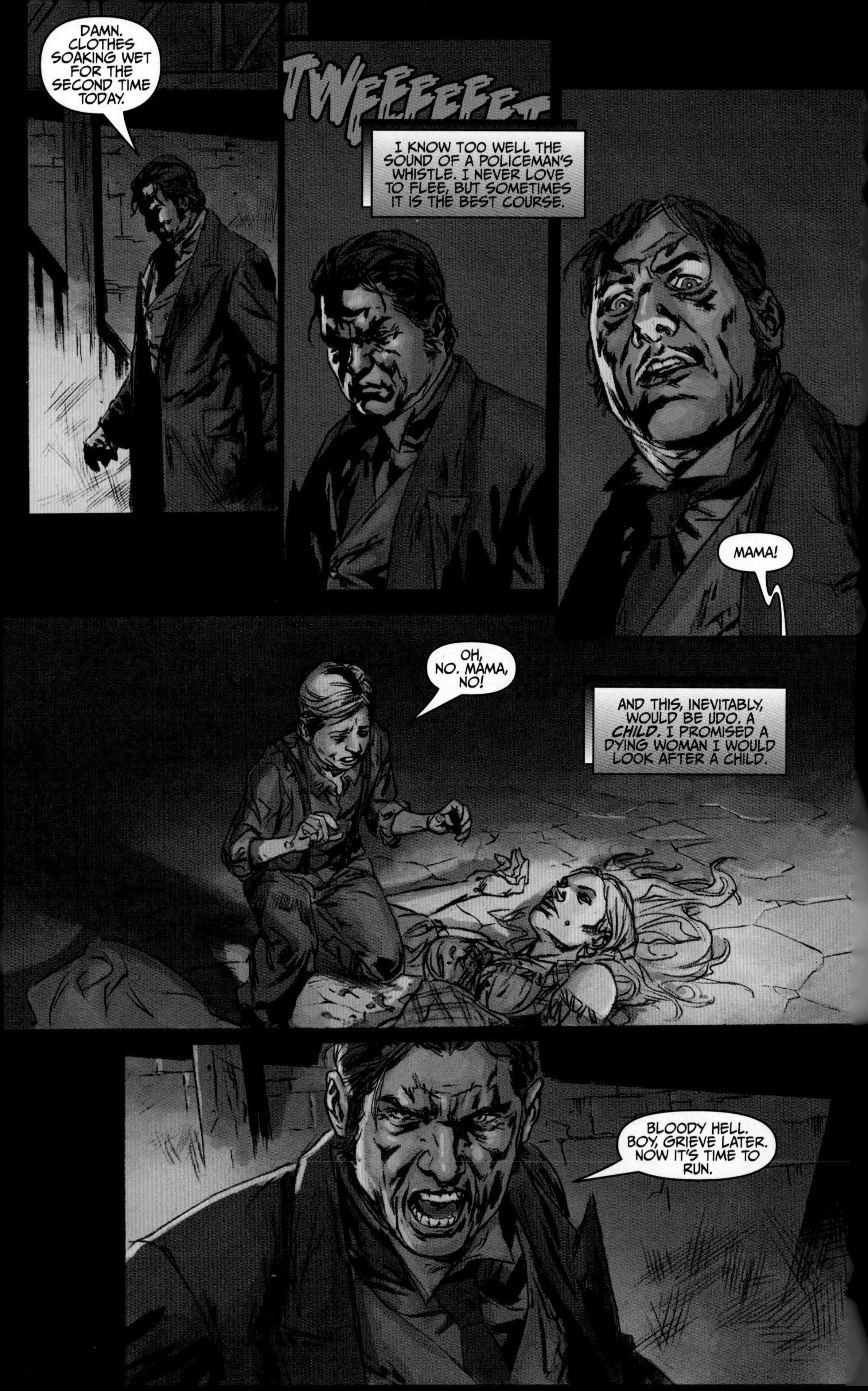
DAMN. CLOTHES SOAKING WET FOR THE SECOND TIME TODAY.
TWEEEEEEET
I KNOW TOO WELL THE SOUND OF A POLICEMAN'S WHISTLE. I NEVER LOVE TO FLEE, BUT SOMETIMES IT IS THE BEST COURSE.
MAMA!
OH, NO. MAMA, NO!
AND THIS, INEVITABLY, WOULD BE UDO. A *CHILD*. I PROMISED A DYING WOMAN I WOULD LOOK AFTER A CHILD.
BLOODY HELL. BOY, GRIEVE LATER. NOW IT'S TIME TO RUN.

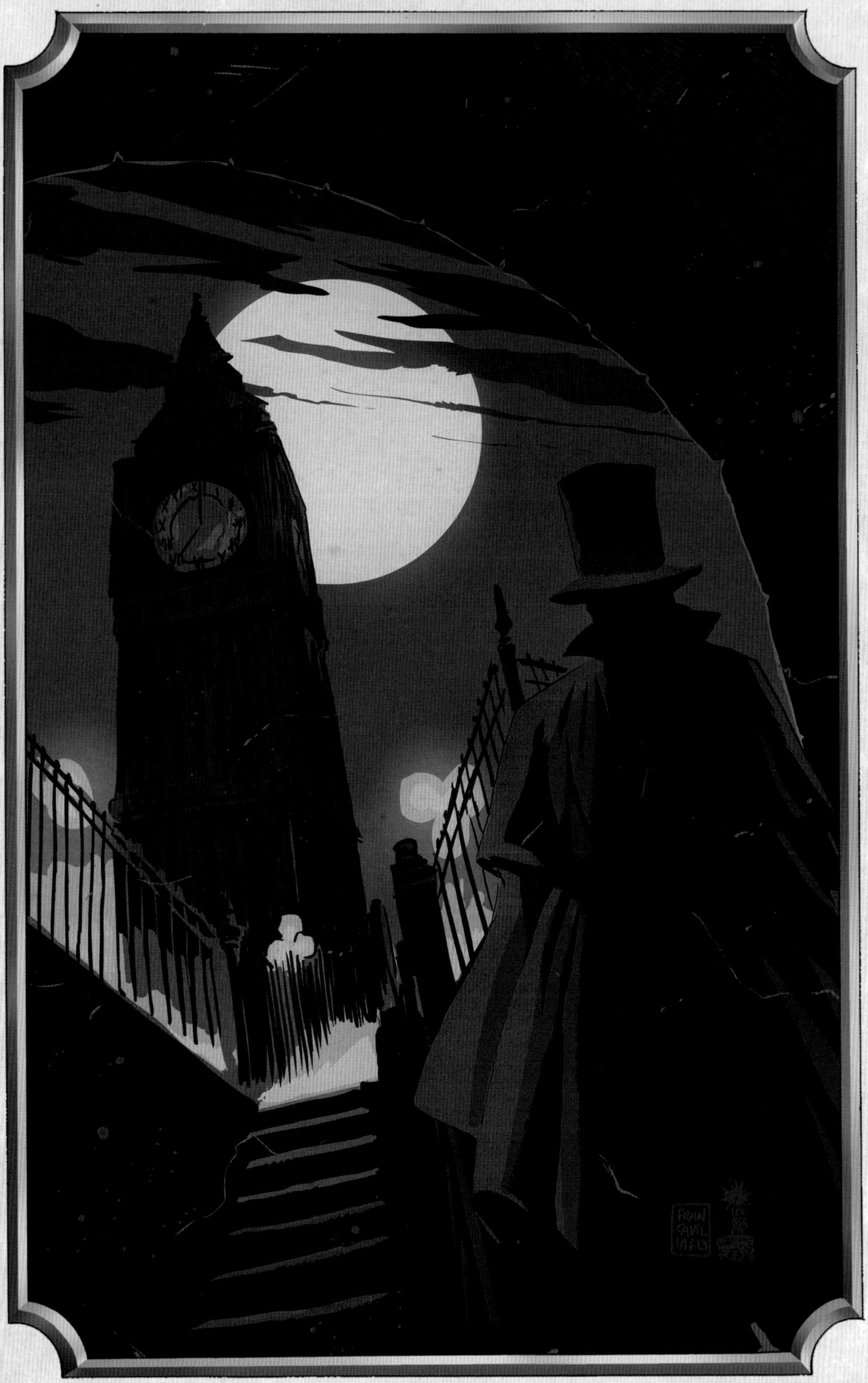

Issue two cover by
Francesco Francavilla

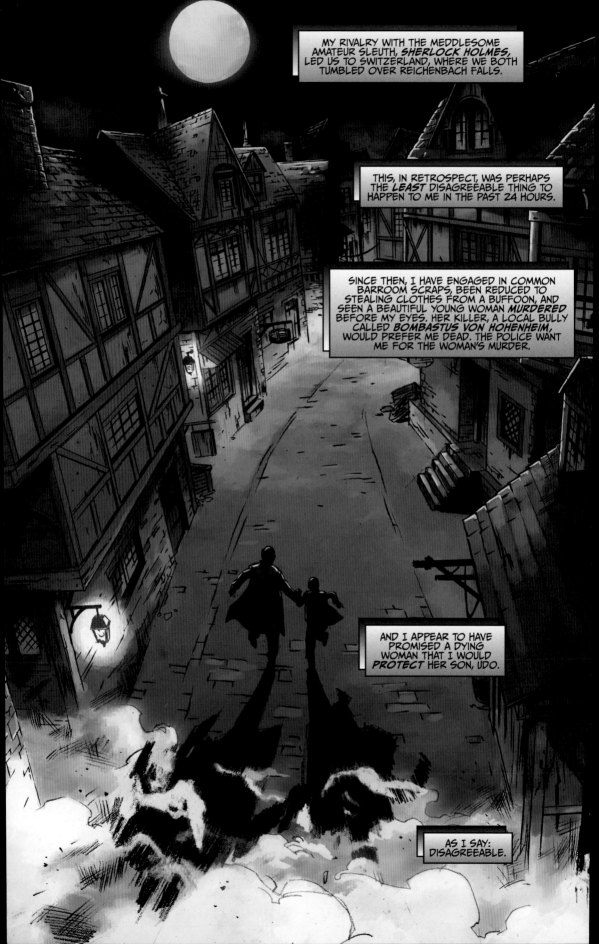

MY RIVALRY WITH THE MEDDLESOME AMATEUR SLEUTH, *SHERLOCK HOLMES*, LED US TO SWITZERLAND, WHERE WE BOTH TUMBLED OVER REICHENBACH FALLS.

THIS, IN RETROSPECT, WAS PERHAPS THE *LEAST* DISAGREEABLE THING TO HAPPEN TO ME IN THE PAST 24 HOURS.

SINCE THEN, I HAVE ENGAGED IN COMMON BARROOM SCRAPS, BEEN REDUCED TO STEALING CLOTHES FROM A BUFFOON, AND SEEN A BEAUTIFUL YOUNG WOMAN *MURDERED* BEFORE MY EYES. HER KILLER, A LOCAL BULLY CALLED *BOMBASTUS VON HOHENHEIM*, WOULD PREFER ME DEAD. THE POLICE WANT ME FOR THE WOMAN'S MURDER.

AND I APPEAR TO HAVE PROMISED A DYING WOMAN THAT I WOULD *PROTECT* HER SON, UDO.

AS I SAY: DISAGREEABLE.

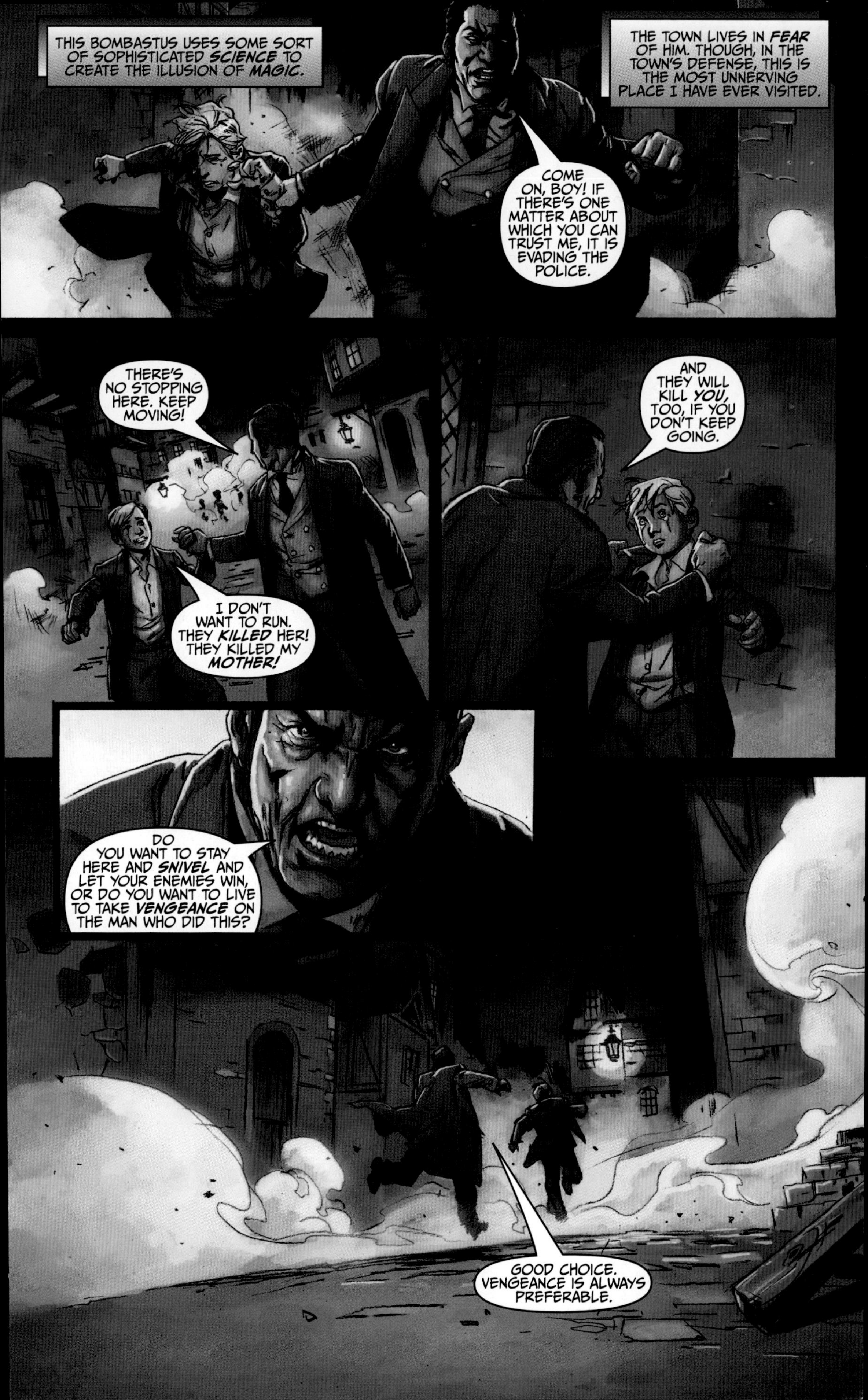
THIS BOMBASTUS USES SOME SORT OF SOPHISTICATED SCIENCE TO CREATE THE ILLUSION OF MAGIC.
THE TOWN LIVES IN FEAR OF HIM. THOUGH, IN THE TOWN'S DEFENSE, THIS IS THE MOST UNNERVING PLACE I HAVE EVER VISITED.
COME ON, BOY! IF THERE'S ONE MATTER ABOUT WHICH YOU CAN TRUST ME, IT IS EVADING THE POLICE.
THERE'S NO STOPPING HERE. KEEP MOVING!
I DON'T WANT TO RUN. THEY KILLED HER! THEY KILLED MY MOTHER!
AND THEY WILL KILL YOU, TOO, IF YOU DON'T KEEP GOING.
DO YOU WANT TO STAY HERE AND SNIVEL AND LET YOUR ENEMIES WIN, OR DO YOU WANT TO LIVE TO TAKE VENGEANCE ON THE MAN WHO DID THIS?
GOOD CHOICE. VENGEANCE IS ALWAYS PREFERABLE.

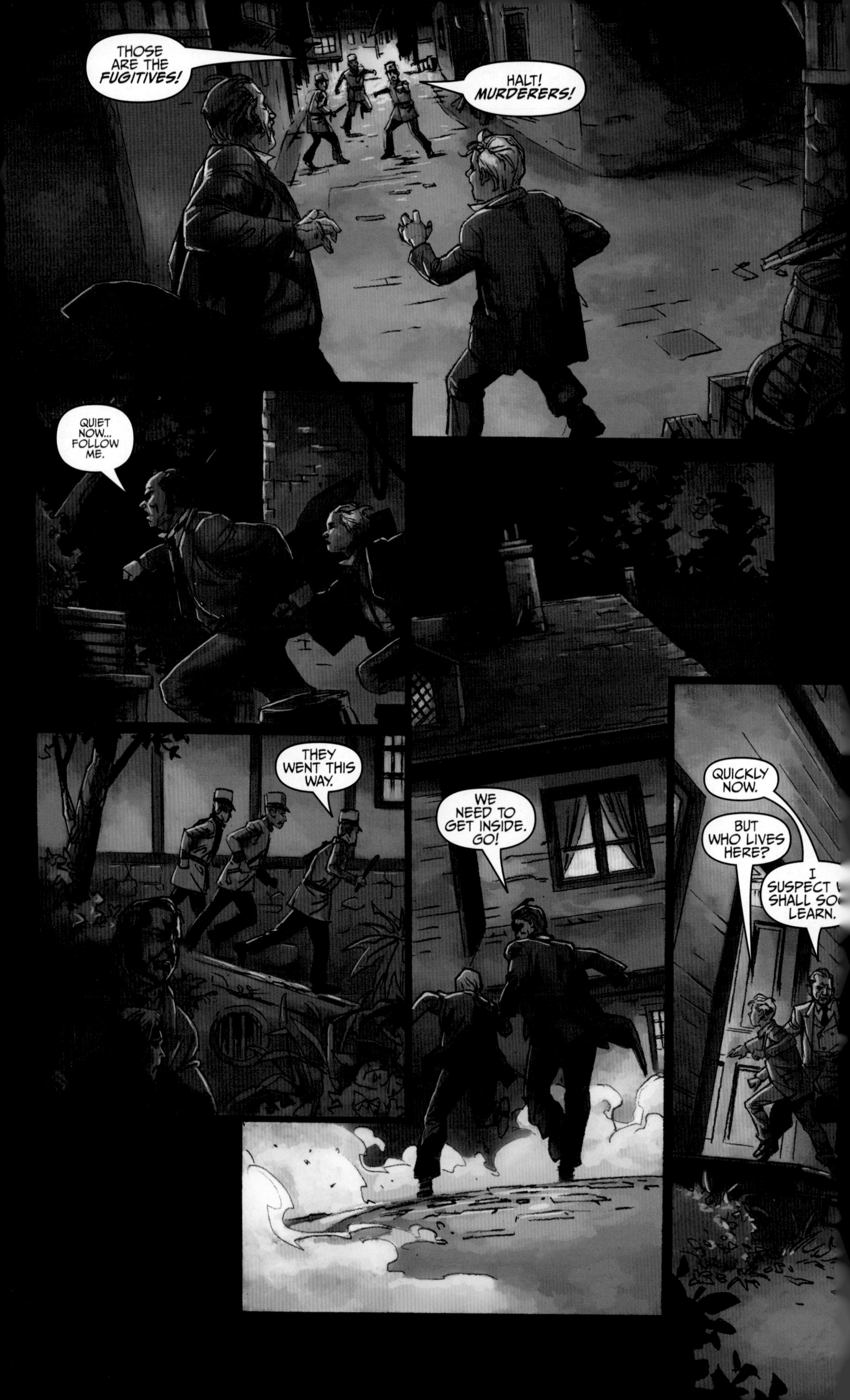
THOSE ARE THE FUGITIVES!
HALT! MURDERERS!
QUIET NOW... FOLLOW ME.
THEY WENT THIS WAY.
WE NEED TO GET INSIDE. GO!
QUICKLY NOW.
BUT WHO LIVES HERE?
I SUSPECT SHALL SO LEARN.

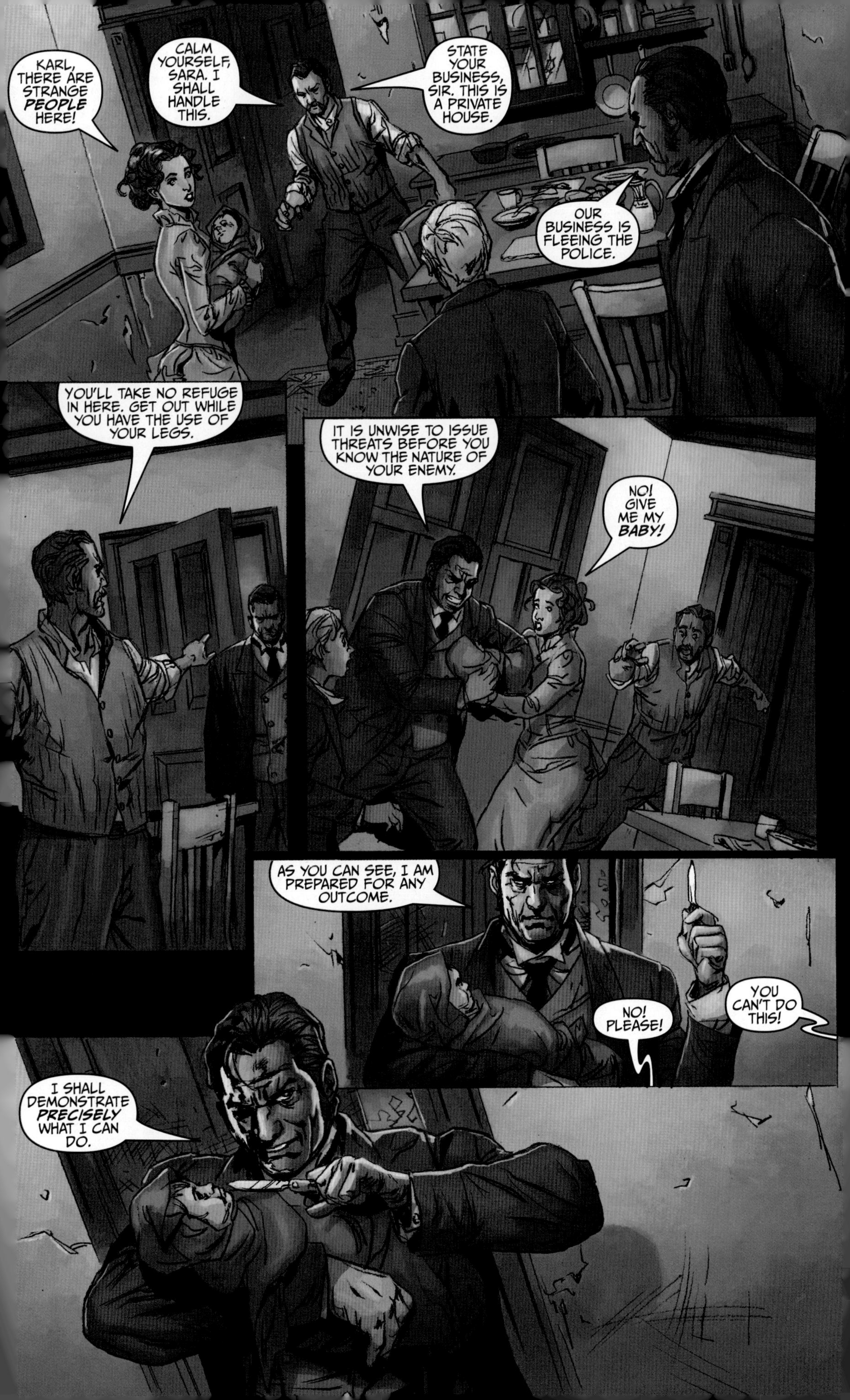
KARL, THERE ARE STRANGE *PEOPLE* HERE!
CALM YOURSELF, SARA. I SHALL HANDLE THIS.
STATE YOUR BUSINESS, SIR. THIS IS A PRIVATE HOUSE.
OUR BUSINESS IS FLEEING THE POLICE.
YOU'LL TAKE NO REFUGE IN HERE. GET OUT WHILE YOU HAVE THE USE OF YOUR LEGS.
IT IS UNWISE TO ISSUE THREATS BEFORE YOU KNOW THE NATURE OF YOUR ENEMY.
NO! GIVE ME MY *BABY!*
AS YOU CAN SEE, I AM PREPARED FOR ANY OUTCOME.
NO! PLEASE!
YOU CAN'T DO THIS!
I SHALL DEMONSTRATE *PRECISELY* WHAT I CAN DO.

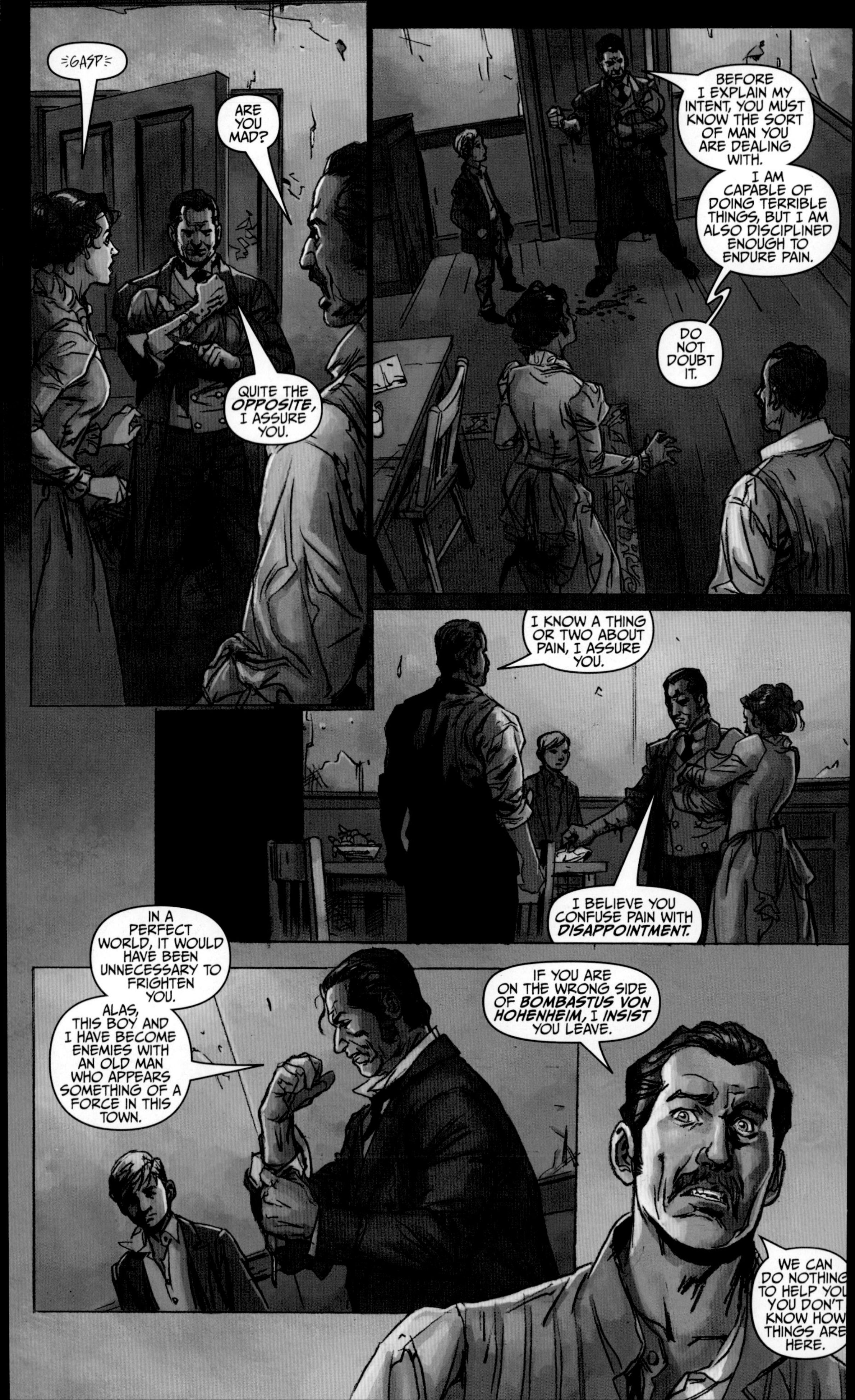
GASP
ARE YOU MAD?
QUITE THE OPPOSITE, I ASSURE YOU.
BEFORE I EXPLAIN MY INTENT, YOU MUST KNOW THE SORT OF MAN YOU ARE DEALING WITH.
I AM CAPABLE OF DOING TERRIBLE THINGS, BUT I AM ALSO DISCIPLINED ENOUGH TO ENDURE PAIN.
DO NOT DOUBT IT.
I KNOW A THING OR TWO ABOUT PAIN, I ASSURE YOU.
I BELIEVE YOU CONFUSE PAIN WITH DISAPPOINTMENT.
IN A PERFECT WORLD, IT WOULD HAVE BEEN UNNECESSARY TO FRIGHTEN YOU.
ALAS, THIS BOY AND I HAVE BECOME ENEMIES WITH AN OLD MAN WHO APPEARS SOMETHING OF A FORCE IN THIS TOWN.
IF YOU ARE ON THE WRONG SIDE OF BOMBASTUS VON HOHENHEIM, I INSIST YOU LEAVE.
WE CAN DO NOTHING TO HELP YOU. YOU DON'T KNOW HOW THINGS ARE HERE.

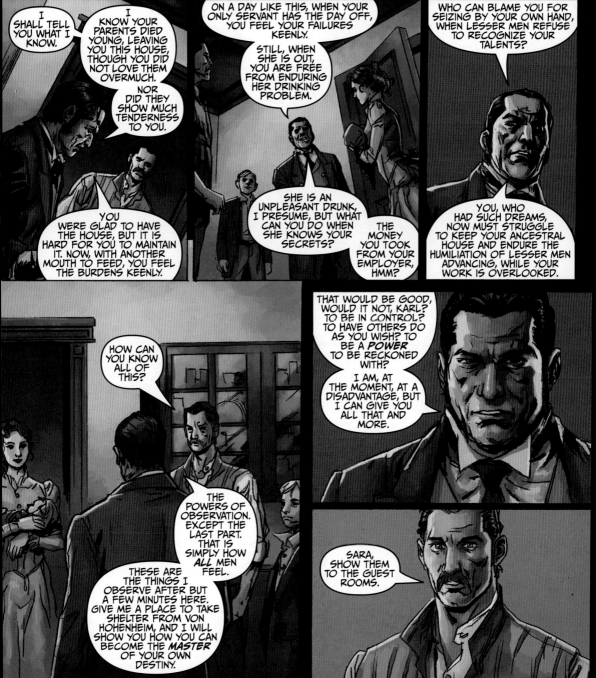

I SHALL TELL YOU WHAT I KNOW.

I KNOW YOUR PARENTS DIED YOUNG, LEAVING YOU THIS HOUSE, THOUGH YOU DID NOT LOVE THEM OVERMUCH.

NOR DID THEY SHOW MUCH TENDERNESS TO YOU.

YOU WERE GLAD TO HAVE THE HOUSE, BUT IT IS HARD FOR YOU TO MAINTAIN IT. NOW, WITH ANOTHER MOUTH TO FEED, YOU FEEL THE BURDENS KEENLY.

ON A DAY LIKE THIS, WHEN YOUR ONLY SERVANT HAS THE DAY OFF, YOU FEEL YOUR FAILURES KEENLY.

STILL, WHEN SHE IS OUT, YOU ARE FREE FROM ENDURING HER DRINKING PROBLEM.

SHE IS AN UNPLEASANT DRUNK, I PRESUME, BUT WHAT CAN YOU DO WHEN SHE KNOWS YOUR SECRETS?

THE MONEY YOU TOOK FROM YOUR EMPLOYER, HMM?

WHO CAN BLAME YOU FOR SEIZING BY YOUR OWN HAND, WHEN LESSER MEN REFUSE TO RECOGNIZE YOUR TALENTS?

YOU, WHO HAD SUCH DREAMS, NOW MUST STRUGGLE TO KEEP YOUR ANCESTRAL HOUSE AND ENDURE THE HUMILIATION OF LESSER MEN ADVANCING, WHILE YOUR WORK IS OVERLOOKED.

HOW CAN YOU KNOW ALL OF THIS?

THE POWERS OF OBSERVATION. EXCEPT THE LAST PART. THAT IS SIMPLY HOW ALL MEN FEEL.

THESE ARE THE THINGS I OBSERVE AFTER BUT A FEW MINUTES HERE. GIVE ME A PLACE TO TAKE SHELTER FROM VON HOHENHEIM, AND I WILL SHOW YOU HOW YOU CAN BECOME THE MASTER OF YOUR OWN DESTINY.

THAT WOULD BE GOOD, WOULD IT NOT, KARL? TO BE IN CONTROL? TO HAVE OTHERS DO AS YOU WISH? TO BE A POWER TO BE RECKONED WITH?

I AM, AT THE MOMENT, AT A DISADVANTAGE, BUT I CAN GIVE YOU ALL THAT AND MORE.

SARA, SHOW THEM TO THE GUEST ROOMS.

THIS WAY.

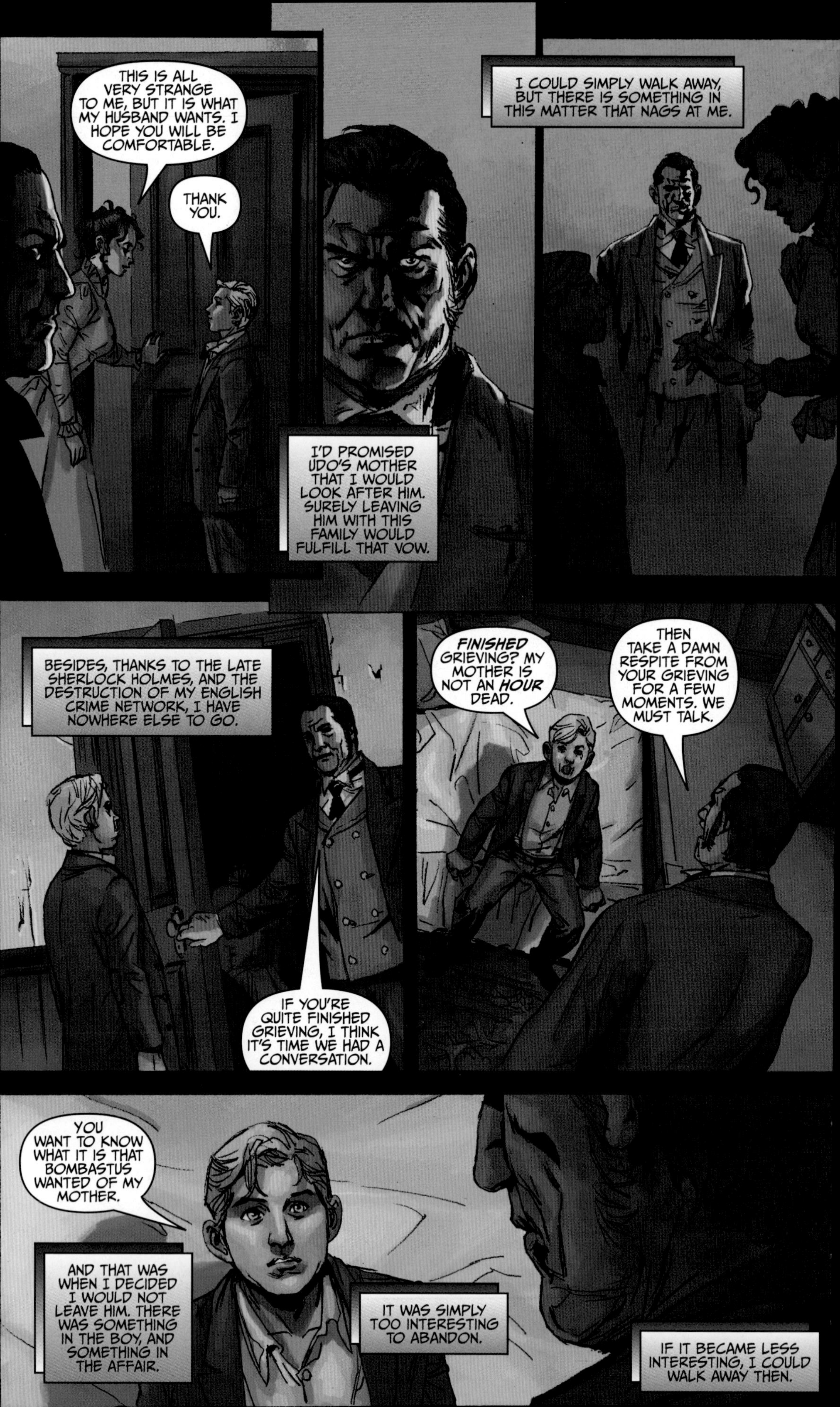
THIS IS ALL VERY STRANGE TO ME, BUT IT IS WHAT MY HUSBAND WANTS. I HOPE YOU WILL BE COMFORTABLE.
THANK YOU.
I'D PROMISED UDO'S MOTHER THAT I WOULD LOOK AFTER HIM. SURELY LEAVING HIM WITH THIS FAMILY WOULD FULFILL THAT VOW.
I COULD SIMPLY WALK AWAY, BUT THERE IS SOMETHING IN THIS MATTER THAT NAGS AT ME.
BESIDES, THANKS TO THE LATE SHERLOCK HOLMES, AND THE DESTRUCTION OF MY ENGLISH CRIME NETWORK, I HAVE NOWHERE ELSE TO GO.
IF YOU'RE QUITE FINISHED GRIEVING, I THINK IT'S TIME WE HAD A CONVERSATION.
FINISHED GRIEVING? MY MOTHER IS NOT AN HOUR DEAD.
THEN TAKE A DAMN RESPITE FROM YOUR GRIEVING FOR A FEW MOMENTS. WE MUST TALK.
YOU WANT TO KNOW WHAT IT IS THAT BOMBASTUS WANTED OF MY MOTHER.
AND THAT WAS WHEN I DECIDED I WOULD NOT LEAVE HIM. THERE WAS SOMETHING IN THE BOY, AND SOMETHING IN THE AFFAIR.
IT WAS SIMPLY TOO INTERESTING TO ABANDON.
IF IT BECAME LESS INTERESTING, I COULD WALK AWAY THEN.

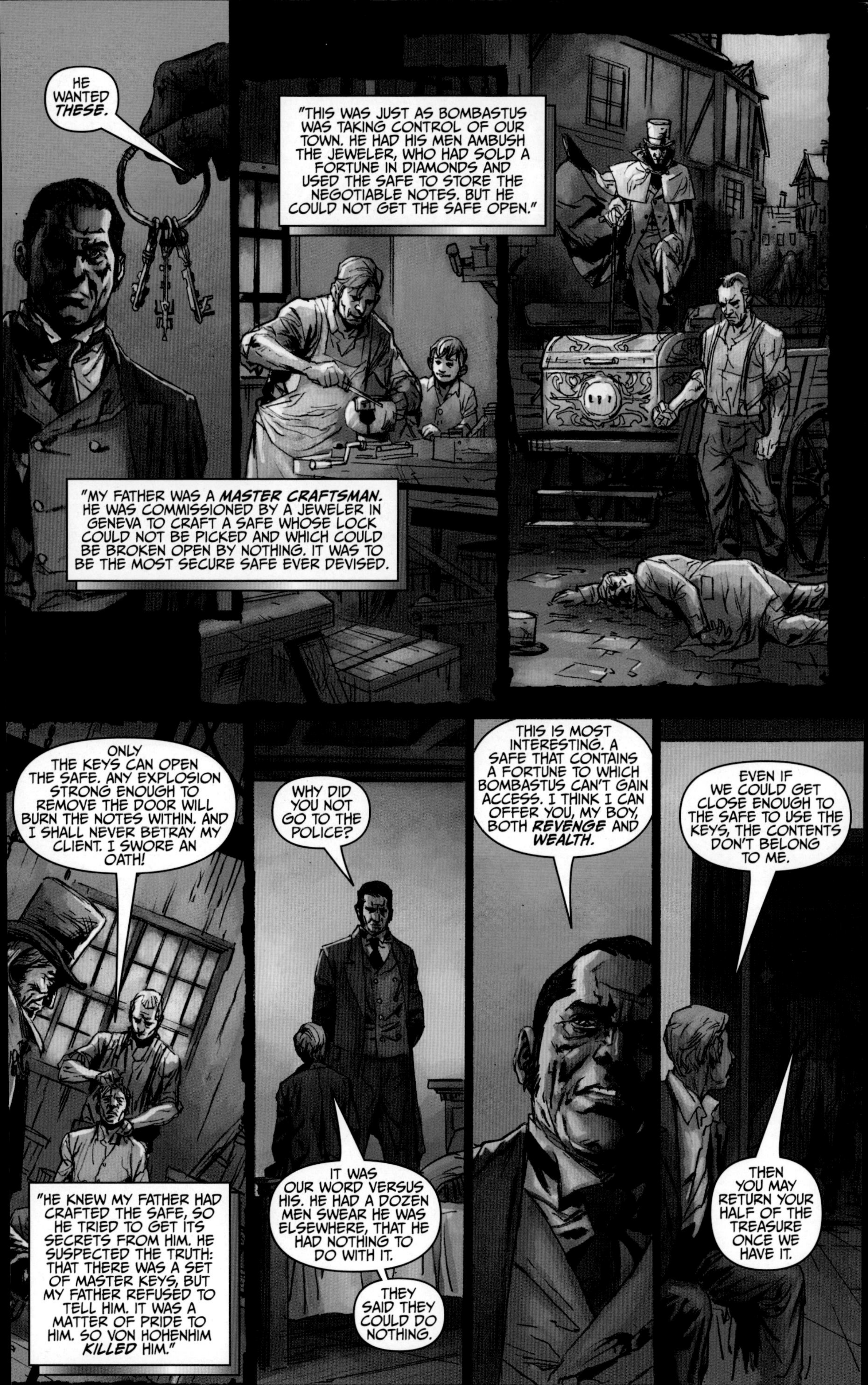
HE WANTED *THESE.*
"THIS WAS JUST AS BOMBASTUS WAS TAKING CONTROL OF OUR TOWN. HE HAD HIS MEN AMBUSH THE JEWELER, WHO HAD SOLD A FORTUNE IN DIAMONDS AND USED THE SAFE TO STORE THE NEGOTIABLE NOTES. BUT HE COULD NOT GET THE SAFE OPEN."
"MY FATHER WAS A *MASTER CRAFTSMAN.* HE WAS COMMISSIONED BY A JEWELER IN GENEVA TO CRAFT A SAFE WHOSE LOCK COULD NOT BE PICKED AND WHICH COULD BE BROKEN OPEN BY NOTHING. IT WAS TO BE THE MOST SECURE SAFE EVER DEVISED.
ONLY THE KEYS CAN OPEN THE SAFE. ANY EXPLOSION STRONG ENOUGH TO REMOVE THE DOOR WILL BURN THE NOTES WITHIN. AND I SHALL NEVER BETRAY MY CLIENT. I SWORE AN OATH!
"HE KNEW MY FATHER HAD CRAFTED THE SAFE, SO HE TRIED TO GET ITS SECRETS FROM HIM. HE SUSPECTED THE TRUTH: THAT THERE WAS A SET OF MASTER KEYS, BUT MY FATHER REFUSED TO TELL HIM. IT WAS A MATTER OF PRIDE TO HIM. SO VON HOHENHIM *KILLED* HIM."
WHY DID YOU NOT GO TO THE POLICE?
IT WAS OUR WORD VERSUS HIS. HE HAD A DOZEN MEN SWEAR HE WAS ELSEWHERE, THAT HE HAD NOTHING TO DO WITH IT.
THEY SAID THEY COULD DO NOTHING.
THIS IS MOST INTERESTING. A SAFE THAT CONTAINS A FORTUNE TO WHICH BOMBASTUS CAN'T GAIN ACCESS. I THINK I CAN OFFER YOU, MY BOY, BOTH *REVENGE* AND *WEALTH.*
EVEN IF WE COULD GET CLOSE ENOUGH TO THE SAFE TO USE THE KEYS, THE CONTENTS DON'T BELONG TO ME.
THEN YOU MAY RETURN YOUR HALF OF THE TREASURE ONCE WE HAVE IT.

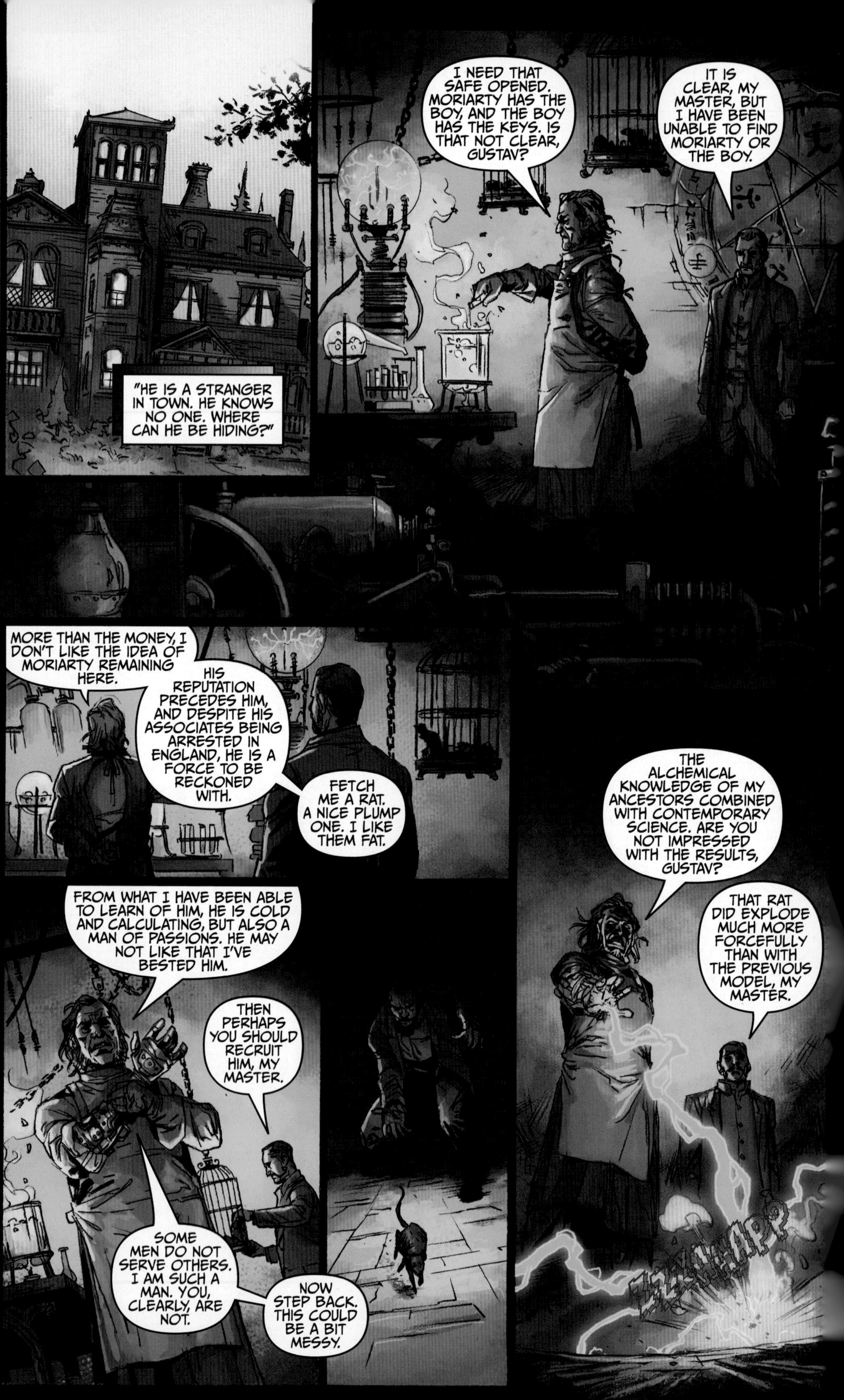
"HE IS A STRANGER IN TOWN. HE KNOWS NO ONE. WHERE CAN HE BE HIDING?"
I NEED THAT SAFE OPENED. MORIARTY HAS THE BOY, AND THE BOY HAS THE KEYS. IS THAT NOT CLEAR, GUSTAV?
IT IS CLEAR, MY MASTER, BUT I HAVE BEEN UNABLE TO FIND MORIARTY OR THE BOY.
MORE THAN THE MONEY, I DON'T LIKE THE IDEA OF MORIARTY REMAINING HERE.
HIS REPUTATION PRECEDES HIM, AND DESPITE HIS ASSOCIATES BEING ARRESTED IN ENGLAND, HE IS A FORCE TO BE RECKONED WITH.
FETCH ME A RAT. A NICE PLUMP ONE. I LIKE THEM FAT.
FROM WHAT I HAVE BEEN ABLE TO LEARN OF HIM, HE IS COLD AND CALCULATING, BUT ALSO A MAN OF PASSIONS. HE MAY NOT LIKE THAT I'VE BESTED HIM.
THEN PERHAPS YOU SHOULD RECRUIT HIM, MY MASTER.
SOME MEN DO NOT SERVE OTHERS. I AM SUCH A MAN. YOU, CLEARLY, ARE NOT.
NOW STEP BACK. THIS COULD BE A BIT MESSY.
THE ALCHEMICAL KNOWLEDGE OF MY ANCESTORS COMBINED WITH CONTEMPORARY SCIENCE. ARE YOU NOT IMPRESSED WITH THE RESULTS, GUSTAV?
THAT RAT DID EXPLODE MUCH MORE FORCEFULLY THAN WITH THE PREVIOUS MODEL, MY MASTER.

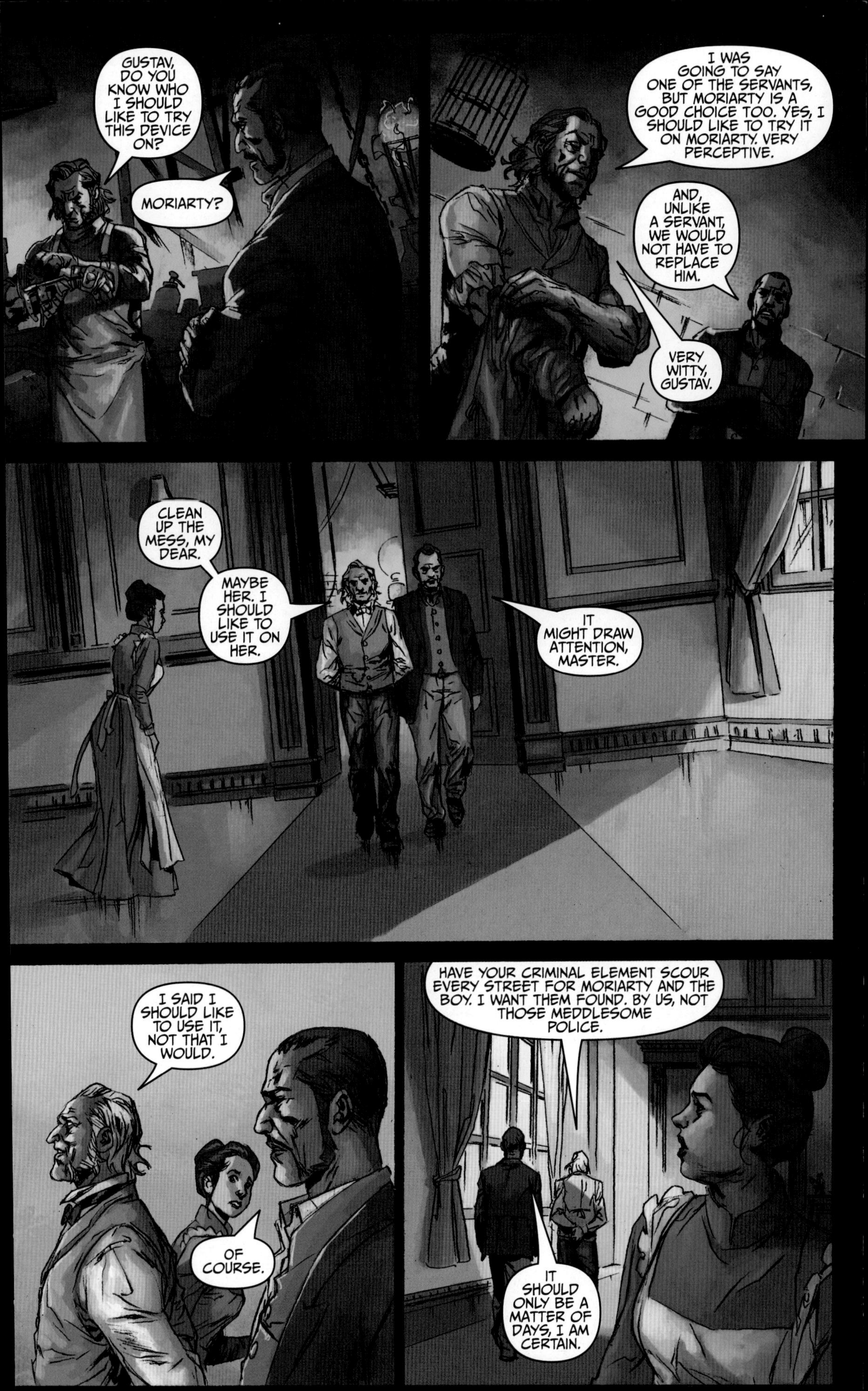
GUSTAV, DO YOU KNOW WHO I SHOULD LIKE TO TRY THIS DEVICE ON?
MORIARTY?
I WAS GOING TO SAY ONE OF THE SERVANTS, BUT MORIARTY IS A GOOD CHOICE TOO. YES, I SHOULD LIKE TO TRY IT ON MORIARTY. VERY PERCEPTIVE.
AND, UNLIKE A SERVANT, WE WOULD NOT HAVE TO REPLACE HIM.
VERY WITTY, GUSTAV.
CLEAN UP THE MESS, MY DEAR.
MAYBE HER. I SHOULD LIKE TO USE IT ON HER.
IT MIGHT DRAW ATTENTION, MASTER.
I SAID I SHOULD LIKE TO USE IT, NOT THAT I WOULD.
OF COURSE.
HAVE YOUR CRIMINAL ELEMENT SCOUR EVERY STREET FOR MORIARTY AND THE BOY. I WANT THEM FOUND. BY US, NOT THOSE MEDDLESOME POLICE.
IT SHOULD ONLY BE A MATTER OF DAYS, I AM CERTAIN.

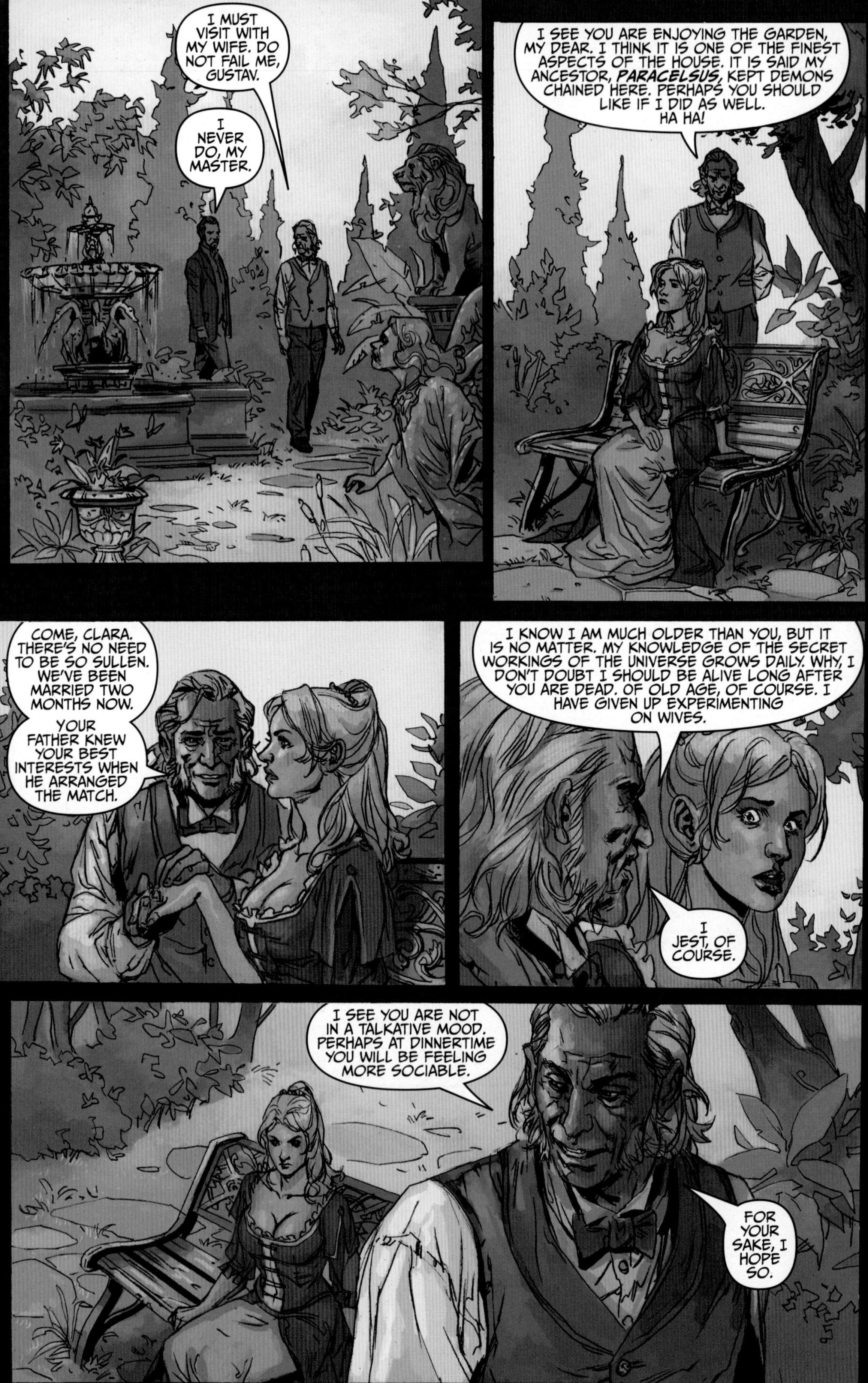

I MUST VISIT WITH MY WIFE. DO NOT FAIL ME, GUSTAV.
I NEVER DO, MY MASTER.
I SEE YOU ARE ENJOYING THE GARDEN, MY DEAR. I THINK IT IS ONE OF THE FINEST ASPECTS OF THE HOUSE. IT IS SAID MY ANCESTOR, ***PARACELSUS,*** KEPT DEMONS CHAINED HERE. PERHAPS YOU SHOULD LIKE IF I DID AS WELL. HA HA!
COME, CLARA. THERE'S NO NEED TO BE SO SULLEN. WE'VE BEEN MARRIED TWO MONTHS NOW.
YOUR FATHER KNEW YOUR BEST INTERESTS WHEN HE ARRANGED THE MATCH.
I KNOW I AM MUCH OLDER THAN YOU, BUT IT IS NO MATTER. MY KNOWLEDGE OF THE SECRET WORKINGS OF THE UNIVERSE GROWS DAILY. WHY, I DON'T DOUBT I SHOULD BE ALIVE LONG AFTER YOU ARE DEAD. OF OLD AGE, OF COURSE. I HAVE GIVEN UP EXPERIMENTING ON WIVES.
I JEST, OF COURSE.
I SEE YOU ARE NOT IN A TALKATIVE MOOD. PERHAPS AT DINNERTIME YOU WILL BE FEELING MORE SOCIABLE.
FOR YOUR SAKE, I HOPE SO.

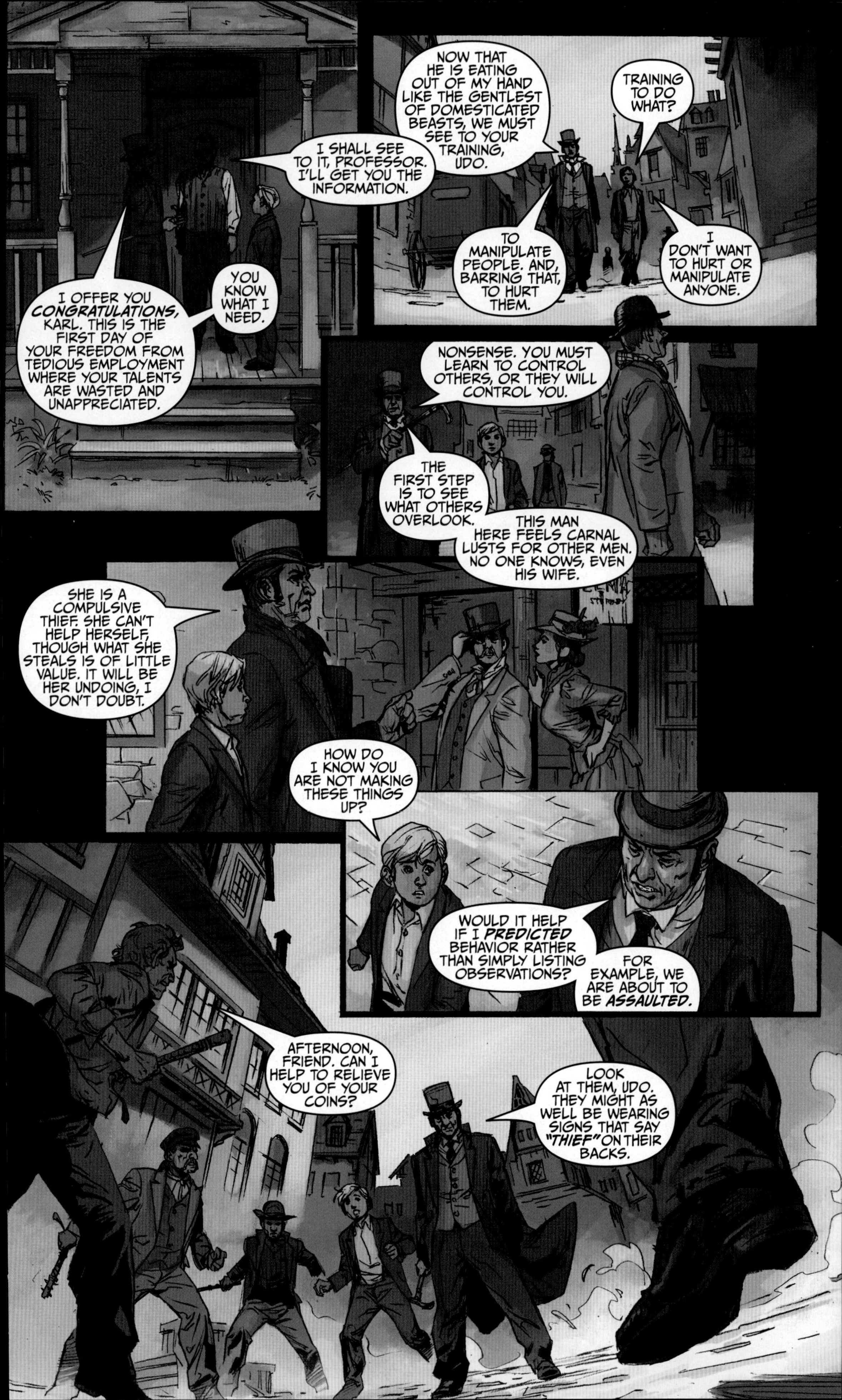
I SHALL SEE TO IT, PROFESSOR. I'LL GET YOU THE INFORMATION.
I OFFER YOU CONGRATULATIONS, KARL. THIS IS THE FIRST DAY OF YOUR FREEDOM FROM TEDIOUS EMPLOYMENT WHERE YOUR TALENTS ARE WASTED AND UNAPPRECIATED.
YOU KNOW WHAT I NEED.
NOW THAT HE IS EATING OUT OF MY HAND LIKE THE GENTLEST OF DOMESTICATED BEASTS, WE MUST SEE TO YOUR TRAINING, UDO.
TRAINING TO DO WHAT?
TO MANIPULATE PEOPLE. AND, BARRING THAT, TO HURT THEM.
I DON'T WANT TO HURT OR MANIPULATE ANYONE.
NONSENSE. YOU MUST LEARN TO CONTROL OTHERS, OR THEY WILL CONTROL YOU.
THE FIRST STEP IS TO SEE WHAT OTHERS OVERLOOK.
THIS MAN HERE FEELS CARNAL LUSTS FOR OTHER MEN. NO ONE KNOWS, EVEN HIS WIFE.
SHE IS A COMPULSIVE THIEF. SHE CAN'T HELP HERSELF, THOUGH WHAT SHE STEALS IS OF LITTLE VALUE. IT WILL BE HER UNDOING, I DON'T DOUBT.
HOW DO I KNOW YOU ARE NOT MAKING THESE THINGS UP?
WOULD IT HELP IF I PREDICTED BEHAVIOR RATHER THAN SIMPLY LISTING OBSERVATIONS?
FOR EXAMPLE, WE ARE ABOUT TO BE ASSAULTED.
AFTERNOON, FRIEND. CAN I HELP TO RELIEVE YOU OF YOUR COINS?
LOOK AT THEM, UDO. THEY MIGHT AS WELL BE WEARING SIGNS THAT SAY "THIEF" ON THEIR BACKS.

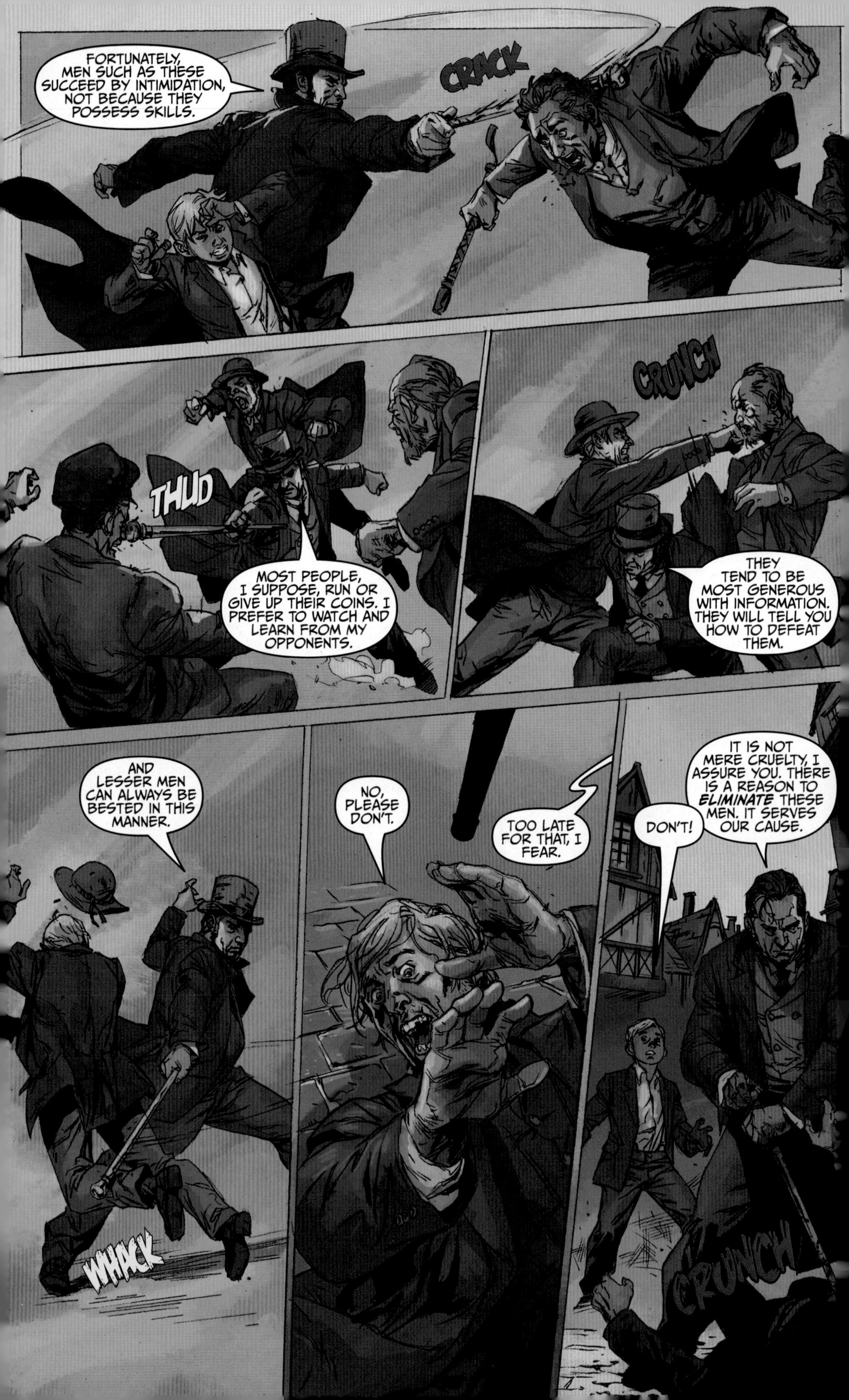
FORTUNATELY, MEN SUCH AS THESE SUCCEED BY INTIMIDATION, NOT BECAUSE THEY POSSESS SKILLS.
CRACK
THUD
MOST PEOPLE, I SUPPOSE, RUN OR GIVE UP THEIR COINS. I PREFER TO WATCH AND LEARN FROM MY OPPONENTS.
CRUNCH
THEY TEND TO BE MOST GENEROUS WITH INFORMATION. THEY WILL TELL YOU HOW TO DEFEAT THEM.
AND LESSER MEN CAN ALWAYS BE BESTED IN THIS MANNER.
WHACK
NO, PLEASE DON'T.
TOO LATE FOR THAT, I FEAR.
DON'T!
IT IS NOT MERE CRUELTY, I ASSURE YOU. THERE IS A REASON TO *ELIMINATE* THESE MEN. IT SERVES OUR CAUSE.
CRUNCH

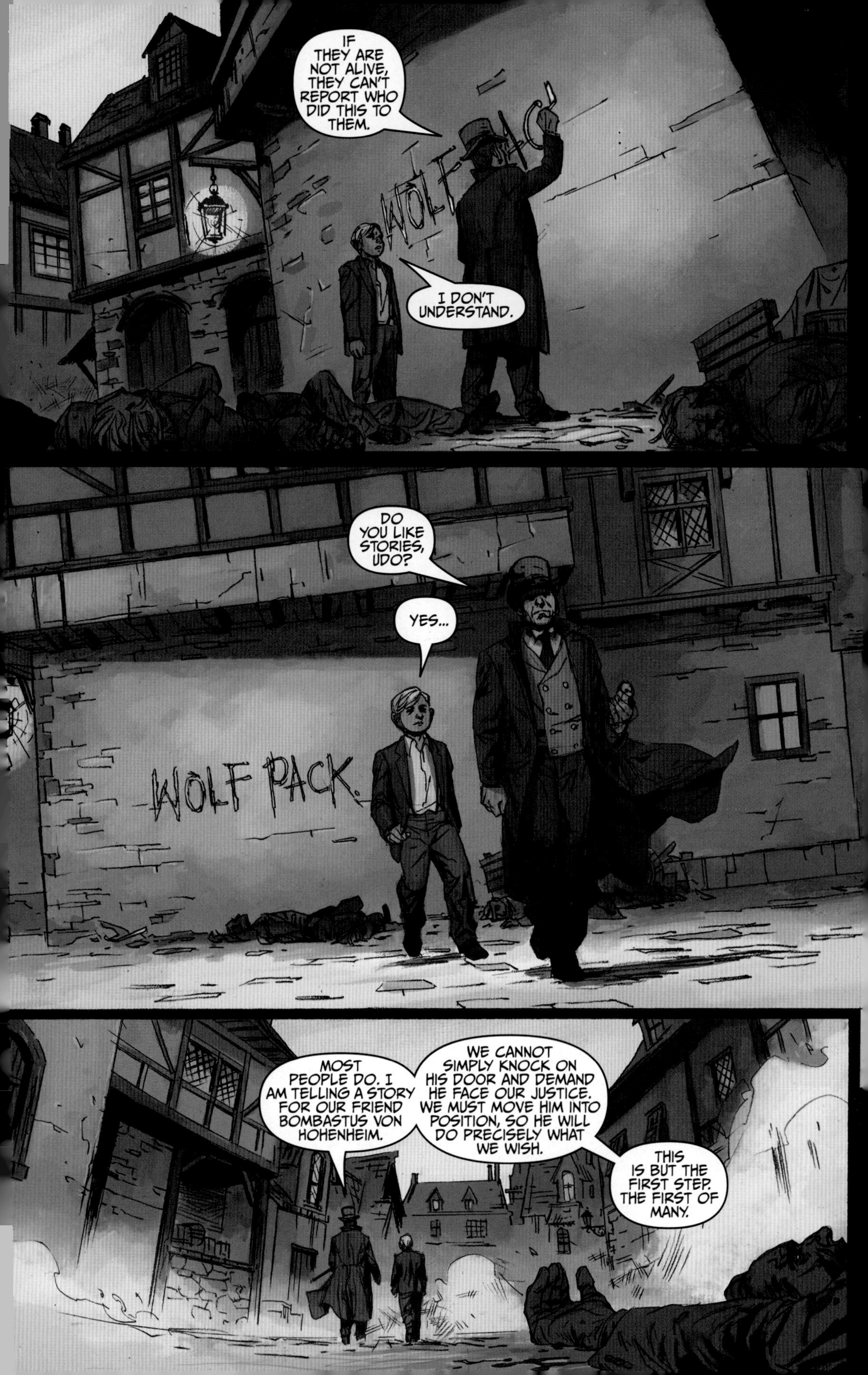
IF THEY ARE NOT ALIVE, THEY CAN'T REPORT WHO DID THIS TO THEM.
I DON'T UNDERSTAND.
WOLF PACK
DO YOU LIKE STORIES, UDO?
YES...
WOLF PACK.
MOST PEOPLE DO. I AM TELLING A STORY FOR OUR FRIEND BOMBASTUS VON HOHENHEIM.
WE CANNOT SIMPLY KNOCK ON HIS DOOR AND DEMAND HE FACE OUR JUSTICE. WE MUST MOVE HIM INTO POSITION, SO HE WILL DO PRECISELY WHAT WE WISH.
THIS IS BUT THE FIRST STEP. THE FIRST OF MANY.

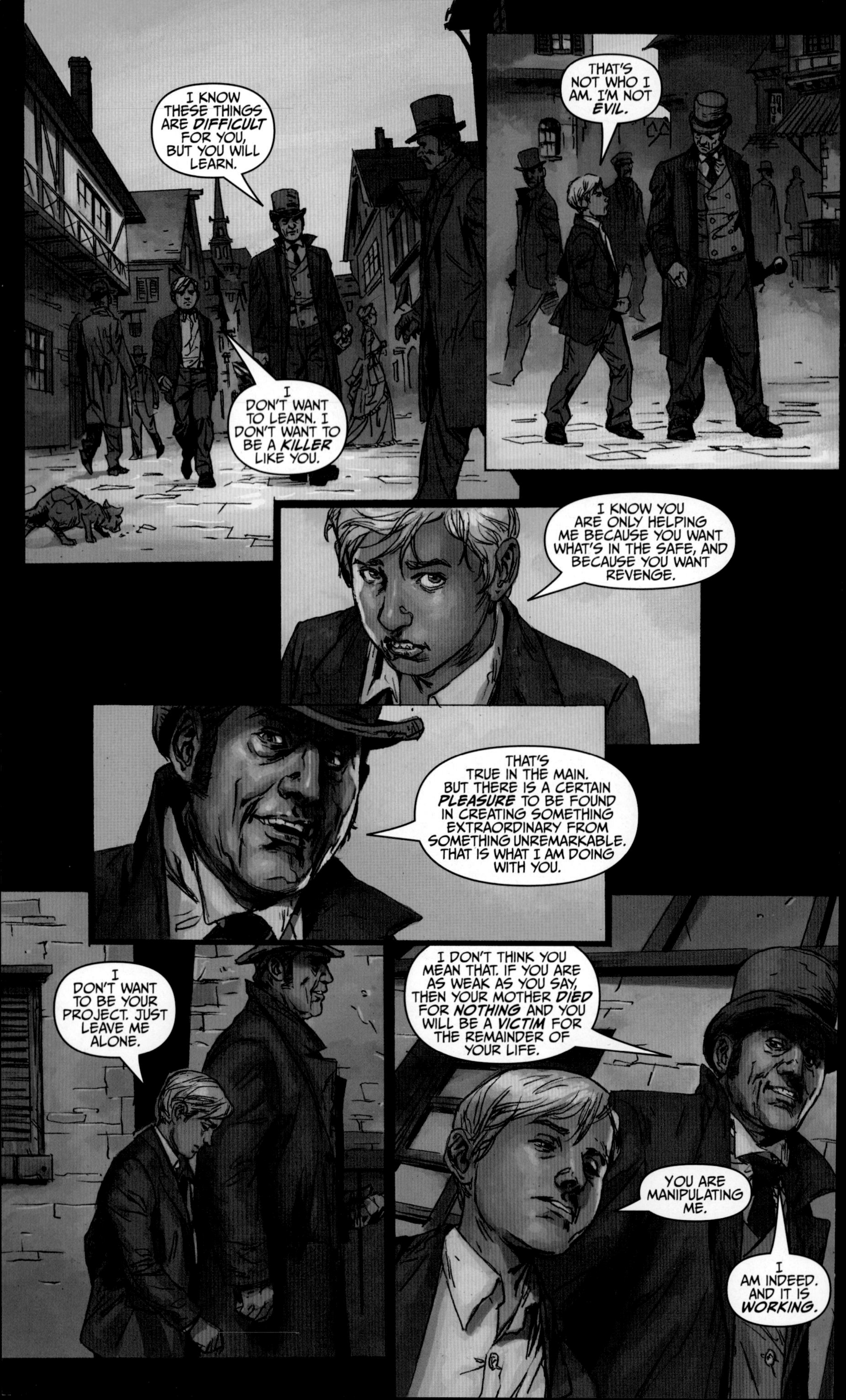
I KNOW THESE THINGS ARE DIFFICULT FOR YOU, BUT YOU WILL LEARN.
I DON'T WANT TO LEARN. I DON'T WANT TO BE A KILLER LIKE YOU.
THAT'S NOT WHO I AM. I'M NOT EVIL.
I KNOW YOU ARE ONLY HELPING ME BECAUSE YOU WANT WHAT'S IN THE SAFE, AND BECAUSE YOU WANT REVENGE.
THAT'S TRUE IN THE MAIN. BUT THERE IS A CERTAIN PLEASURE TO BE FOUND IN CREATING SOMETHING EXTRAORDINARY FROM SOMETHING UNREMARKABLE. THAT IS WHAT I AM DOING WITH YOU.
I DON'T WANT TO BE YOUR PROJECT. JUST LEAVE ME ALONE.
I DON'T THINK YOU MEAN THAT. IF YOU ARE AS WEAK AS YOU SAY, THEN YOUR MOTHER DIED FOR NOTHING AND YOU WILL BE A VICTIM FOR THE REMAINDER OF YOUR LIFE.
YOU ARE MANIPULATING ME.
I AM INDEED. AND IT IS WORKING.

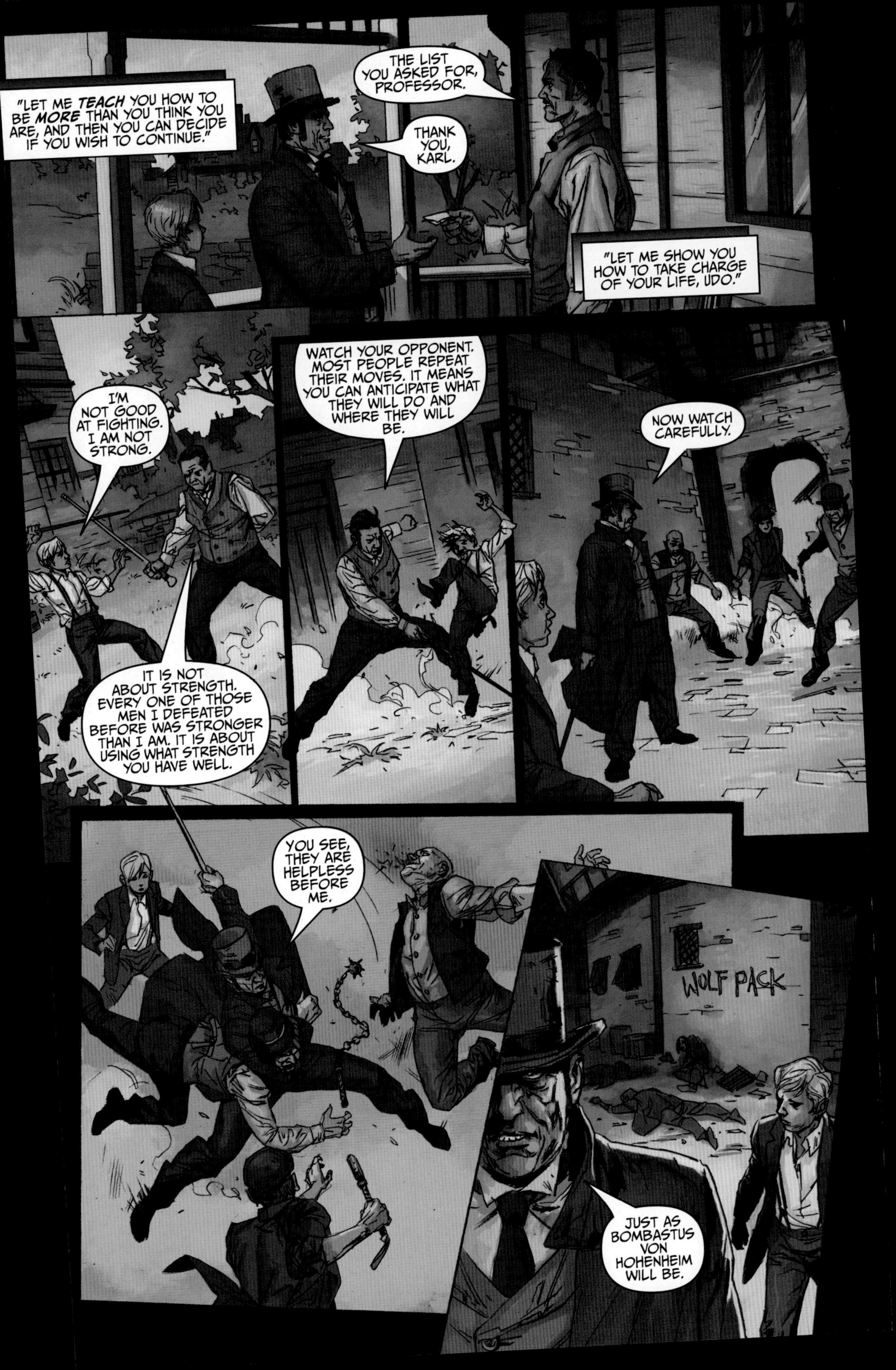
"LET ME TEACH YOU HOW TO BE MORE THAN YOU THINK YOU ARE, AND THEN YOU CAN DECIDE IF YOU WISH TO CONTINUE."
THE LIST YOU ASKED FOR, PROFESSOR.
THANK YOU, KARL.
"LET ME SHOW YOU HOW TO TAKE CHARGE OF YOUR LIFE, UDO."
I'M NOT GOOD AT FIGHTING. I AM NOT STRONG.
IT IS NOT ABOUT STRENGTH. EVERY ONE OF THOSE MEN I DEFEATED BEFORE WAS STRONGER THAN I AM. IT IS ABOUT USING WHAT STRENGTH YOU HAVE WELL.
WATCH YOUR OPPONENT. MOST PEOPLE REPEAT THEIR MOVES. IT MEANS YOU CAN ANTICIPATE WHAT THEY WILL DO AND WHERE THEY WILL BE.
NOW WATCH CAREFULLY.
YOU SEE, THEY ARE HELPLESS BEFORE ME.
WOLF PACK
JUST AS BOMBASTUS VON HOHENHEIM WILL BE.

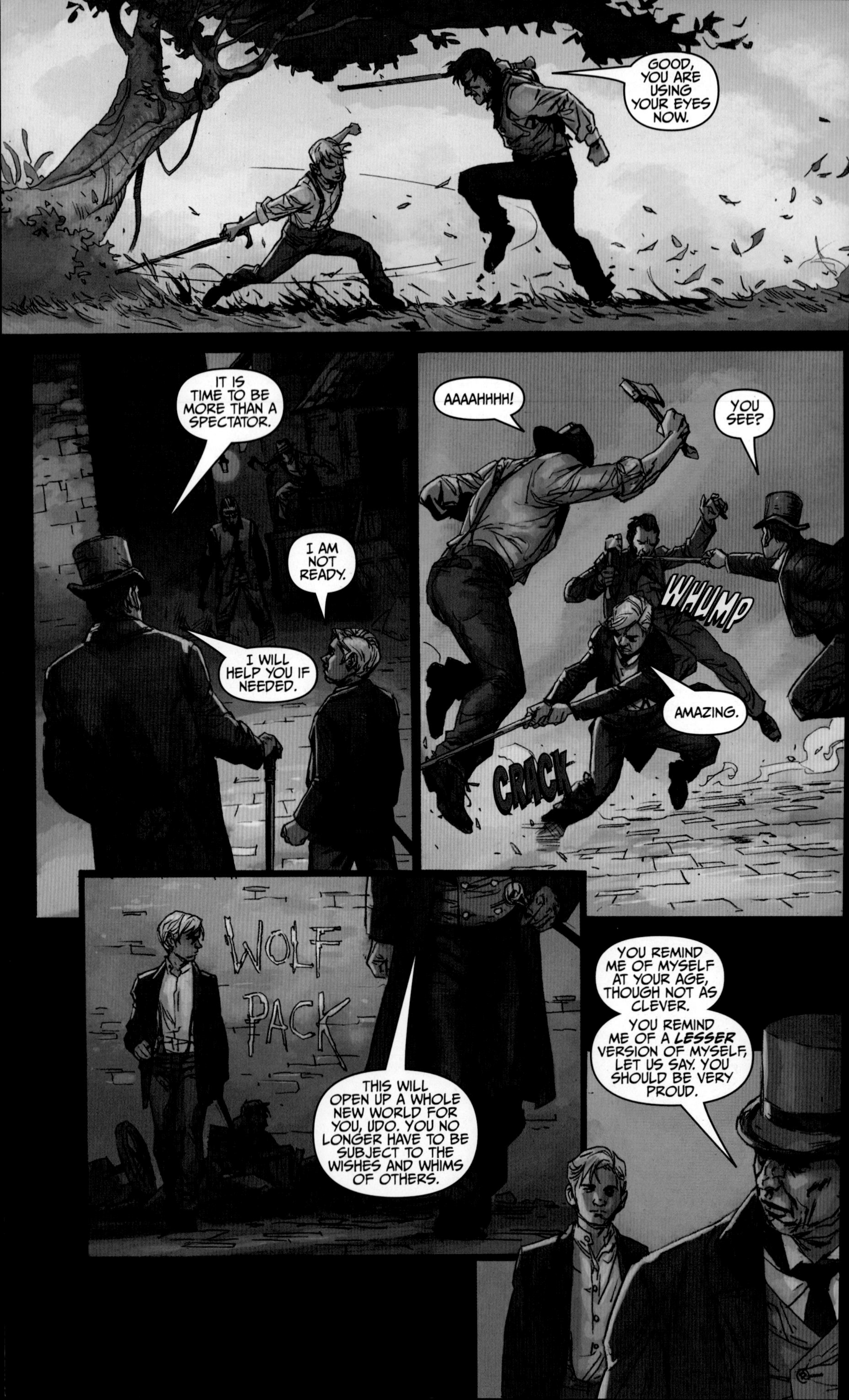
GOOD, YOU ARE USING YOUR EYES NOW.
IT IS TIME TO BE MORE THAN A SPECTATOR.
I AM NOT READY.
I WILL HELP YOU IF NEEDED.
AAAAHHHH!
YOU SEE?
WHUMP
AMAZING.
CRACK
WOLF PACK
THIS WILL OPEN UP A WHOLE NEW WORLD FOR YOU, UDO. YOU NO LONGER HAVE TO BE SUBJECT TO THE WISHES AND WHIMS OF OTHERS.
YOU REMIND ME OF MYSELF AT YOUR AGE, THOUGH NOT AS CLEVER.
YOU REMIND ME OF A LESSER VERSION OF MYSELF, LET US SAY. YOU SHOULD BE VERY PROUD.

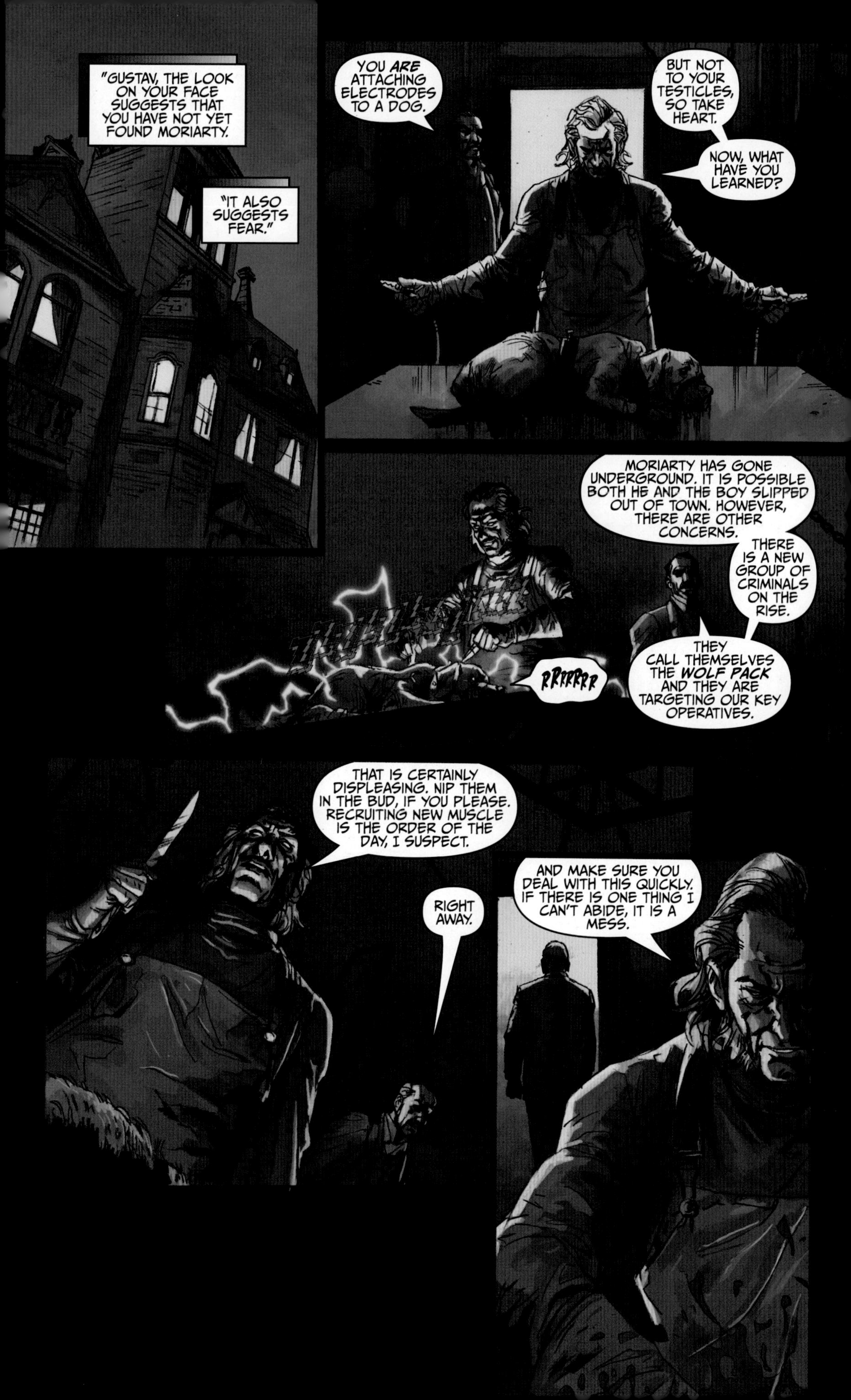
"GUSTAV, THE LOOK ON YOUR FACE SUGGESTS THAT YOU HAVE NOT YET FOUND MORIARTY.
"IT ALSO SUGGESTS FEAR."
YOU ARE ATTACHING ELECTRODES TO A DOG.
BUT NOT TO YOUR TESTICLES, SO TAKE HEART.
NOW, WHAT HAVE YOU LEARNED?
MORIARTY HAS GONE UNDERGROUND. IT IS POSSIBLE BOTH HE AND THE BOY SLIPPED OUT OF TOWN. HOWEVER, THERE ARE OTHER CONCERNS.
THERE IS A NEW GROUP OF CRIMINALS ON THE RISE.
RRRRRRR
THEY CALL THEMSELVES THE WOLF PACK AND THEY ARE TARGETING OUR KEY OPERATIVES.
THAT IS CERTAINLY DISPLEASING. NIP THEM IN THE BUD, IF YOU PLEASE. RECRUITING NEW MUSCLE IS THE ORDER OF THE DAY, I SUSPECT.
RIGHT AWAY.
AND MAKE SURE YOU DEAL WITH THIS QUICKLY. IF THERE IS ONE THING I CAN'T ABIDE, IT IS A MESS.

"YOU SEE, UDO. I HAVE SET EVENTS IN MOTION TO MY LIKING."

NOW I MUST TAKE ADVANTAGE OF THEM.

BUT HOW DID YOU KNOW WHAT THEY WOULD DO?

AS A SPECIES, PEOPLE ARE UTTERLY PREDICTABLE. PEOPLE WHOM YOU HAVE OBSERVED ARE EVEN MORE SO.

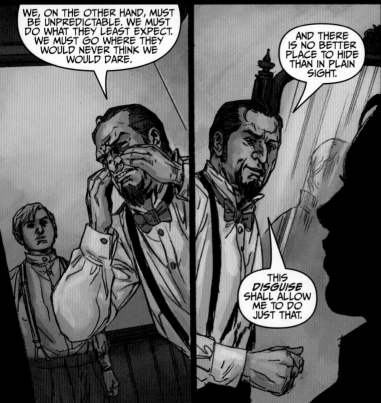

WE, ON THE OTHER HAND, MUST BE UNPREDICTABLE. WE MUST DO WHAT THEY LEAST EXPECT. WE MUST GO WHERE THEY WOULD NEVER THINK WE WOULD DARE.

AND THERE IS NO BETTER PLACE TO HIDE THAN IN PLAIN SIGHT.

THIS DISGUISE SHALL ALLOW ME TO DO JUST THAT.

"AND SO, UNRECOGNIZABLE TO MY ENEMY, I SHALL MANEUVER CLOSE ENOUGH FOR THE KILL."

YOU'LL DO.

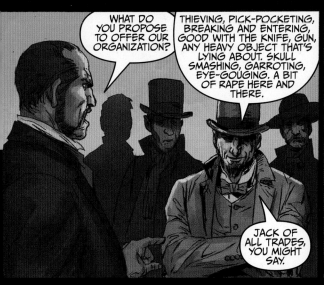

WHAT DO YOU PROPOSE TO OFFER OUR ORGANIZATION?

THIEVING, PICK-POCKETING, BREAKING AND ENTERING, GOOD WITH THE KNIFE, GUN, ANY HEAVY OBJECT THAT'S LYING ABOUT. SKULL SMASHING, GARROTING, EYE-GOUGING. A BIT OF RAPE HERE AND THERE.

JACK OF ALL TRADES, YOU MIGHT SAY.

AND MASTER OF NONE, I AM SURE. YOU LOOK TOO UNIMPOSING, IF I MAY SAY SO. I IMAGINE YOU ARE NOT AS SKILLED IN A FIGHT AS YOU SAY.

YOU KNOW WHAT MY DEAR, LATE MOTHER ALWAYS TOLD ME?

IMAGINATION GETS YOU INTO TROUBLE.

VERY WISE, YOUR MOTHER. I THINK, PERHAPS, YOU WILL DO AFTER ALL. BUT DON'T THINK TO STRIKE ME AGAIN.

MERELY MAKING A POINT, SIR.

FROM NOW ON, YOU HAVE MY COMPLETE LOYALTY.

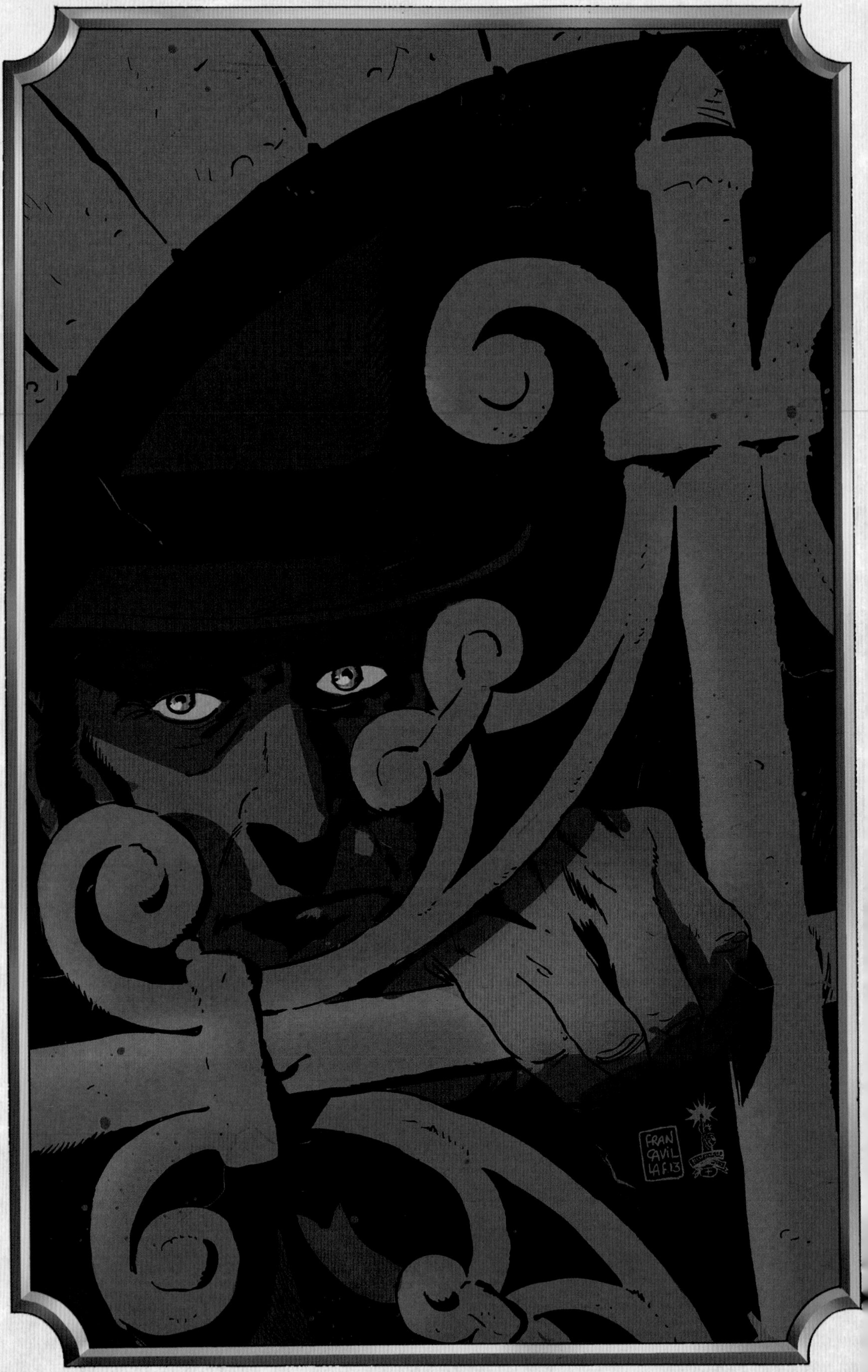
FRAN
CAVIL
LA F.13

Issue three cover by
Francesco Francavilla

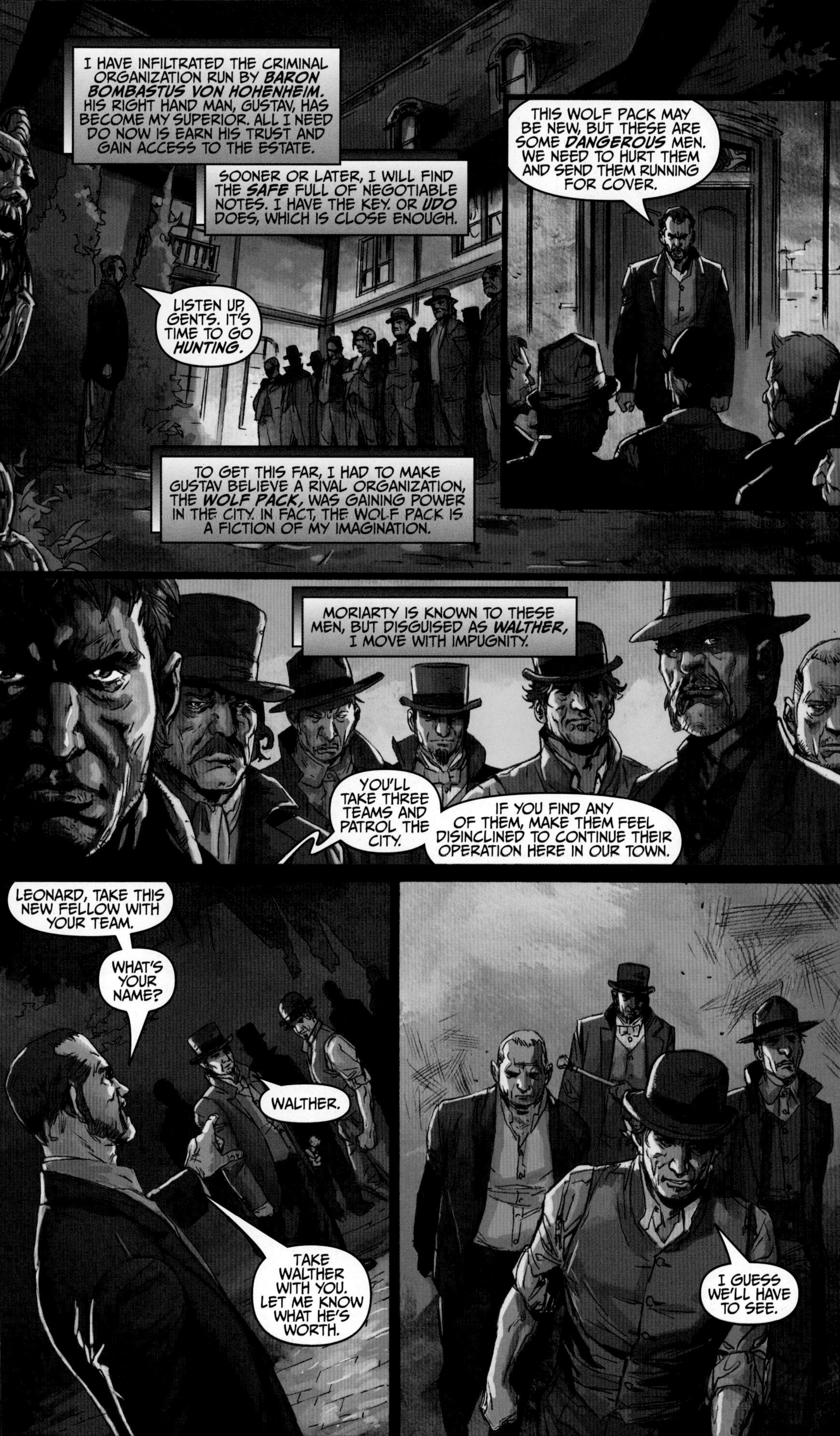
I HAVE INFILTRATED THE CRIMINAL ORGANIZATION RUN BY BARON BOMBASTUS VON HOHENHEIM. HIS RIGHT HAND MAN, GUSTAV, HAS BECOME MY SUPERIOR. ALL I NEED DO NOW IS EARN HIS TRUST AND GAIN ACCESS TO THE ESTATE.
SOONER OR LATER, I WILL FIND THE SAFE FULL OF NEGOTIABLE NOTES. I HAVE THE KEY. OR UDO DOES, WHICH IS CLOSE ENOUGH.
LISTEN UP, GENTS. IT'S TIME TO GO HUNTING.
TO GET THIS FAR, I HAD TO MAKE GUSTAV BELIEVE A RIVAL ORGANIZATION, THE WOLF PACK, WAS GAINING POWER IN THE CITY. IN FACT, THE WOLF PACK IS A FICTION OF MY IMAGINATION.
THIS WOLF PACK MAY BE NEW, BUT THESE ARE SOME DANGEROUS MEN. WE NEED TO HURT THEM AND SEND THEM RUNNING FOR COVER.
MORIARTY IS KNOWN TO THESE MEN, BUT DISGUISED AS WALTHER, I MOVE WITH IMPUGNITY.
YOU'LL TAKE THREE TEAMS AND PATROL THE CITY.
IF YOU FIND ANY OF THEM, MAKE THEM FEEL DISINCLINED TO CONTINUE THEIR OPERATION HERE IN OUR TOWN.
LEONARD, TAKE THIS NEW FELLOW WITH YOUR TEAM.
WHAT'S YOUR NAME?
WALTHER.
TAKE WALTHER WITH YOU. LET ME KNOW WHAT HE'S WORTH.
I GUESS WE'LL HAVE TO SEE.

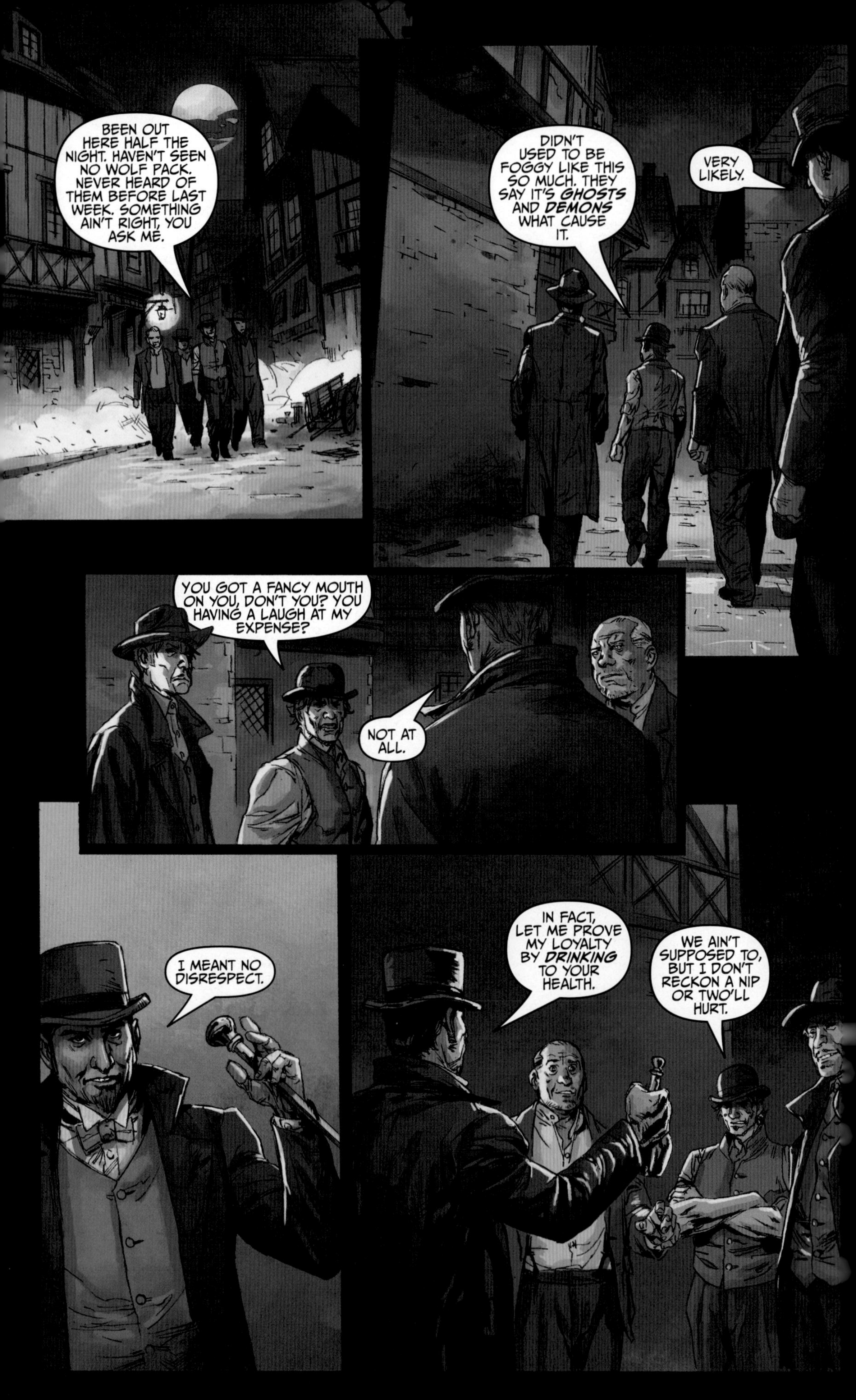
BEEN OUT HERE HALF THE NIGHT. HAVEN'T SEEN NO WOLF PACK. NEVER HEARD OF THEM BEFORE LAST WEEK. SOMETHING AIN'T RIGHT, YOU ASK ME.
DIDN'T USED TO BE FOGGY LIKE THIS SO MUCH. THEY SAY IT'S GHOSTS AND DEMONS WHAT CAUSE IT.
VERY LIKELY.
YOU GOT A FANCY MOUTH ON YOU, DON'T YOU? YOU HAVING A LAUGH AT MY EXPENSE?
NOT AT ALL.
I MEANT NO DISRESPECT.
IN FACT, LET ME PROVE MY LOYALTY BY DRINKING TO YOUR HEALTH.
WE AIN'T SUPPOSED TO, BUT I DON'T RECKON A NIP OR TWO'LL HURT.

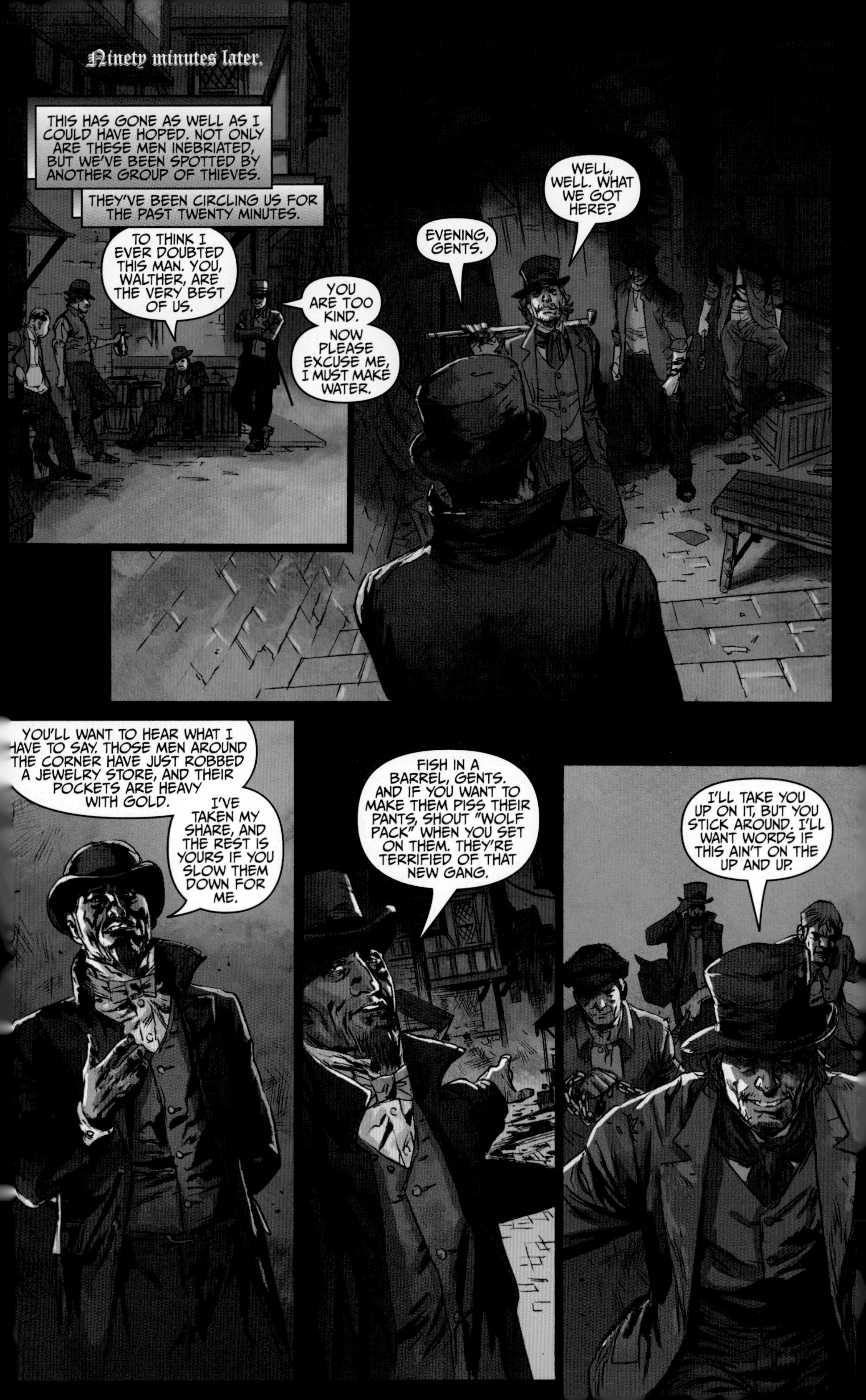
Ninety minutes later.
THIS HAS GONE AS WELL AS I COULD HAVE HOPED. NOT ONLY ARE THESE MEN INEBRIATED, BUT WE'VE BEEN SPOTTED BY ANOTHER GROUP OF THIEVES.
THEY'VE BEEN CIRCLING US FOR THE PAST TWENTY MINUTES.
TO THINK I EVER DOUBTED THIS MAN. YOU, WALTHER, ARE THE VERY BEST OF US.
YOU ARE TOO KIND.
NOW PLEASE EXCUSE ME, I MUST MAKE WATER.
EVENING, GENTS.
WELL, WELL. WHAT WE GOT HERE?
YOU'LL WANT TO HEAR WHAT I HAVE TO SAY. THOSE MEN AROUND THE CORNER HAVE JUST ROBBED A JEWELRY STORE, AND THEIR POCKETS ARE HEAVY WITH GOLD.
I'VE TAKEN MY SHARE, AND THE REST IS YOURS IF YOU SLOW THEM DOWN FOR ME.
FISH IN A BARREL, GENTS. AND IF YOU WANT TO MAKE THEM PISS THEIR PANTS, SHOUT "WOLF PACK" WHEN YOU SET ON THEM. THEY'RE TERRIFIED OF THAT NEW GANG.
I'LL TAKE YOU UP ON IT, BUT YOU STICK AROUND. I'LL WANT WORDS IF THIS AIN'T ON THE UP AND UP.

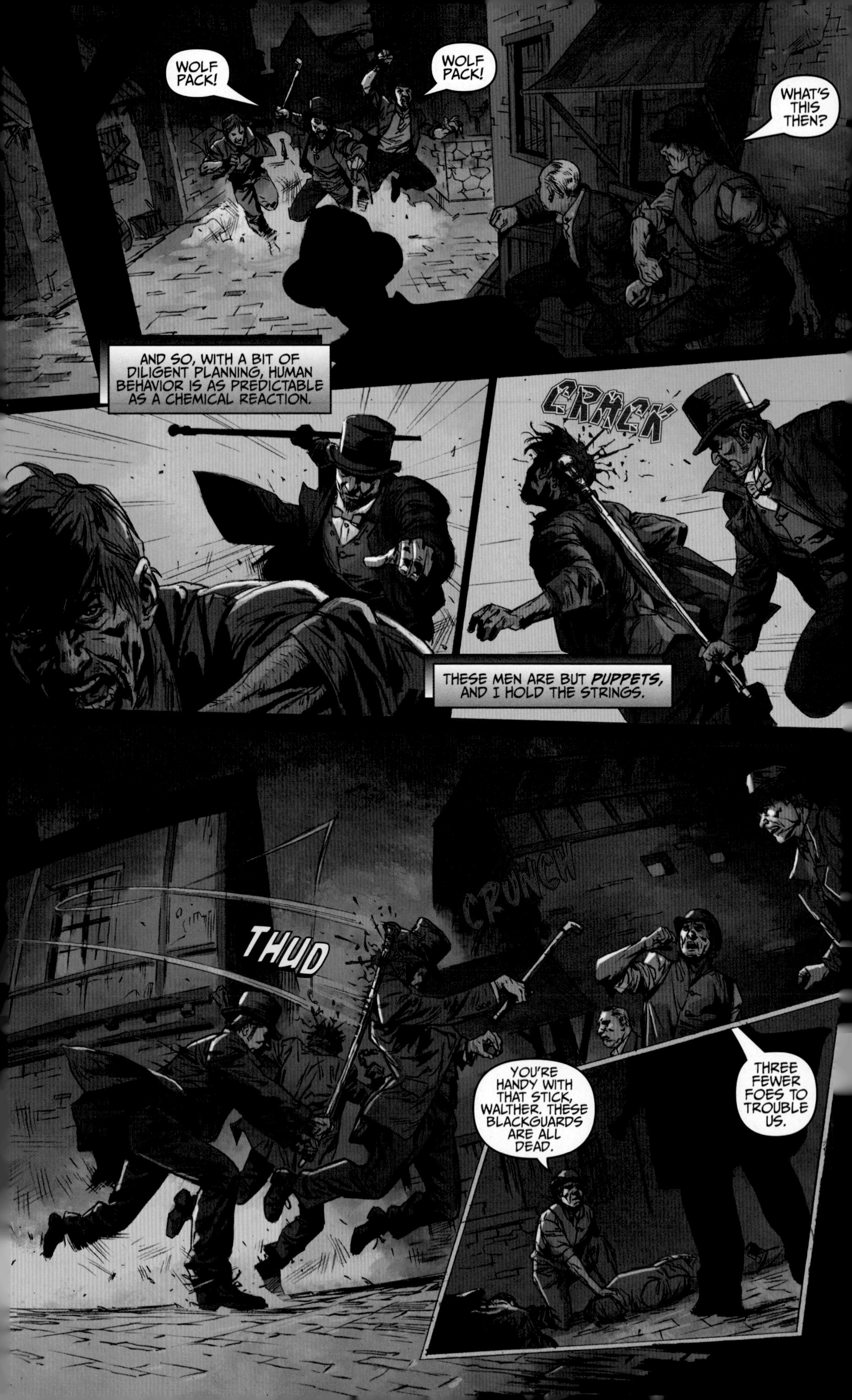
WOLF PACK!
WOLF PACK!
WHAT'S THIS THEN?
AND SO, WITH A BIT OF DILIGENT PLANNING, HUMAN BEHAVIOR IS AS PREDICTABLE AS A CHEMICAL REACTION.
CRACK
THESE MEN ARE BUT *PUPPETS,* AND I HOLD THE STRINGS.
THUD
CRUNCH
YOU'RE HANDY WITH THAT STICK, WALTHER. THESE BLACKGUARDS ARE ALL DEAD.
THREE FEWER FOES TO TROUBLE US.

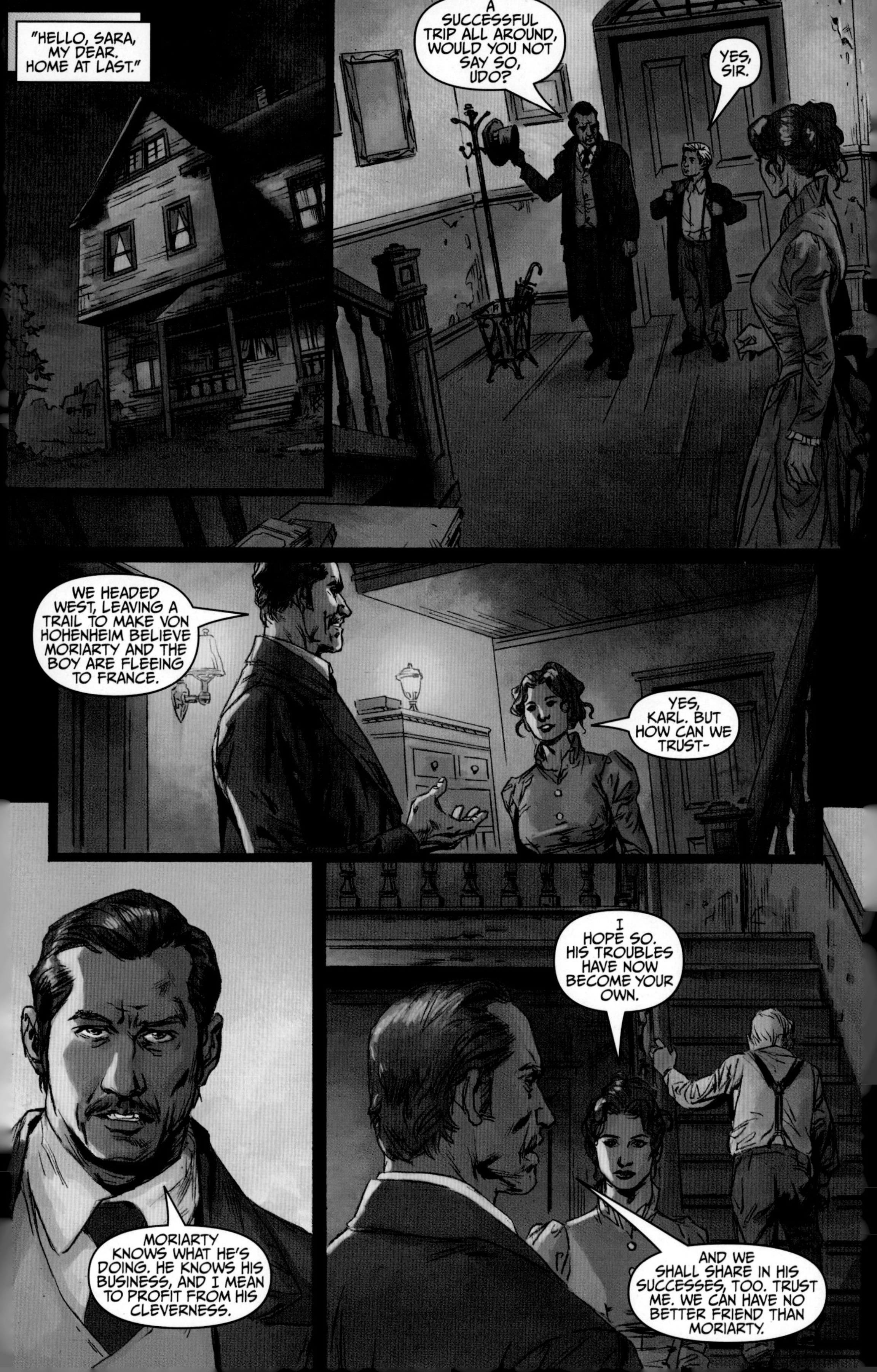
"HELLO, SARA, MY DEAR. HOME AT LAST."
A SUCCESSFUL TRIP ALL AROUND, WOULD YOU NOT SAY SO, UDO?
YES, SIR.
WE HEADED WEST, LEAVING A TRAIL TO MAKE VON HOHENHEIM BELIEVE MORIARTY AND THE BOY ARE FLEEING TO FRANCE.
YES, KARL. BUT HOW CAN WE TRUST-
MORIARTY KNOWS WHAT HE'S DOING. HE KNOWS HIS BUSINESS, AND I MEAN TO PROFIT FROM HIS CLEVERNESS.
I HOPE SO. HIS TROUBLES HAVE NOW BECOME YOUR OWN.
AND WE SHALL SHARE IN HIS SUCCESSES, TOO. TRUST ME. WE CAN HAVE NO BETTER FRIEND THAN MORIARTY.

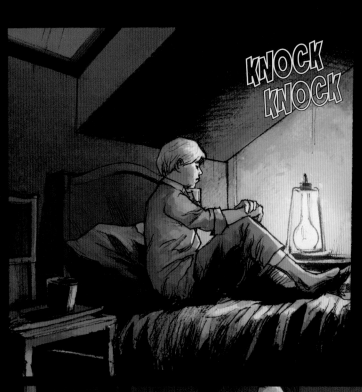

KNOCK KNOCK

I HOPE I'M NOT DISTURBING YOU, UDO.

IT'S FINE.

I DON'T KNOW WHAT TO MAKE OF THIS. A MAN COMES INTO OUR HOUSE, THREATENS OUR BABY, AND NOW KARL OBEYS HIS EVERY WHIM.

I AM JUST THE WIFE. I CANNOT TELL HIM WHAT TO DO, BUT I DON'T UNDERSTAND IT.

YOU SEEM LIKE SUCH A SWEET AND CLEVER BOY. DO YOU *TRUST* THIS MORIARTY?

I TRUST HIM TO DO WHAT IS IN HIS BEST INTEREST.

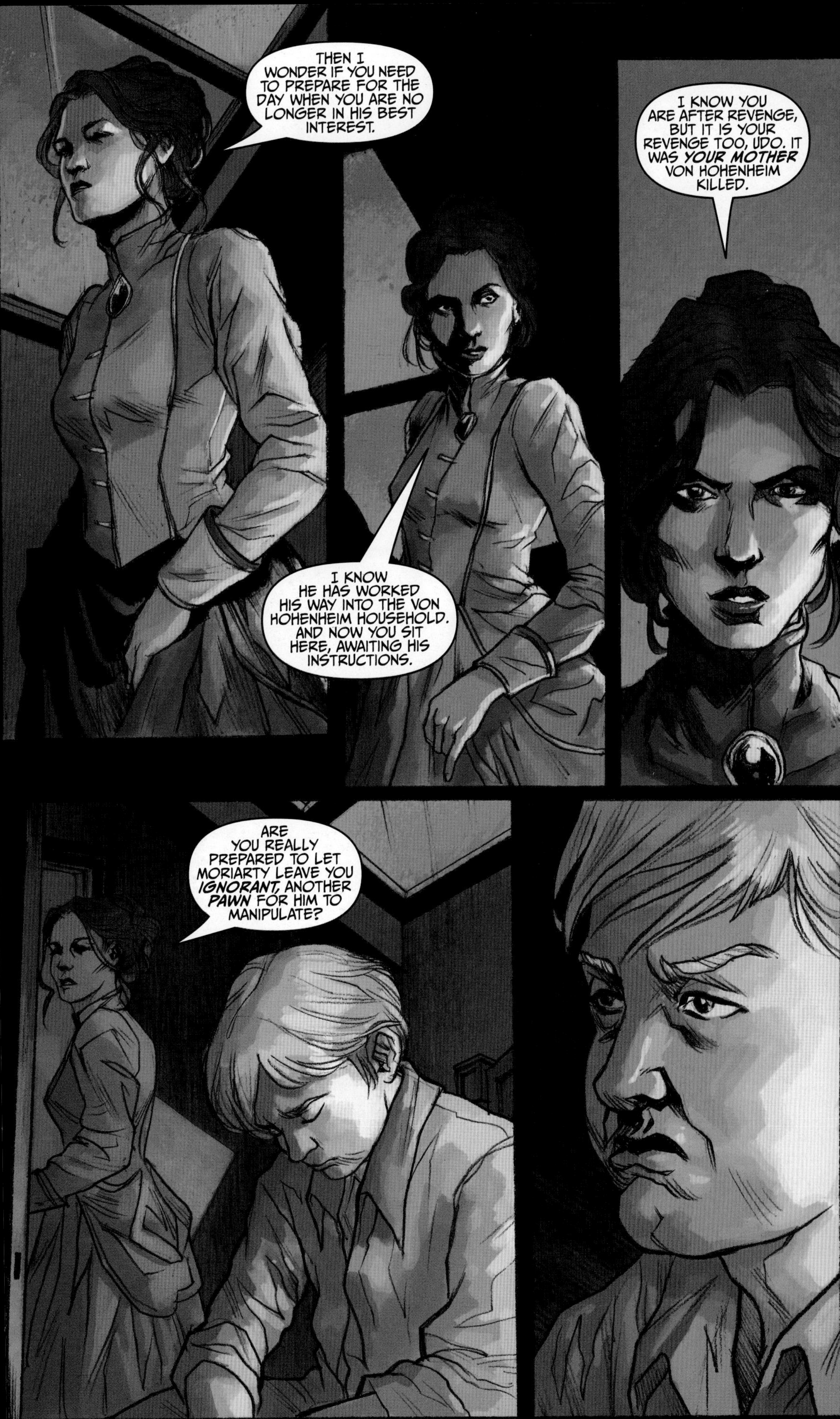
THEN I WONDER IF YOU NEED TO PREPARE FOR THE DAY WHEN YOU ARE NO LONGER IN HIS BEST INTEREST.
I KNOW HE HAS WORKED HIS WAY INTO THE VON HOHENHEIM HOUSEHOLD. AND NOW YOU SIT HERE, AWAITING HIS INSTRUCTIONS.
I KNOW YOU ARE AFTER REVENGE, BUT IT IS YOUR REVENGE TOO, UDO. IT WAS ***YOUR MOTHER*** VON HOHENHEIM KILLED.
ARE YOU REALLY PREPARED TO LET MORIARTY LEAVE YOU *IGNORANT,* ANOTHER ***PAWN*** FOR HIM TO MANIPULATE?

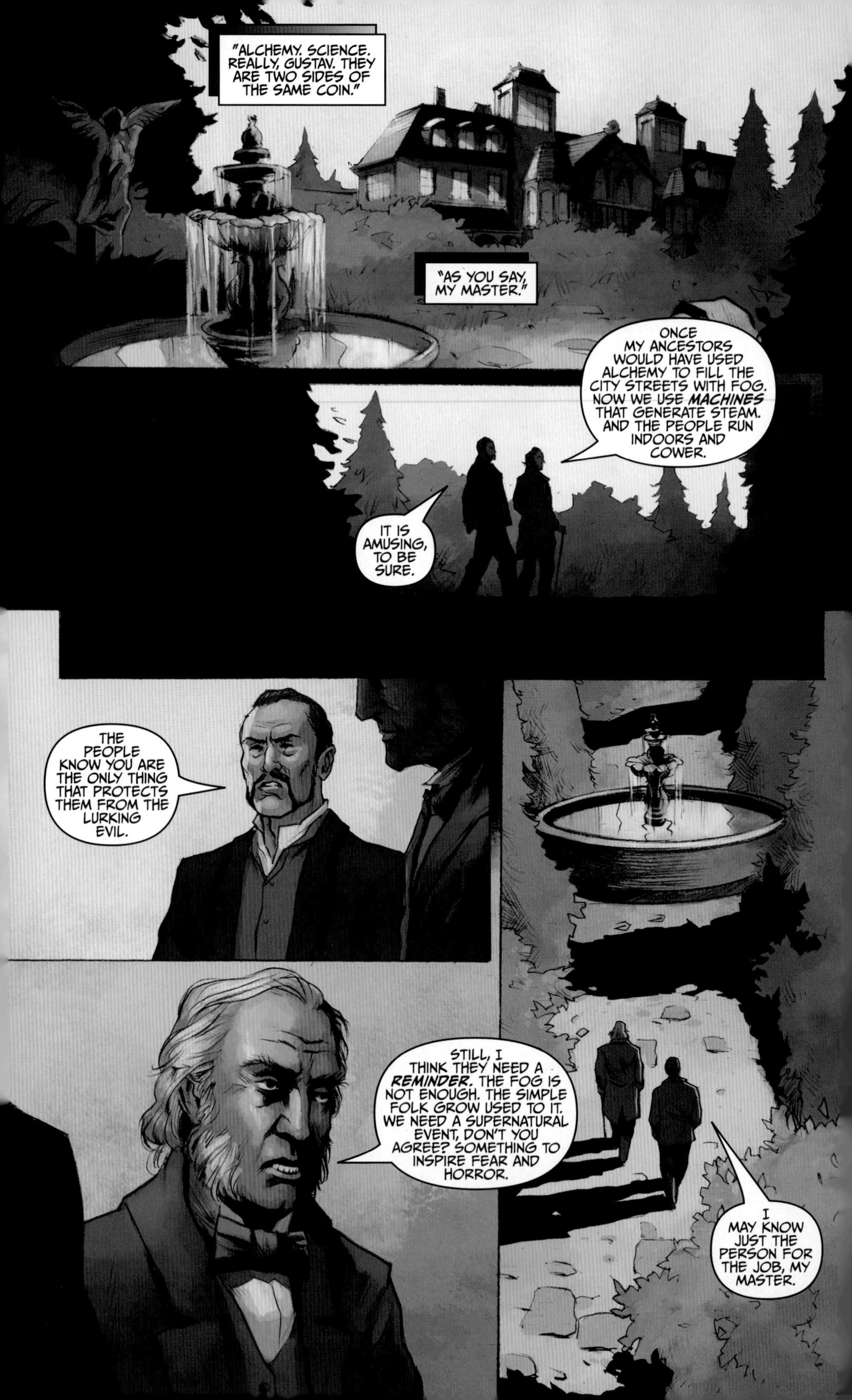
"ALCHEMY. SCIENCE. REALLY, GUSTAV. THEY ARE TWO SIDES OF THE SAME COIN."
"AS YOU SAY, MY MASTER."
ONCE MY ANCESTORS WOULD HAVE USED ALCHEMY TO FILL THE CITY STREETS WITH FOG. NOW WE USE MACHINES THAT GENERATE STEAM. AND THE PEOPLE RUN INDOORS AND COWER.
IT IS AMUSING, TO BE SURE.
THE PEOPLE KNOW YOU ARE THE ONLY THING THAT PROTECTS THEM FROM THE LURKING EVIL.
STILL, I THINK THEY NEED A REMINDER. THE FOG IS NOT ENOUGH. THE SIMPLE FOLK GROW USED TO IT. WE NEED A SUPERNATURAL EVENT, DON'T YOU AGREE? SOMETHING TO INSPIRE FEAR AND HORROR.
I MAY KNOW JUST THE PERSON FOR THE JOB, MY MASTER.

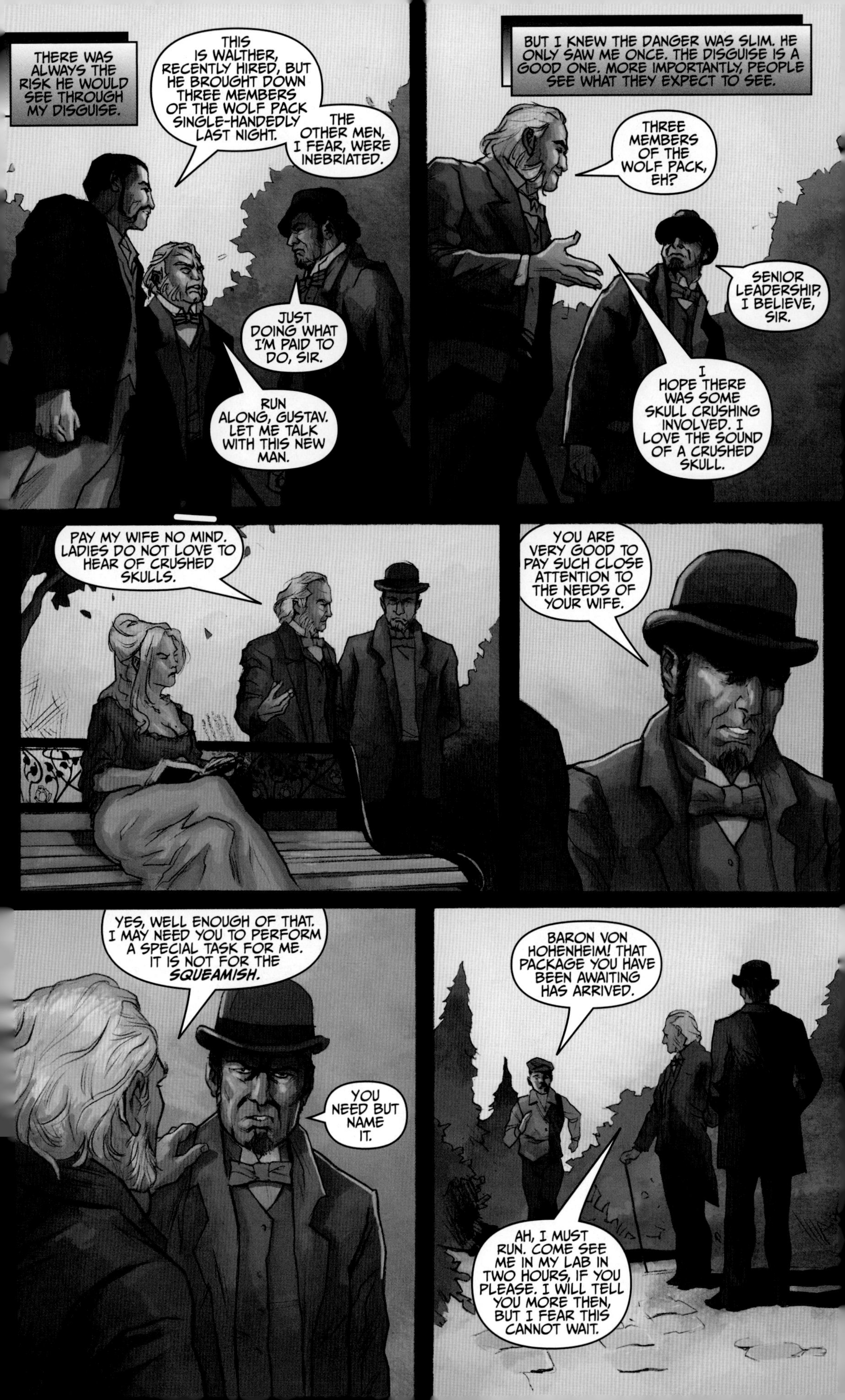
THERE WAS ALWAYS THE RISK HE WOULD SEE THROUGH MY DISGUISE.
THIS IS WALTHER, RECENTLY HIRED, BUT HE BROUGHT DOWN THREE MEMBERS OF THE WOLF PACK SINGLE-HANDEDLY LAST NIGHT.
THE OTHER MEN, I FEAR, WERE INEBRIATED.
JUST DOING WHAT I'M PAID TO DO, SIR.
RUN ALONG, GUSTAV. LET ME TALK WITH THIS NEW MAN.
BUT I KNEW THE DANGER WAS SLIM. HE ONLY SAW ME ONCE. THE DISGUISE IS A GOOD ONE. MORE IMPORTANTLY, PEOPLE SEE WHAT THEY EXPECT TO SEE.
THREE MEMBERS OF THE WOLF PACK, EH?
SENIOR LEADERSHIP, I BELIEVE, SIR.
I HOPE THERE WAS SOME SKULL CRUSHING INVOLVED. I LOVE THE SOUND OF A CRUSHED SKULL.
PAY MY WIFE NO MIND. LADIES DO NOT LOVE TO HEAR OF CRUSHED SKULLS.
YOU ARE VERY GOOD TO PAY SUCH CLOSE ATTENTION TO THE NEEDS OF YOUR WIFE.
YES, WELL ENOUGH OF THAT. I MAY NEED YOU TO PERFORM A SPECIAL TASK FOR ME. IT IS NOT FOR THE *SQUEAMISH.*
YOU NEED BUT NAME IT.
BARON VON HOHENHEIM! THAT PACKAGE YOU HAVE BEEN AWAITING HAS ARRIVED.
AH, I MUST RUN. COME SEE ME IN MY LAB IN TWO HOURS, IF YOU PLEASE. I WILL TELL YOU MORE THEN, BUT I FEAR THIS CANNOT WAIT.

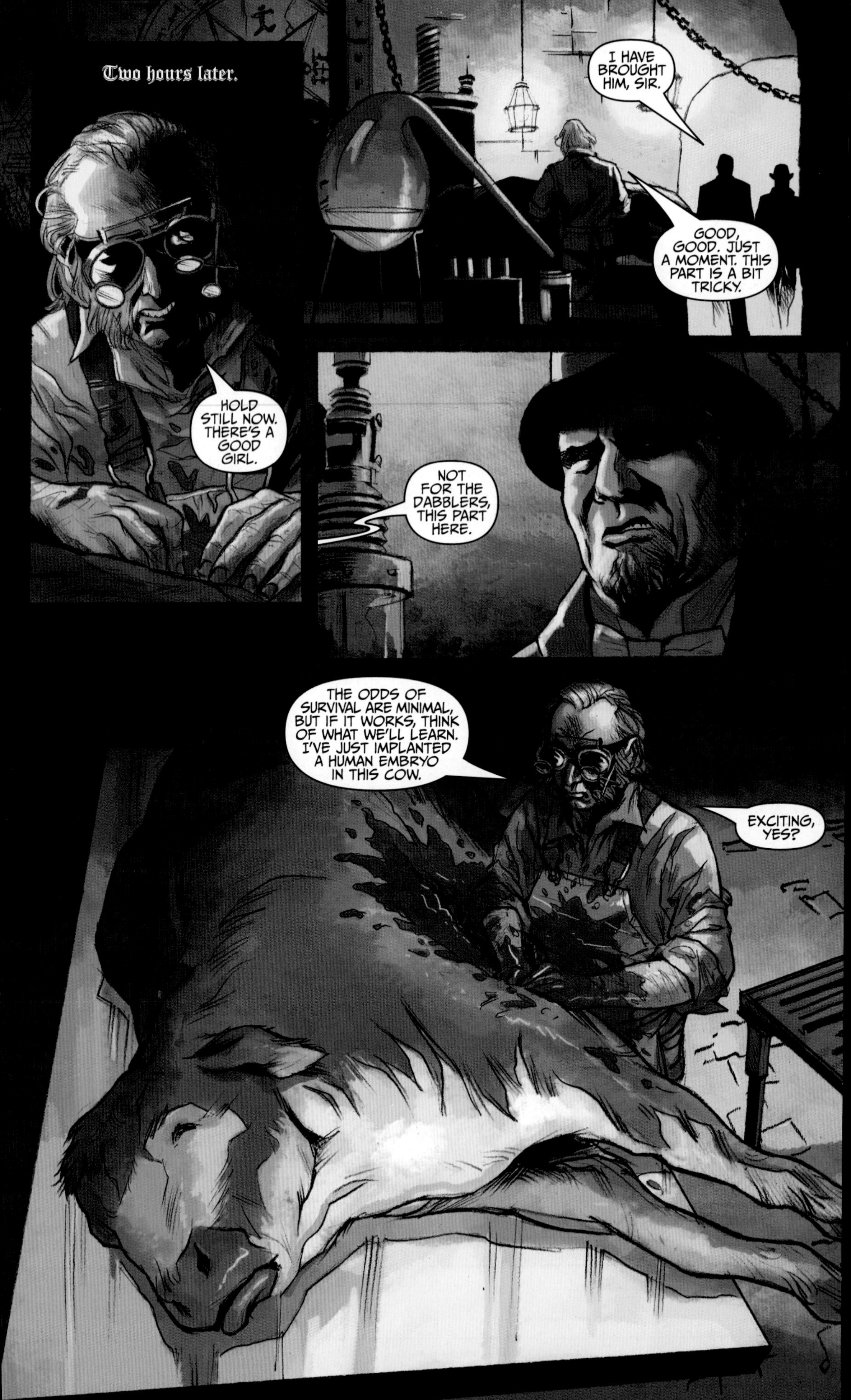
Two hours later.
HOLD STILL NOW. THERE'S A GOOD GIRL.
I HAVE BROUGHT HIM, SIR.
GOOD, GOOD. JUST A MOMENT. THIS PART IS A BIT TRICKY.
NOT FOR THE DABBLERS, THIS PART HERE.
THE ODDS OF SURVIVAL ARE MINIMAL, BUT IF IT WORKS, THINK OF WHAT WE'LL LEARN. I'VE JUST IMPLANTED A HUMAN EMBRYO IN THIS COW.
EXCITING, YES?

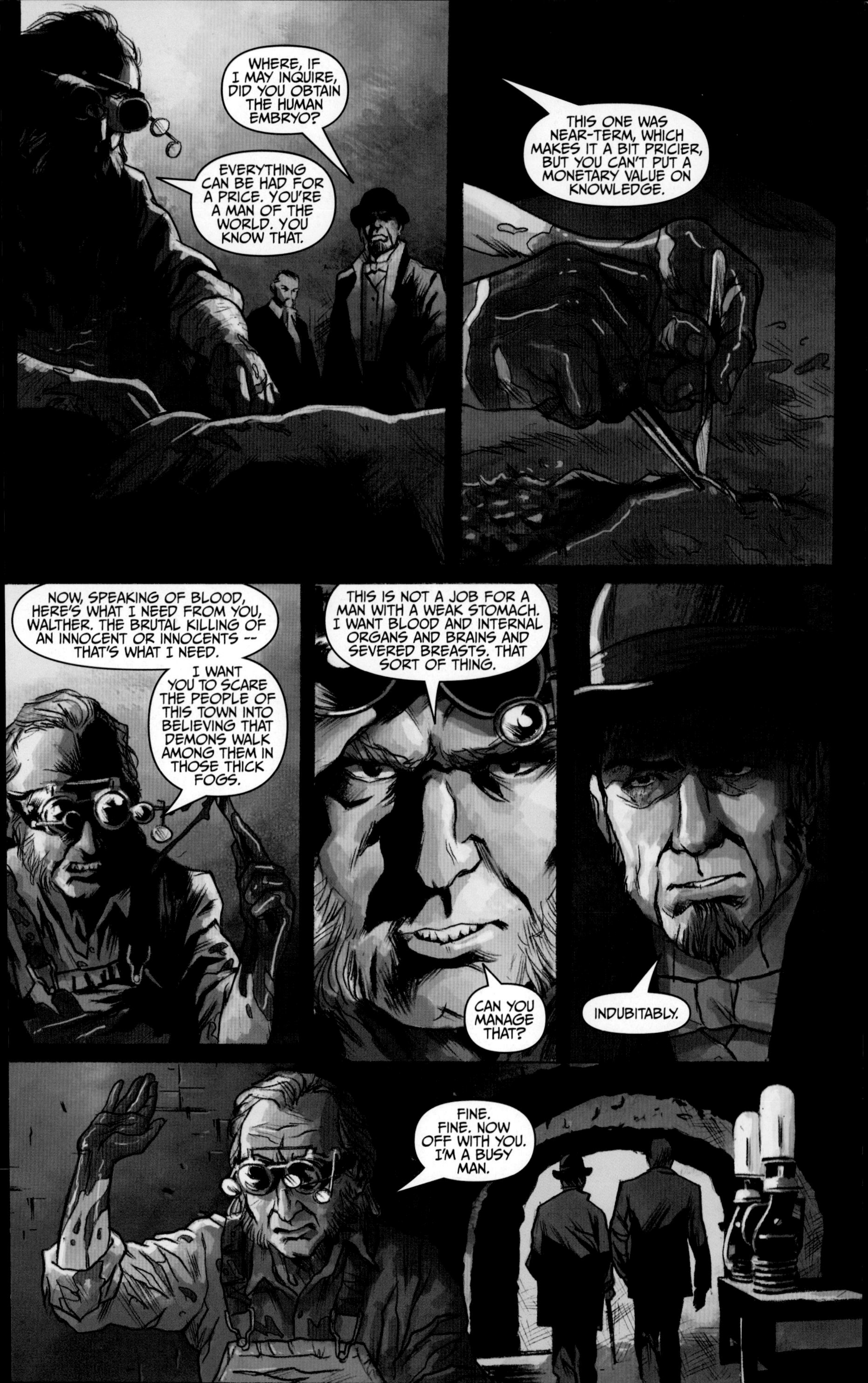
WHERE, IF I MAY INQUIRE, DID YOU OBTAIN THE HUMAN EMBRYO?
EVERYTHING CAN BE HAD FOR A PRICE. YOU'RE A MAN OF THE WORLD. YOU KNOW THAT.
THIS ONE WAS NEAR-TERM, WHICH MAKES IT A BIT PRICIER, BUT YOU CAN'T PUT A MONETARY VALUE ON KNOWLEDGE.
NOW, SPEAKING OF BLOOD, HERE'S WHAT I NEED FROM YOU, WALTHER. THE BRUTAL KILLING OF AN INNOCENT OR INNOCENTS -- THAT'S WHAT I NEED.
I WANT YOU TO SCARE THE PEOPLE OF THIS TOWN INTO BELIEVING THAT DEMONS WALK AMONG THEM IN THOSE THICK FOGS.
THIS IS NOT A JOB FOR A MAN WITH A WEAK STOMACH. I WANT BLOOD AND INTERNAL ORGANS AND BRAINS AND SEVERED BREASTS. THAT SORT OF THING.
CAN YOU MANAGE THAT?
INDUBITABLY.
FINE. FINE. NOW OFF WITH YOU. I'M A BUSY MAN.

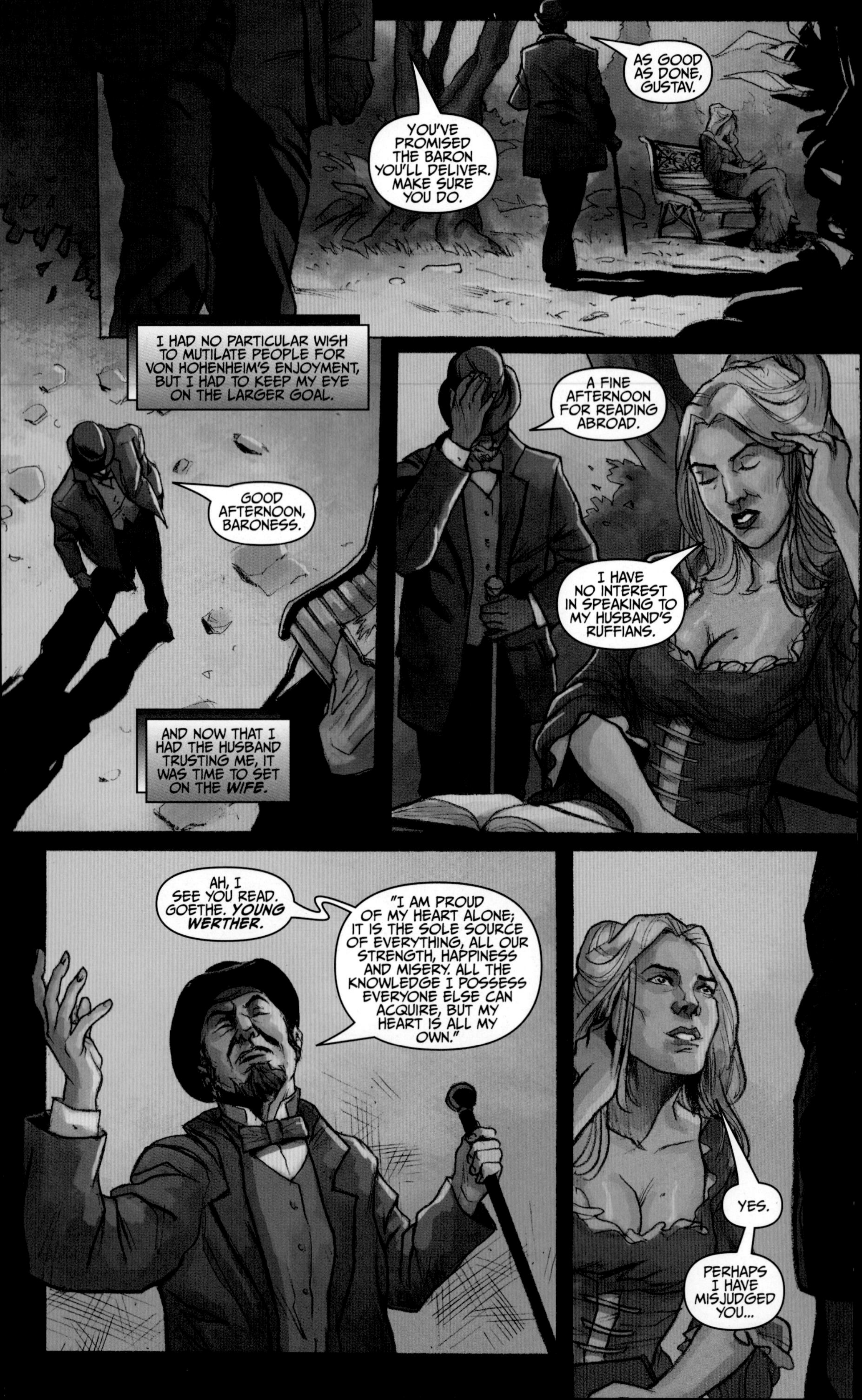
AS GOOD AS DONE, GUSTAV.
YOU'VE PROMISED THE BARON YOU'LL DELIVER. MAKE SURE YOU DO.
I HAD NO PARTICULAR WISH TO MUTILATE PEOPLE FOR VON HOHENHEIM'S ENJOYMENT, BUT I HAD TO KEEP MY EYE ON THE LARGER GOAL.
GOOD AFTERNOON, BARONESS.
AND NOW THAT I HAD THE HUSBAND TRUSTING ME, IT WAS TIME TO SET ON THE *WIFE*.
A FINE AFTERNOON FOR READING ABROAD.
I HAVE NO INTEREST IN SPEAKING TO MY HUSBAND'S RUFFIANS.
AH, I SEE YOU READ. GOETHE. ***YOUNG WERTHER.***
"I AM PROUD OF MY HEART ALONE; IT IS THE SOLE SOURCE OF EVERYTHING, ALL OUR STRENGTH, HAPPINESS AND MISERY. ALL THE KNOWLEDGE I POSSESS EVERYONE ELSE CAN ACQUIRE, BUT MY HEART IS ALL MY OWN."
YES.
PERHAPS I HAVE MISJUDGED YOU...

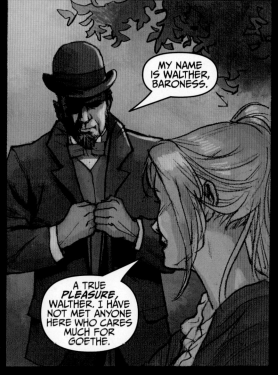

MY NAME IS WALTHER, BARONESS.

A TRUE *PLEASURE*, WALTHER. I HAVE NOT MET ANYONE HERE WHO CARES MUCH FOR GOETHE.

A SHAME, MADAM. HIS WISDOM I FEEL ECHOES THE SENTIMENTS OF MY HEART, ONLY ARTICULATED MORE BEAUTIFULLY THAN COULD A MERE MORTAL.

I HAVE OFTEN FELT THE SAME.

COME, SIT. I MUST HEAR WHAT ELSE YOU LIKE TO READ.

I SHOULD LIKE NOTHING BETTER, BUT I FEAR MY DUTIES CALL ME AWAY.

PERHAPS ANOTHER TIME.

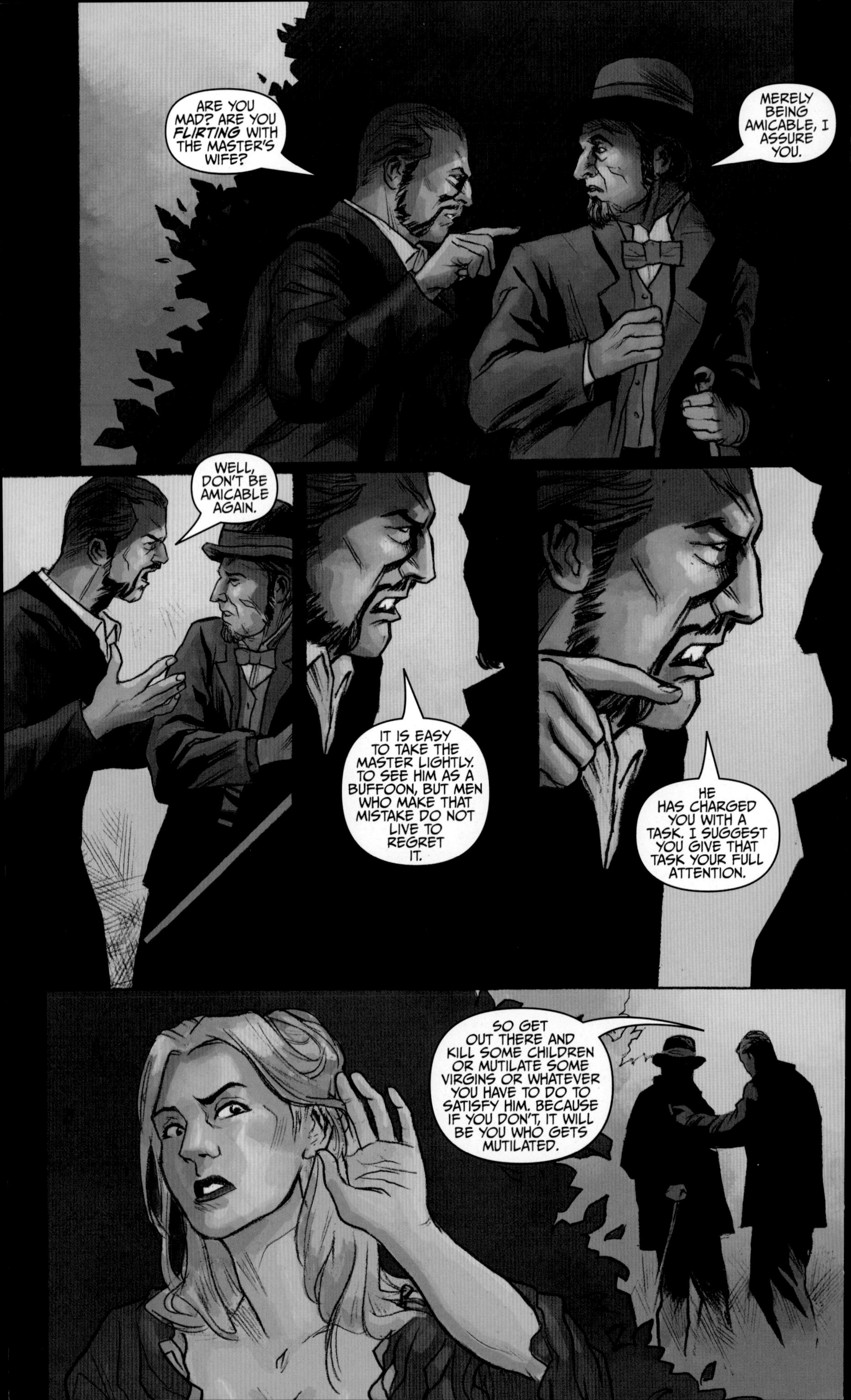
ARE YOU MAD? ARE YOU *FLIRTING* WITH THE MASTER'S WIFE?
MERELY BEING AMICABLE, I ASSURE YOU.
WELL, DON'T BE AMICABLE AGAIN.
IT IS EASY TO TAKE THE MASTER LIGHTLY. TO SEE HIM AS A BUFFOON, BUT MEN WHO MAKE THAT MISTAKE DO NOT LIVE TO REGRET IT.
HE HAS CHARGED YOU WITH A TASK. I SUGGEST YOU GIVE THAT TASK YOUR FULL ATTENTION.
SO GET OUT THERE AND KILL SOME CHILDREN OR MUTILATE SOME VIRGINS OR WHATEVER YOU HAVE TO DO TO SATISFY HIM. BECAUSE IF YOU DON'T, IT WILL BE YOU WHO GETS MUTILATED.

THEY PUT TOGETHER A NICE SPREAD FOR THE HELP. I'LL SAY THAT.

WILL YOU NOW?

Two hours later.

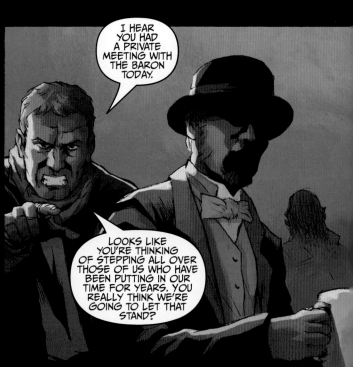

I HEAR YOU HAD A PRIVATE MEETING WITH THE BARON TODAY.

LOOKS LIKE YOU'RE THINKING OF STEPPING ALL OVER THOSE OF US WHO HAVE BEEN PUTTING IN OUR TIME FOR YEARS. YOU REALLY THINK WE'RE GOING TO LET THAT STAND?

CLANG

CRACK

ANYONE ELSE HAVE A COMPLAINT ABOUT THE TRAJECTORY OF MY CAREER ADVANCEMENT?

NOT ME.

NO.

NO PROBLEMS HERE.

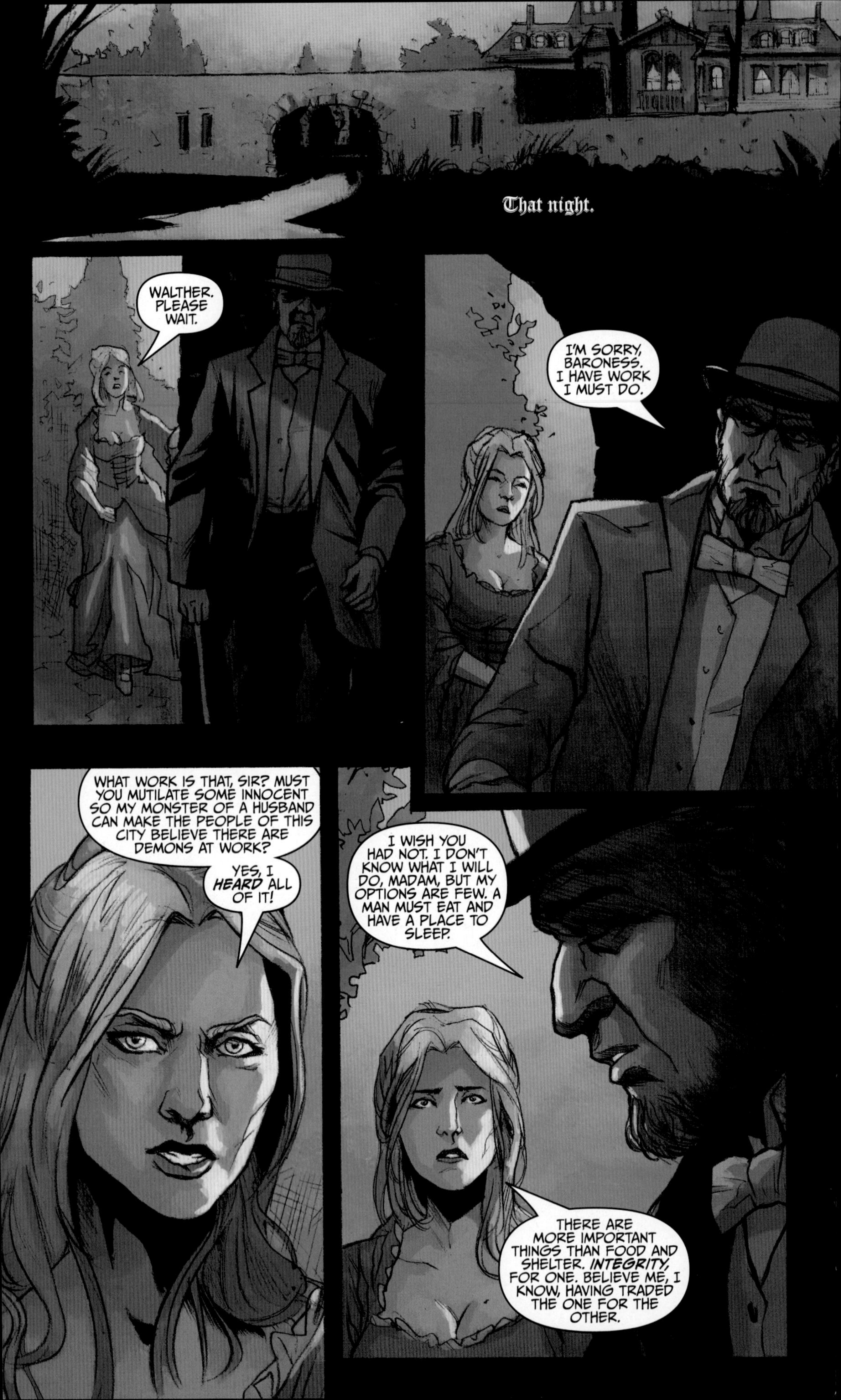
That night.
WALTHER. PLEASE WAIT.
I'M SORRY, BARONESS. I HAVE WORK I MUST DO.
WHAT WORK IS THAT, SIR? MUST YOU MUTILATE SOME INNOCENT SO MY MONSTER OF A HUSBAND CAN MAKE THE PEOPLE OF THIS CITY BELIEVE THERE ARE DEMONS AT WORK?
YES, I *HEARD* ALL OF IT!
I WISH YOU HAD NOT. I DON'T KNOW WHAT I WILL DO, MADAM, BUT MY OPTIONS ARE FEW. A MAN MUST EAT AND HAVE A PLACE TO SLEEP.
THERE ARE MORE IMPORTANT THINGS THAN FOOD AND SHELTER. *INTEGRITY,* FOR ONE. BELIEVE ME, I KNOW, HAVING TRADED THE ONE FOR THE OTHER.

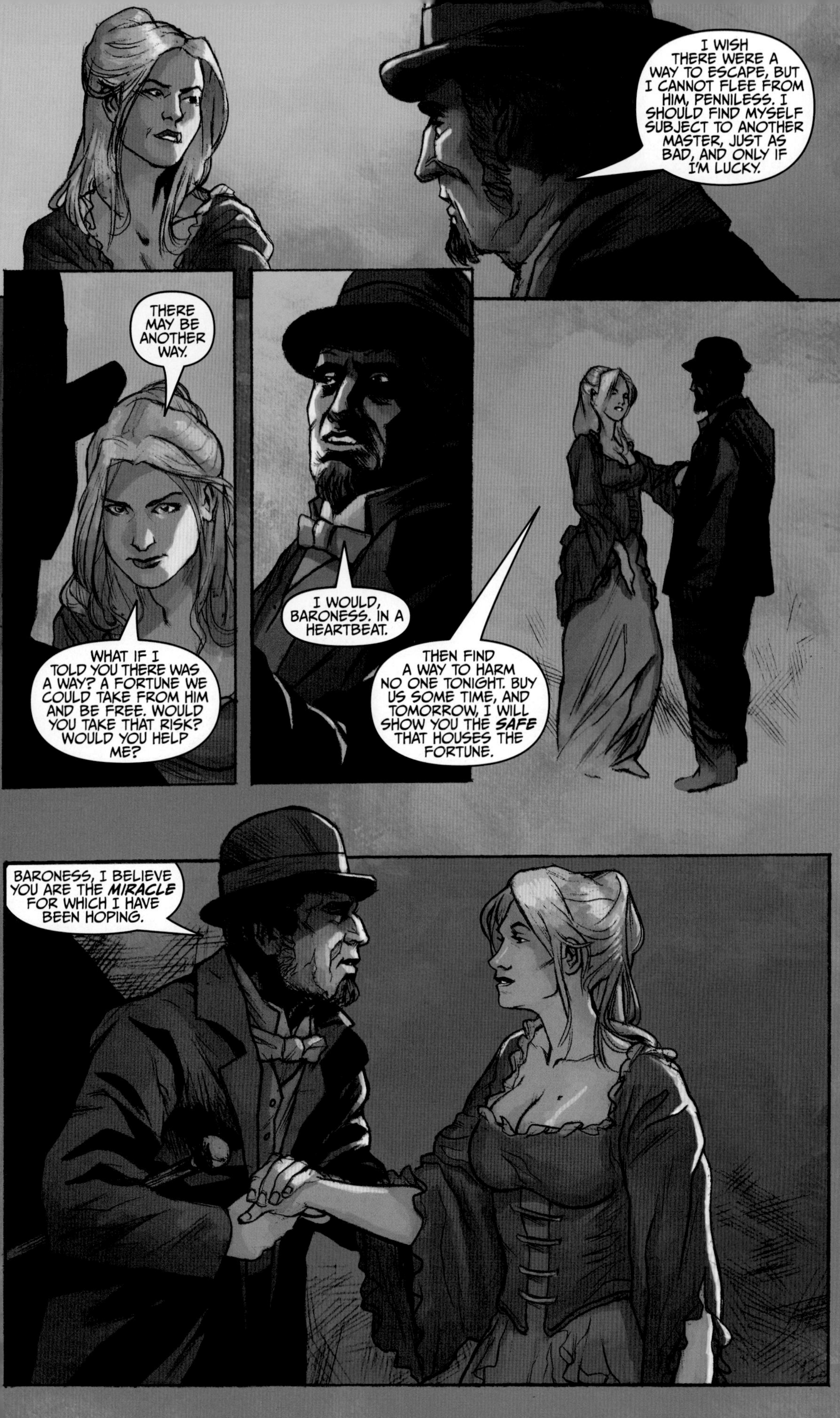
I WISH THERE WERE A WAY TO ESCAPE, BUT I CANNOT FLEE FROM HIM, PENNILESS. I SHOULD FIND MYSELF SUBJECT TO ANOTHER MASTER, JUST AS BAD, AND ONLY IF I'M LUCKY.
THERE MAY BE ANOTHER WAY.
WHAT IF I TOLD YOU THERE WAS A WAY? A FORTUNE WE COULD TAKE FROM HIM AND BE FREE. WOULD YOU TAKE THAT RISK? WOULD YOU HELP ME?
I WOULD, BARONESS. IN A HEARTBEAT.
THEN FIND A WAY TO HARM NO ONE TONIGHT. BUY US SOME TIME, AND TOMORROW, I WILL SHOW YOU THE SAFE THAT HOUSES THE FORTUNE.
BARONESS, I BELIEVE YOU ARE THE MIRACLE FOR WHICH I HAVE BEEN HOPING.

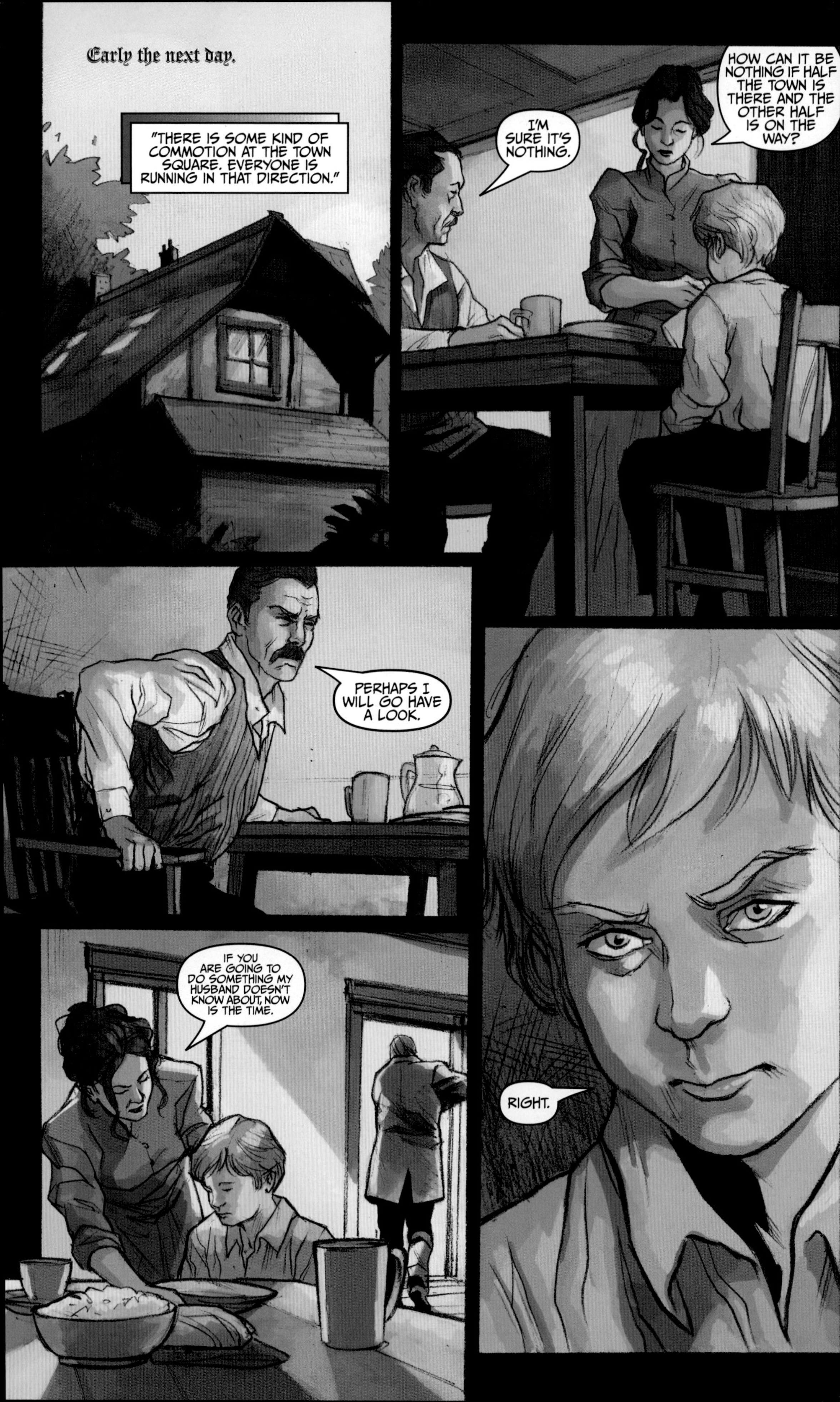
Early the next day.
"THERE IS SOME KIND OF COMMOTION AT THE TOWN SQUARE. EVERYONE IS RUNNING IN THAT DIRECTION."
I'M SURE IT'S NOTHING.
HOW CAN IT BE NOTHING IF HALF THE TOWN IS THERE AND THE OTHER HALF IS ON THE WAY?
PERHAPS I WILL GO HAVE A LOOK.
IF YOU ARE GOING TO DO SOMETHING MY HUSBAND DOESN'T KNOW ABOUT, NOW IS THE TIME.
RIGHT.

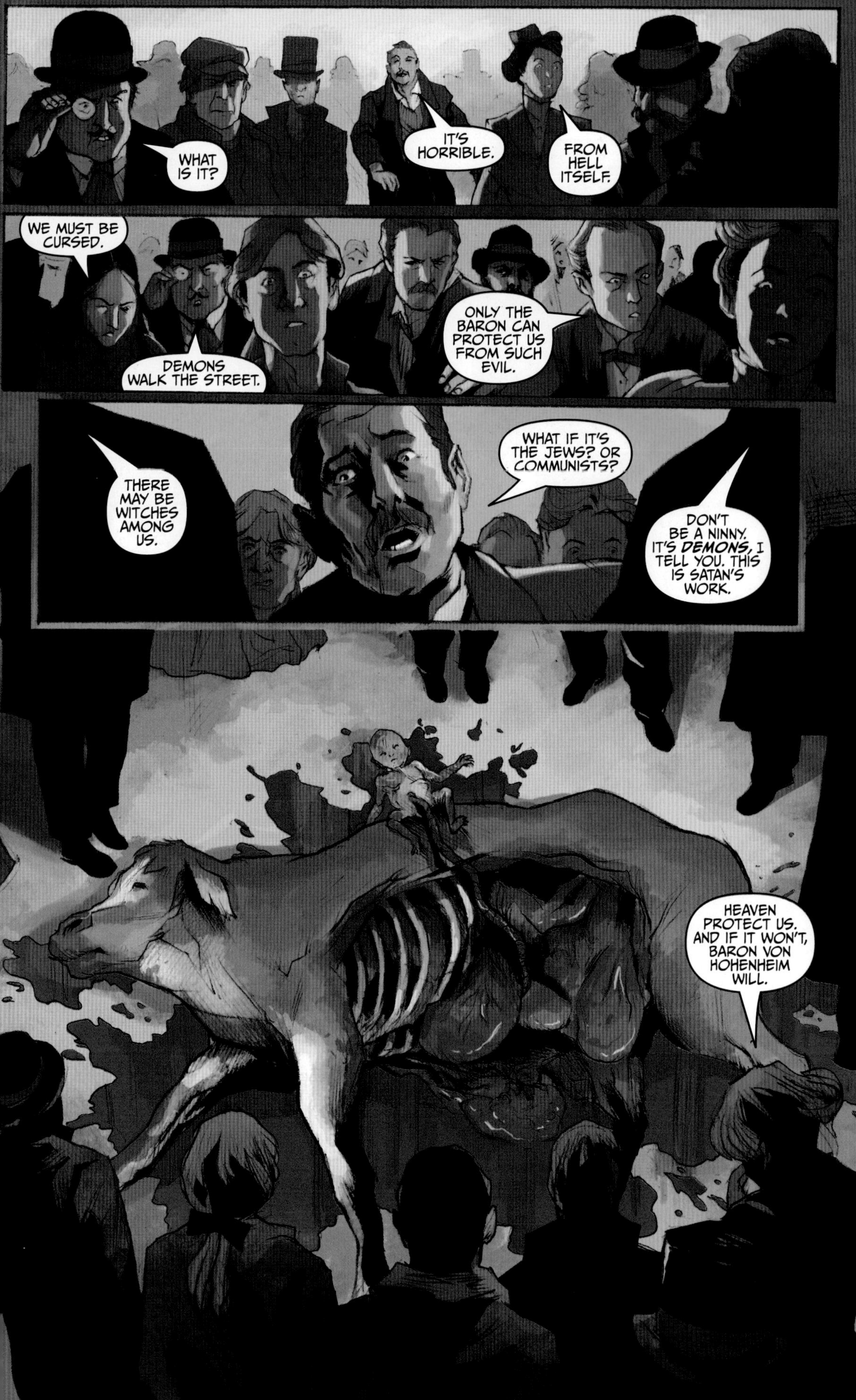
WHAT IS IT?
IT'S HORRIBLE.
FROM HELL ITSELF.
WE MUST BE CURSED.
DEMONS WALK THE STREET.
ONLY THE BARON CAN PROTECT US FROM SUCH EVIL.
THERE MAY BE WITCHES AMONG US.
WHAT IF IT'S THE JEWS? OR COMMUNISTS?
DON'T BE A NINNY. IT'S *DEMONS*, I TELL YOU. THIS IS SATAN'S WORK.
HEAVEN PROTECT US. AND IF IT WON'T, BARON VON HOHENHEIM WILL.

One hour later.

"EVERYONE'S GONE OFF TO SEE THE HULLABALOO IN THE TOWN SQUARE. I DON'T USUALLY STOOP TO MANAGING THE DOMESTIC HELP."

YOU SAY YOU WERE HIRED LAST WEEK AND TOLD TO REPORT TODAY?

YES, SIR. I DON'T RECOLLECT THE LADY'S NAME, BUT SHE SEEMED REAL NASTY.

I'M AFRAID THAT'S EVERYONE WHO WORKS HERE. HA HA!

YOUR NEW KITCHEN BOY IS HERE.

DIDN'T KNOW WE WAS GETTING ONE.

NOT THAT WE'RE COMPLAINING. WE NEED ALL THE HELP WE CAN GET.

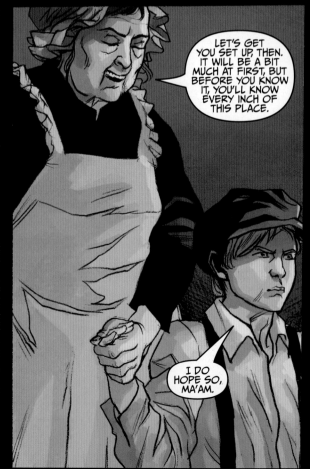

LET'S GET YOU SET UP, THEN. IT WILL BE A BIT MUCH AT FIRST, BUT BEFORE YOU KNOW IT, YOU'LL KNOW EVERY INCH OF THIS PLACE.

I DO HOPE SO, MA'AM.

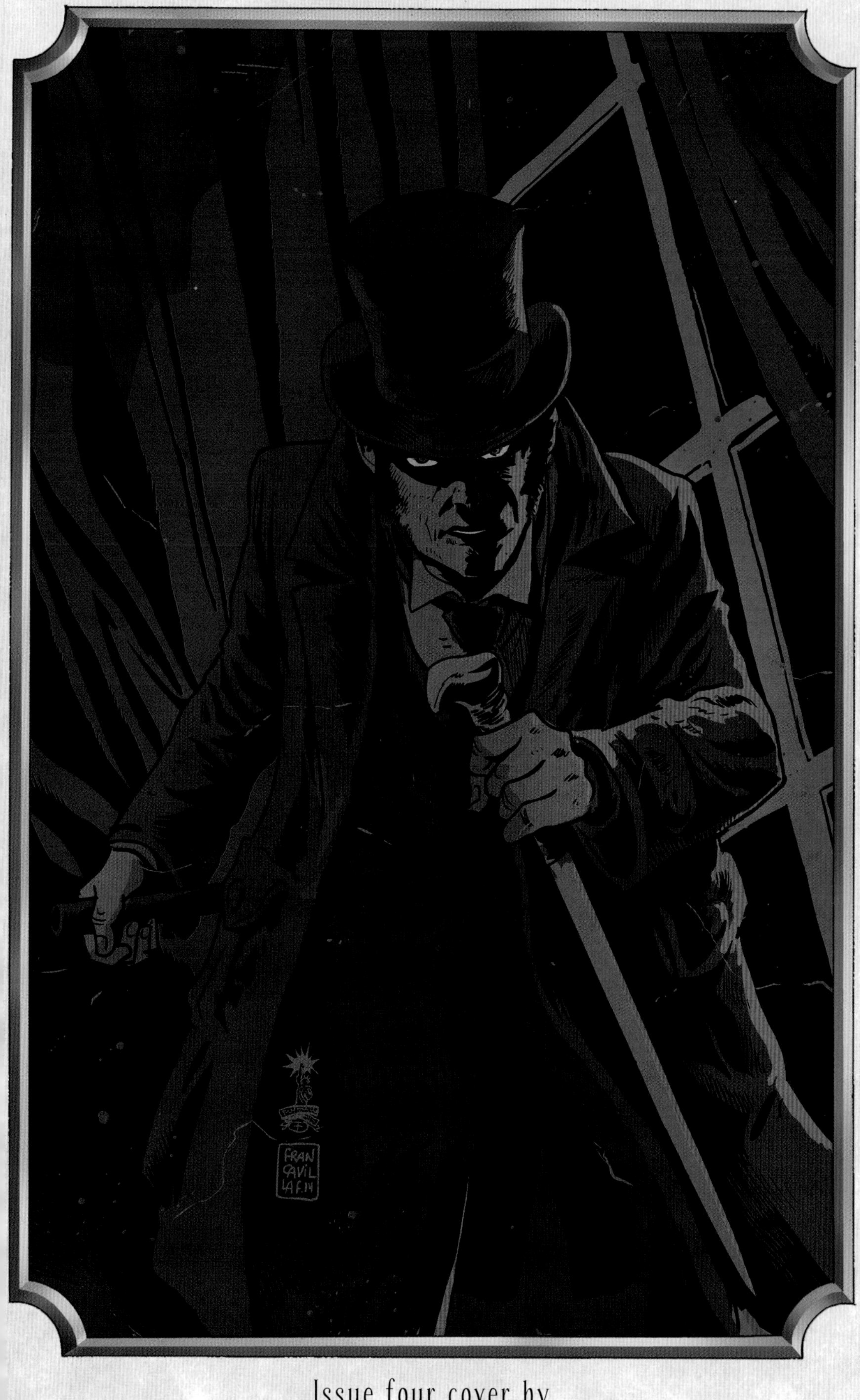

Issue four cover by
Francesco Francavilla

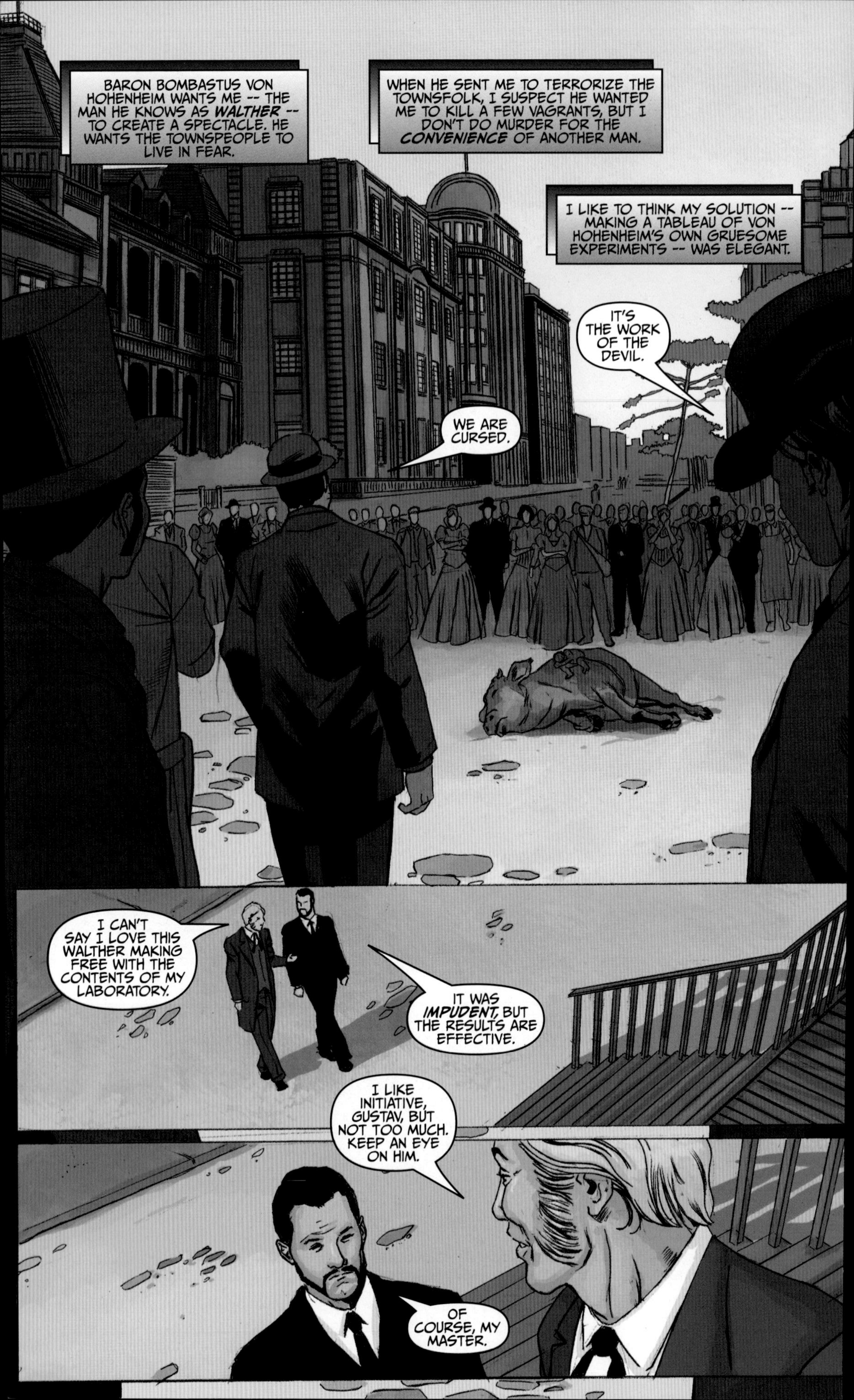

BARON BOMBASTUS VON HOHENHEIM WANTS ME -- THE MAN HE KNOWS AS WALTHER -- TO CREATE A SPECTACLE. HE WANTS THE TOWNSPEOPLE TO LIVE IN FEAR.
WHEN HE SENT ME TO TERRORIZE THE TOWNSFOLK, I SUSPECT HE WANTED ME TO KILL A FEW VAGRANTS, BUT I DON'T DO MURDER FOR THE CONVENIENCE OF ANOTHER MAN.
I LIKE TO THINK MY SOLUTION -- MAKING A TABLEAU OF VON HOHENHEIM'S OWN GRUESOME EXPERIMENTS -- WAS ELEGANT.
IT'S THE WORK OF THE DEVIL.
WE ARE CURSED.
I CAN'T SAY I LOVE THIS WALTHER MAKING FREE WITH THE CONTENTS OF MY LABORATORY.
IT WAS IMPUDENT, BUT THE RESULTS ARE EFFECTIVE.
I LIKE INITIATIVE, GUSTAV, BUT NOT TOO MUCH. KEEP AN EYE ON HIM.
OF COURSE, MY MASTER.

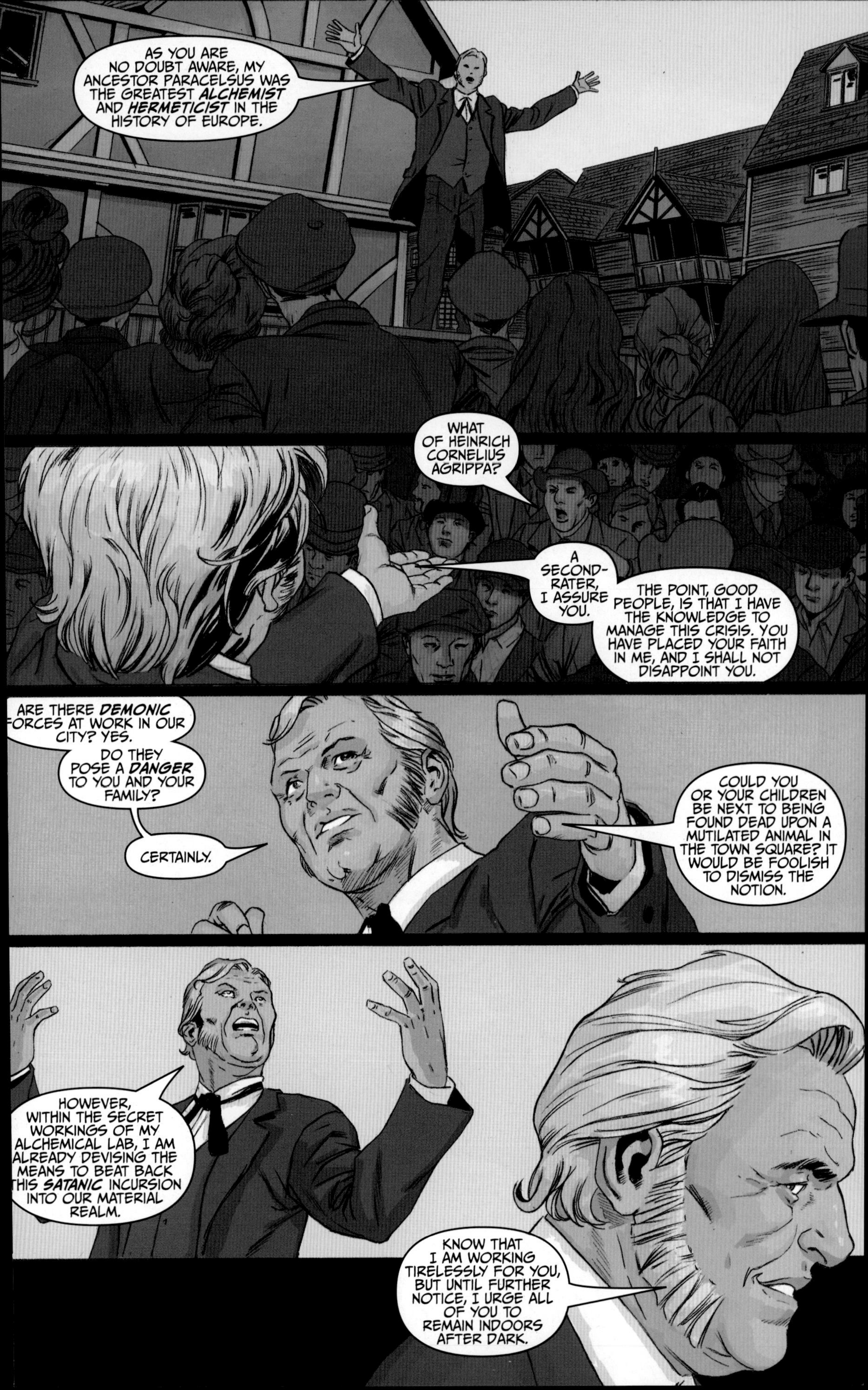
AS YOU ARE NO DOUBT AWARE, MY ANCESTOR PARACELSUS WAS THE GREATEST ALCHEMIST AND HERMETICIST IN THE HISTORY OF EUROPE.
WHAT OF HEINRICH CORNELIUS AGRIPPA?
A SECOND-RATER, I ASSURE YOU.
THE POINT, GOOD PEOPLE, IS THAT I HAVE THE KNOWLEDGE TO MANAGE THIS CRISIS. YOU HAVE PLACED YOUR FAITH IN ME, AND I SHALL NOT DISAPPOINT YOU.
ARE THERE DEMONIC FORCES AT WORK IN OUR CITY? YES.
DO THEY POSE A DANGER TO YOU AND YOUR FAMILY?
CERTAINLY.
COULD YOU OR YOUR CHILDREN BE NEXT TO BEING FOUND DEAD UPON A MUTILATED ANIMAL IN THE TOWN SQUARE? IT WOULD BE FOOLISH TO DISMISS THE NOTION.
HOWEVER, WITHIN THE SECRET WORKINGS OF MY ALCHEMICAL LAB, I AM ALREADY DEVISING THE MEANS TO BEAT BACK THIS SATANIC INCURSION INTO OUR MATERIAL REALM.
KNOW THAT I AM WORKING TIRELESSLY FOR YOU, BUT UNTIL FURTHER NOTICE, I URGE ALL OF YOU TO REMAIN INDOORS AFTER DARK.

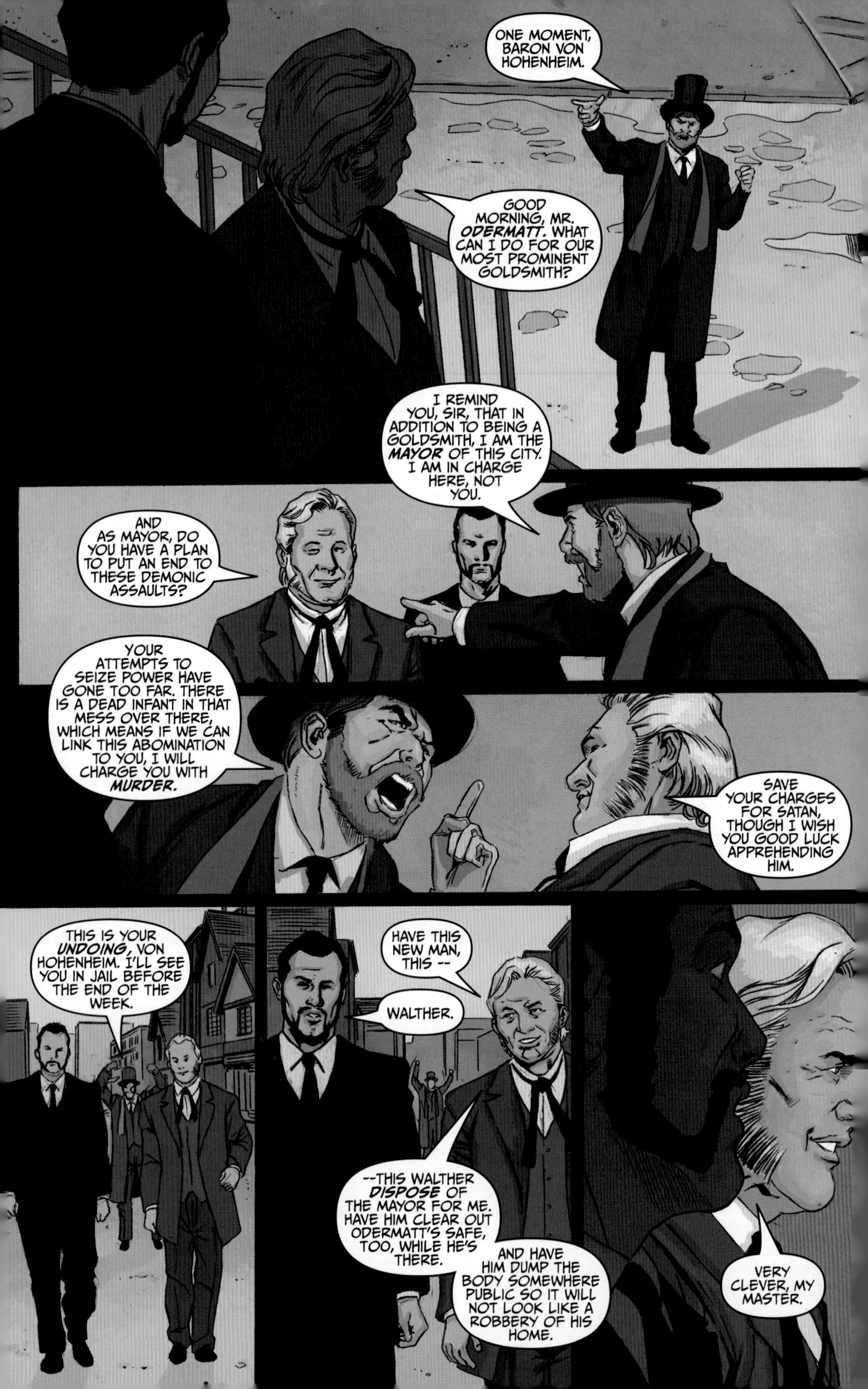
ONE MOMENT, BARON VON HOHENHEIM.
GOOD MORNING, MR. ODERMATT. WHAT CAN I DO FOR OUR MOST PROMINENT GOLDSMITH?
I REMIND YOU, SIR, THAT IN ADDITION TO BEING A GOLDSMITH, I AM THE MAYOR OF THIS CITY. I AM IN CHARGE HERE, NOT YOU.
AND AS MAYOR, DO YOU HAVE A PLAN TO PUT AN END TO THESE DEMONIC ASSAULTS?
YOUR ATTEMPTS TO SEIZE POWER HAVE GONE TOO FAR. THERE IS A DEAD INFANT IN THAT MESS OVER THERE, WHICH MEANS IF WE CAN LINK THIS ABOMINATION TO YOU, I WILL CHARGE YOU WITH MURDER.
SAVE YOUR CHARGES FOR SATAN, THOUGH I WISH YOU GOOD LUCK APPREHENDING HIM.
THIS IS YOUR UNDOING, VON HOHENHEIM. I'LL SEE YOU IN JAIL BEFORE THE END OF THE WEEK.
HAVE THIS NEW MAN, THIS --
WALTHER.
--THIS WALTHER DISPOSE OF THE MAYOR FOR ME. HAVE HIM CLEAR OUT ODERMATT'S SAFE, TOO, WHILE HE'S THERE.
AND HAVE HIM DUMP THE BODY SOMEWHERE PUBLIC SO IT WILL NOT LOOK LIKE A ROBBERY OF HIS HOME.
VERY CLEVER, MY MASTER.

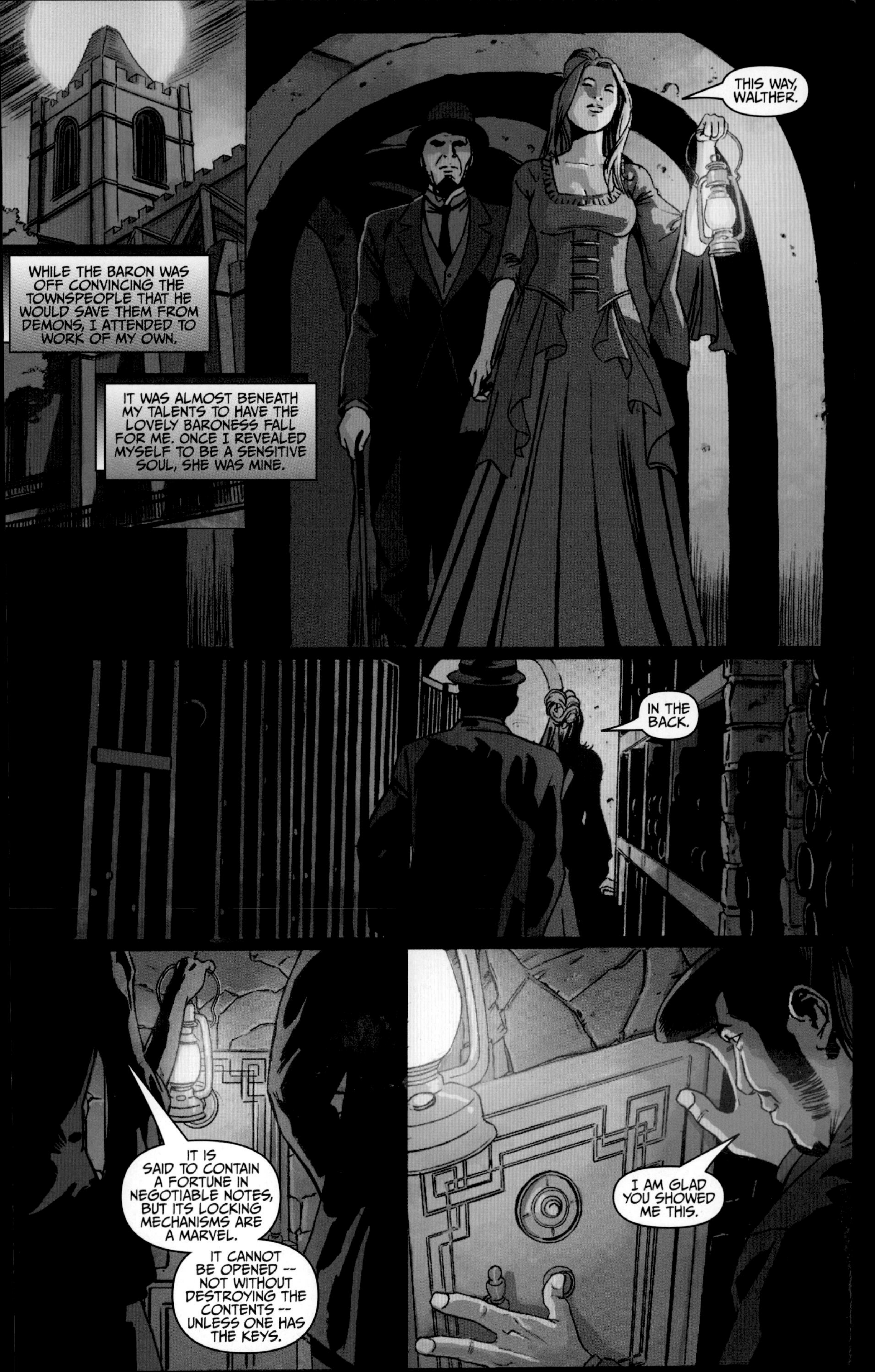
WHILE THE BARON WAS OFF CONVINCING THE TOWNSPEOPLE THAT HE WOULD SAVE THEM FROM DEMONS, I ATTENDED TO WORK OF MY OWN.
IT WAS ALMOST BENEATH MY TALENTS TO HAVE THE LOVELY BARONESS FALL FOR ME. ONCE I REVEALED MYSELF TO BE A SENSITIVE SOUL, SHE WAS MINE.
THIS WAY, WALTHER.
IN THE BACK.
IT IS SAID TO CONTAIN A FORTUNE IN NEGOTIABLE NOTES, BUT ITS LOCKING MECHANISMS ARE A MARVEL.
IT CANNOT BE OPENED -- NOT WITHOUT DESTROYING THE CONTENTS -- UNLESS ONE HAS THE KEYS.
I AM GLAD YOU SHOWED ME THIS.

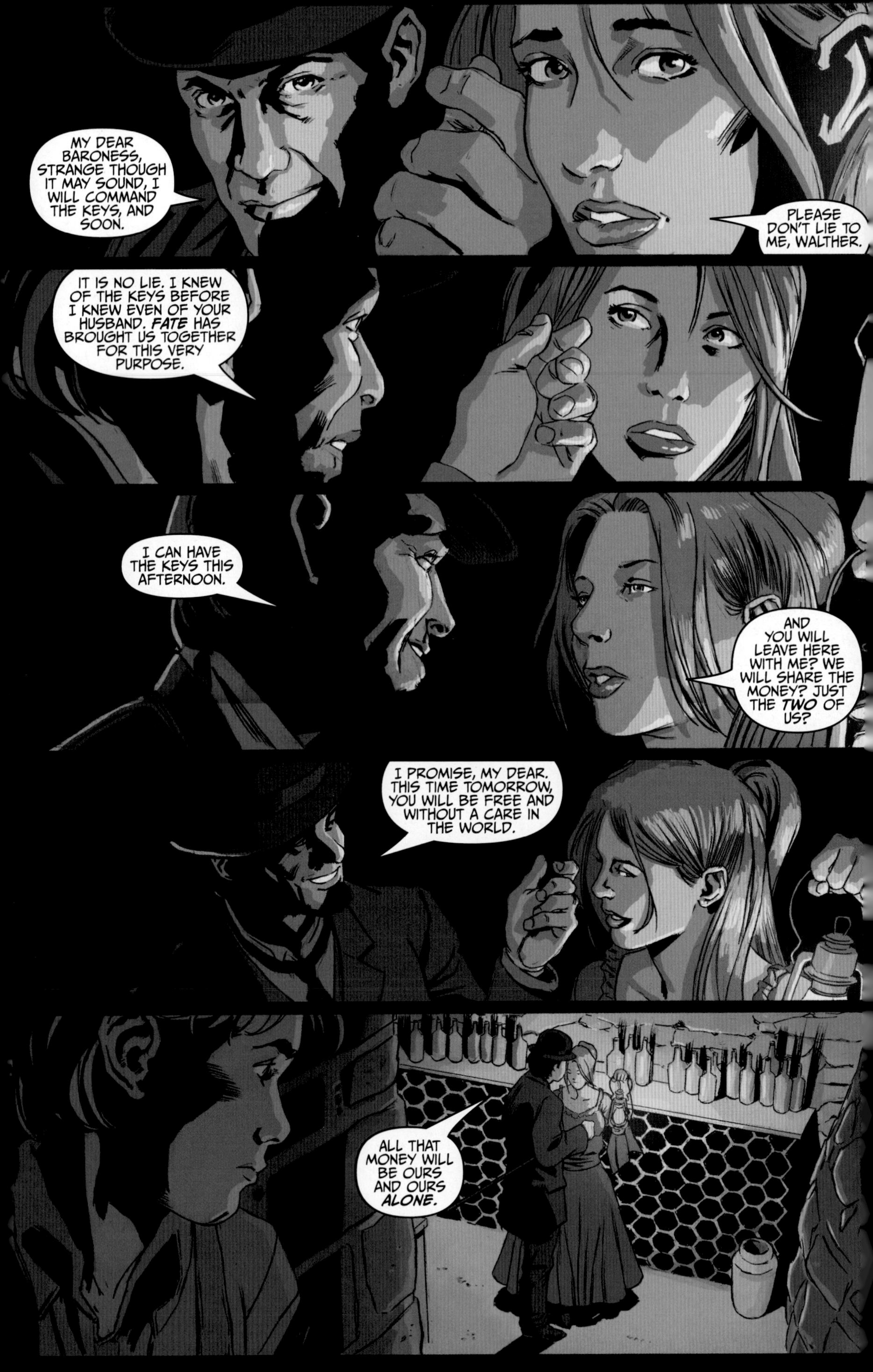
MY DEAR BARONESS, STRANGE THOUGH IT MAY SOUND, I WILL COMMAND THE KEYS, AND SOON.
PLEASE DON'T LIE TO ME, WALTHER.
IT IS NO LIE. I KNEW OF THE KEYS BEFORE I KNEW EVEN OF YOUR HUSBAND. FATE HAS BROUGHT US TOGETHER FOR THIS VERY PURPOSE.
I CAN HAVE THE KEYS THIS AFTERNOON.
AND YOU WILL LEAVE HERE WITH ME? WE WILL SHARE THE MONEY? JUST THE TWO OF US?
I PROMISE, MY DEAR. THIS TIME TOMORROW, YOU WILL BE FREE AND WITHOUT A CARE IN THE WORLD.
ALL THAT MONEY WILL BE OURS AND OURS ALONE.

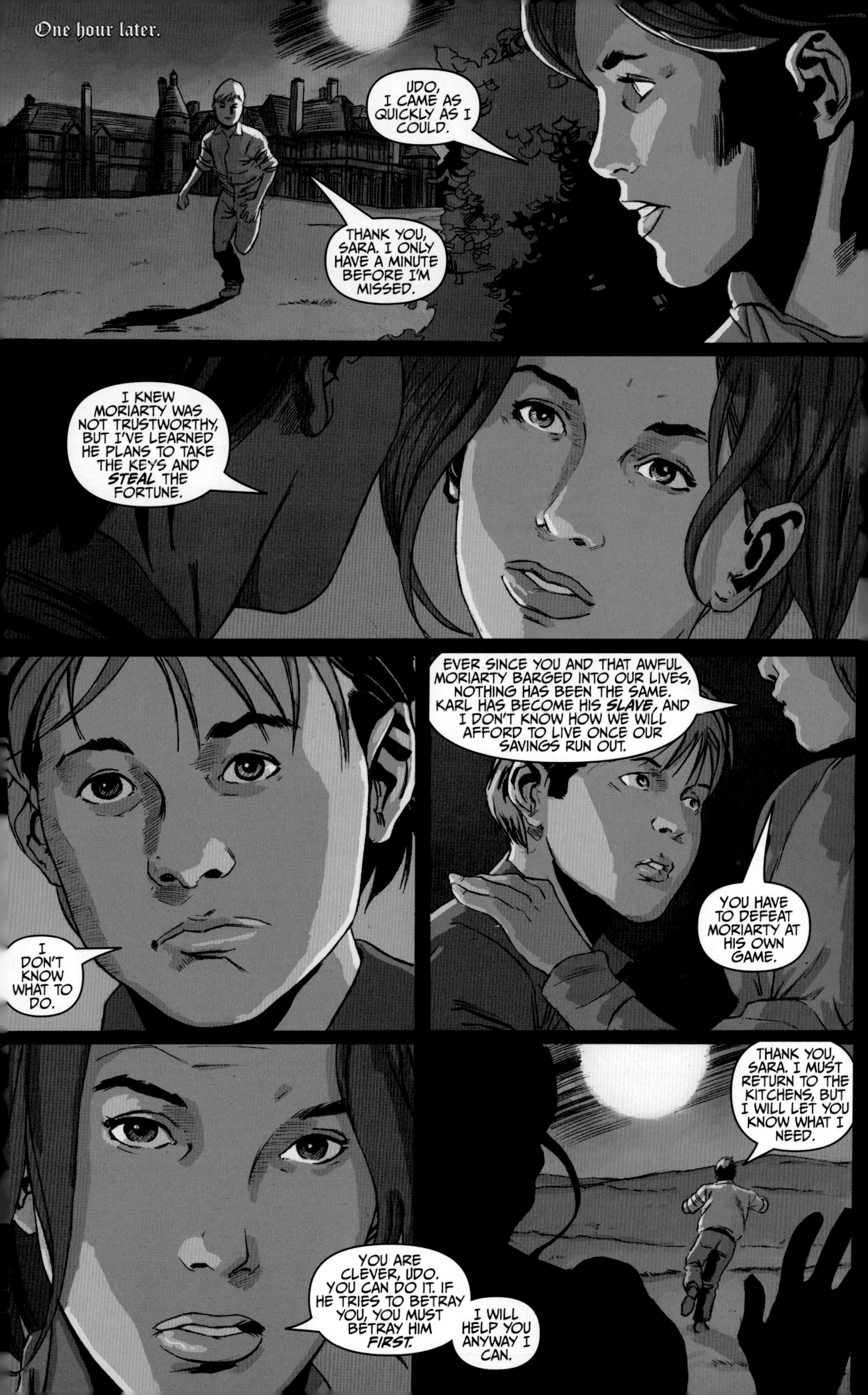
One hour later.
UDO, I CAME AS QUICKLY AS I COULD.
THANK YOU, SARA. I ONLY HAVE A MINUTE BEFORE I'M MISSED.
I KNEW MORIARTY WAS NOT TRUSTWORTHY, BUT I'VE LEARNED HE PLANS TO TAKE THE KEYS AND STEAL THE FORTUNE.
I DON'T KNOW WHAT TO DO.
EVER SINCE YOU AND THAT AWFUL MORIARTY BARGED INTO OUR LIVES, NOTHING HAS BEEN THE SAME. KARL HAS BECOME HIS SLAVE, AND I DON'T KNOW HOW WE WILL AFFORD TO LIVE ONCE OUR SAVINGS RUN OUT.
YOU HAVE TO DEFEAT MORIARTY AT HIS OWN GAME.
YOU ARE CLEVER, UDO. YOU CAN DO IT. IF HE TRIES TO BETRAY YOU, YOU MUST BETRAY HIM FIRST.
I WILL HELP YOU ANYWAY I CAN.
THANK YOU, SARA. I MUST RETURN TO THE KITCHENS, BUT I WILL LET YOU KNOW WHAT I NEED.

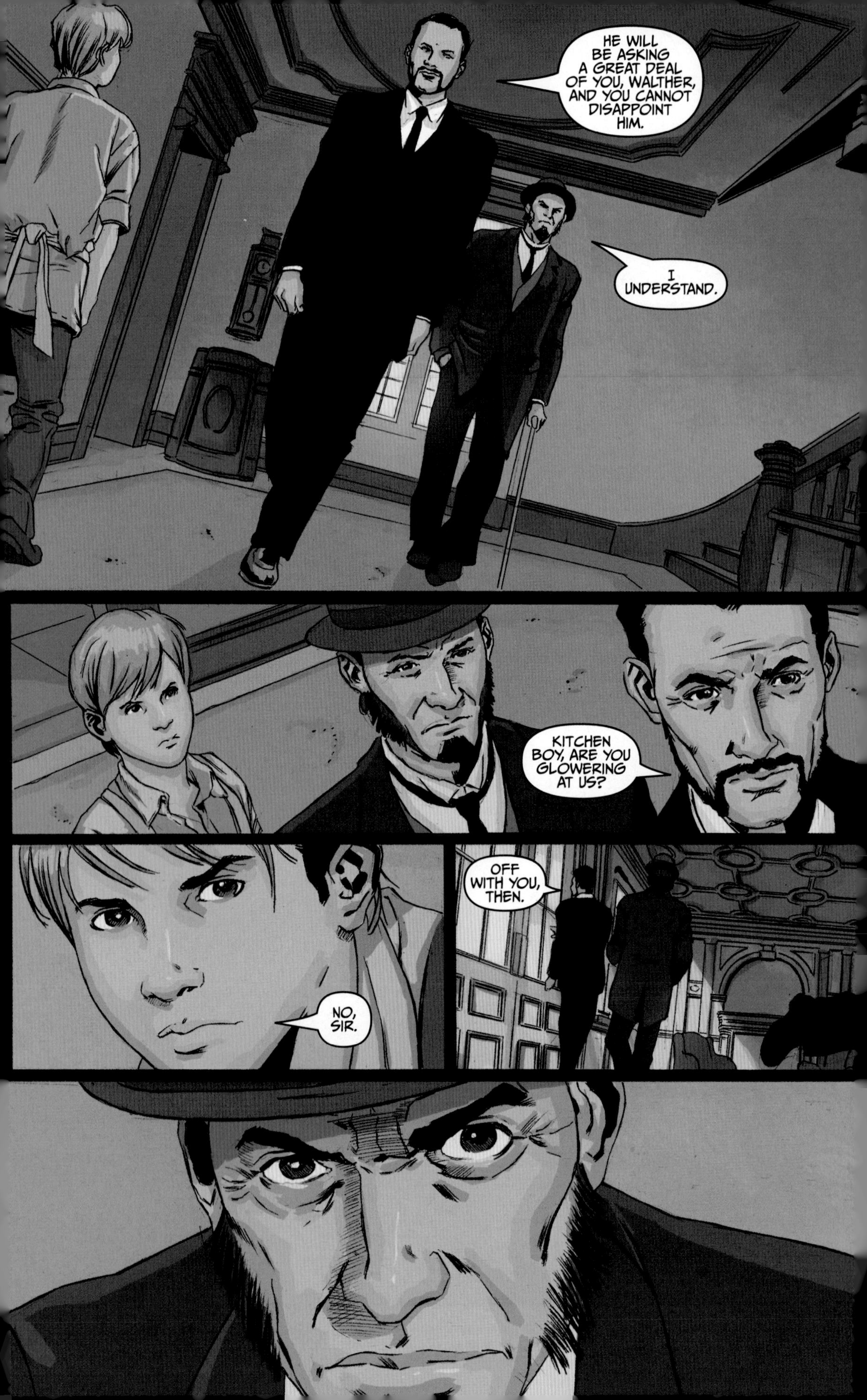
HE WILL BE ASKING A GREAT DEAL OF YOU, WALTHER, AND YOU CANNOT DISAPPOINT HIM.
I UNDERSTAND.
KITCHEN BOY, ARE YOU GLOWERING AT US?
NO, SIR.
OFF WITH YOU, THEN.

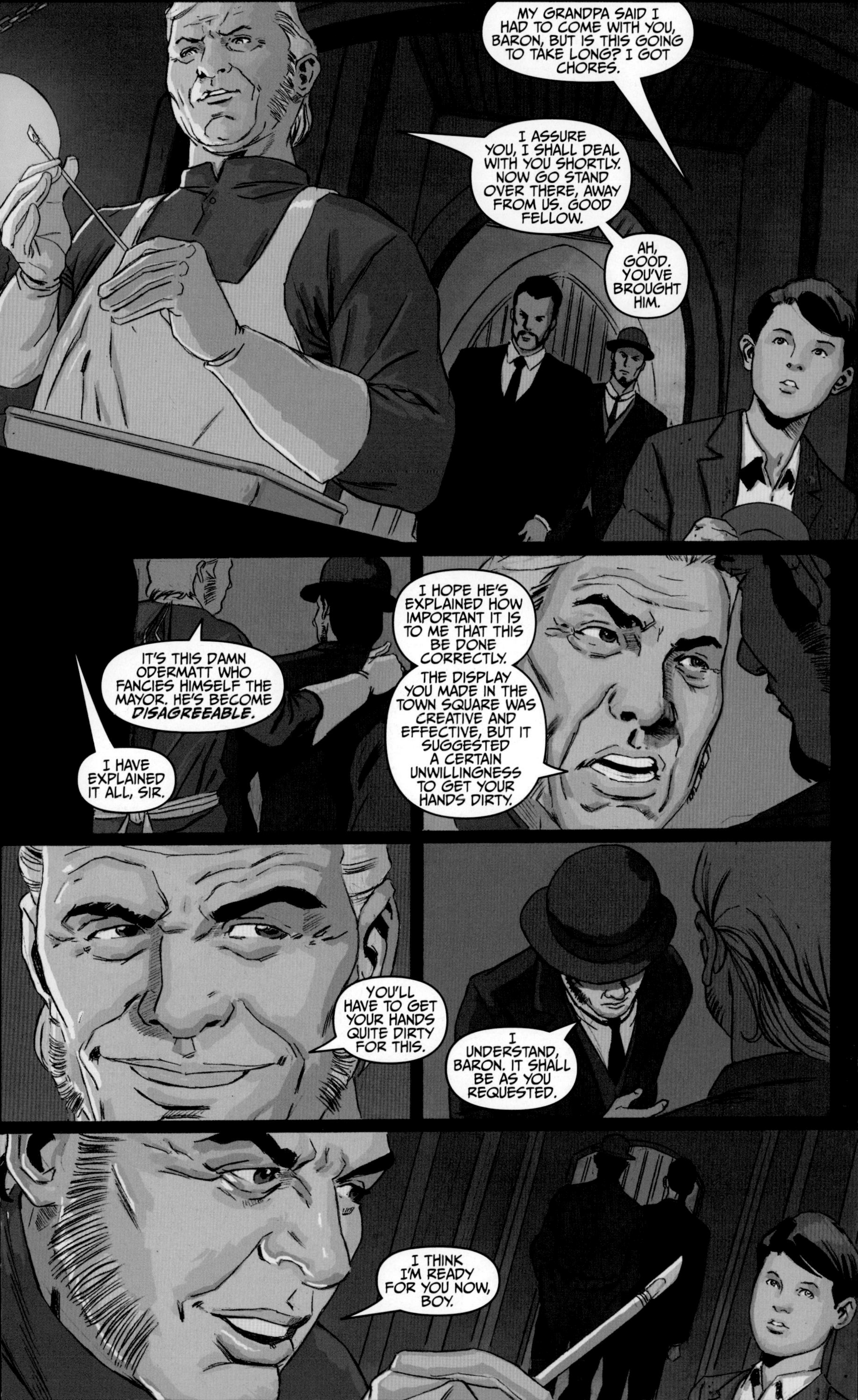
MY GRANDPA SAID I HAD TO COME WITH YOU, BARON, BUT IS THIS GOING TO TAKE LONG? I GOT CHORES.
I ASSURE YOU, I SHALL DEAL WITH YOU SHORTLY. NOW GO STAND OVER THERE, AWAY FROM US. GOOD FELLOW.
AH, GOOD. YOU'VE BROUGHT HIM.
IT'S THIS DAMN ODERMATT WHO FANCIES HIMSELF THE MAYOR. HE'S BECOME *DISAGREEABLE.*
I HAVE EXPLAINED IT ALL, SIR.
I HOPE HE'S EXPLAINED HOW IMPORTANT IT IS TO ME THAT THIS BE DONE CORRECTLY.
THE DISPLAY YOU MADE IN THE TOWN SQUARE WAS CREATIVE AND EFFECTIVE, BUT IT SUGGESTED A CERTAIN UNWILLINGNESS TO GET YOUR HANDS DIRTY.
YOU'LL HAVE TO GET YOUR HANDS QUITE DIRTY FOR THIS.
I UNDERSTAND, BARON. IT SHALL BE AS YOU REQUESTED.
I THINK I'M READY FOR YOU NOW, BOY.

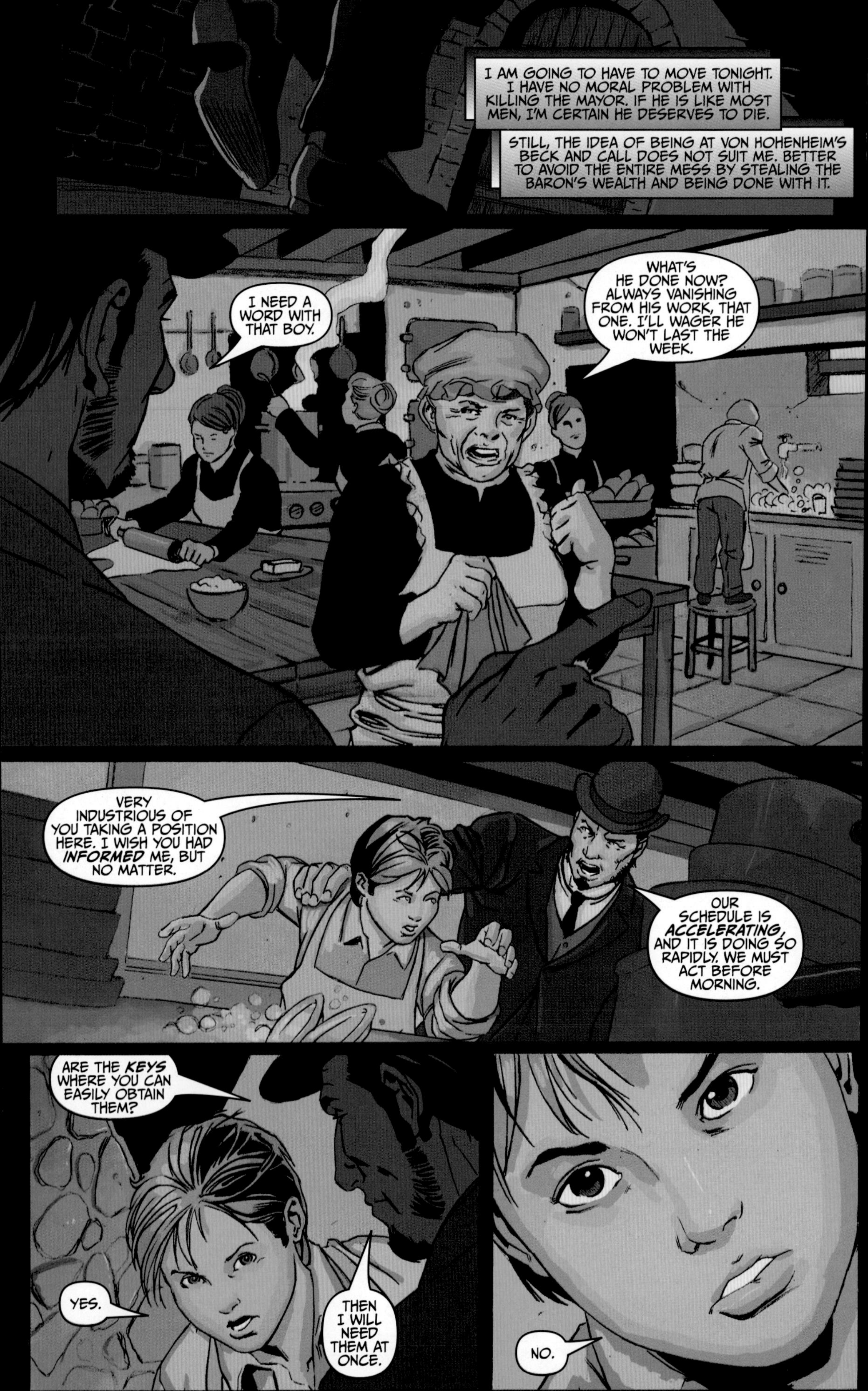
I AM GOING TO HAVE TO MOVE TONIGHT. I HAVE NO MORAL PROBLEM WITH KILLING THE MAYOR. IF HE IS LIKE MOST MEN, I'M CERTAIN HE DESERVES TO DIE.
STILL, THE IDEA OF BEING AT VON HOHENHEIM'S BECK AND CALL DOES NOT SUIT ME. BETTER TO AVOID THE ENTIRE MESS BY STEALING THE BARON'S WEALTH AND BEING DONE WITH IT.
I NEED A WORD WITH THAT BOY.
WHAT'S HE DONE NOW? ALWAYS VANISHING FROM HIS WORK, THAT ONE. I'LL WAGER HE WON'T LAST THE WEEK.
VERY INDUSTRIOUS OF YOU TAKING A POSITION HERE. I WISH YOU HAD *INFORMED* ME, BUT NO MATTER.
OUR SCHEDULE IS *ACCELERATING*, AND IT IS DOING SO RAPIDLY. WE MUST ACT BEFORE MORNING.
ARE THE *KEYS* WHERE YOU CAN EASILY OBTAIN THEM?
YES.
THEN I WILL NEED THEM AT ONCE.
NO.

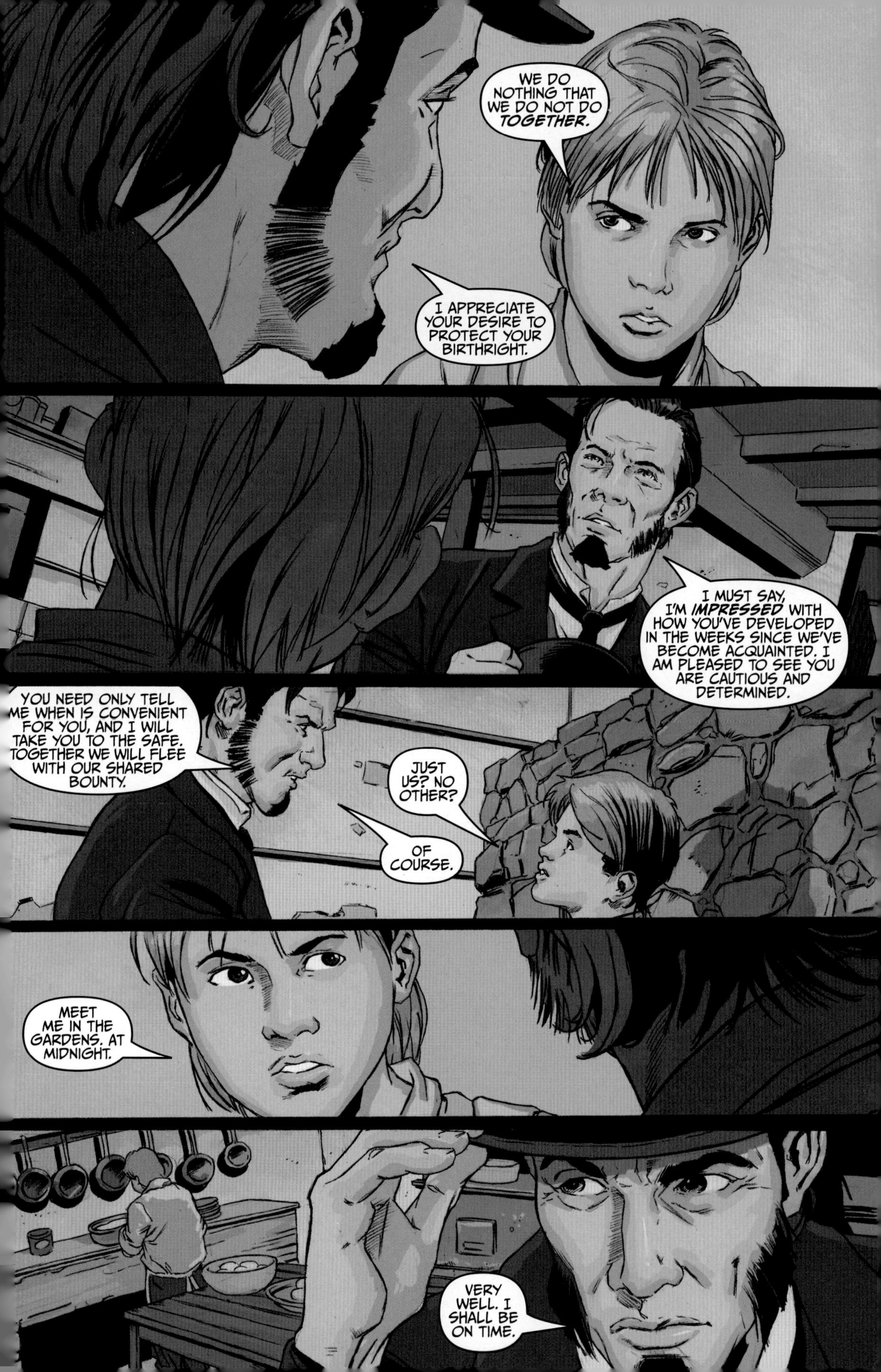

WE DO NOTHING THAT WE DO NOT DO *TOGETHER.*
I APPRECIATE YOUR DESIRE TO PROTECT YOUR BIRTHRIGHT.
I MUST SAY, I'M *IMPRESSED* WITH HOW YOU'VE DEVELOPED IN THE WEEKS SINCE WE'VE BECOME ACQUAINTED. I AM PLEASED TO SEE YOU ARE CAUTIOUS AND DETERMINED.
YOU NEED ONLY TELL ME WHEN IS CONVENIENT FOR YOU, AND I WILL TAKE YOU TO THE SAFE. TOGETHER WE WILL FLEE WITH OUR SHARED BOUNTY.
JUST US? NO OTHER?
OF COURSE.
MEET ME IN THE GARDENS. AT MIDNIGHT.
VERY WELL. I SHALL BE ON TIME.

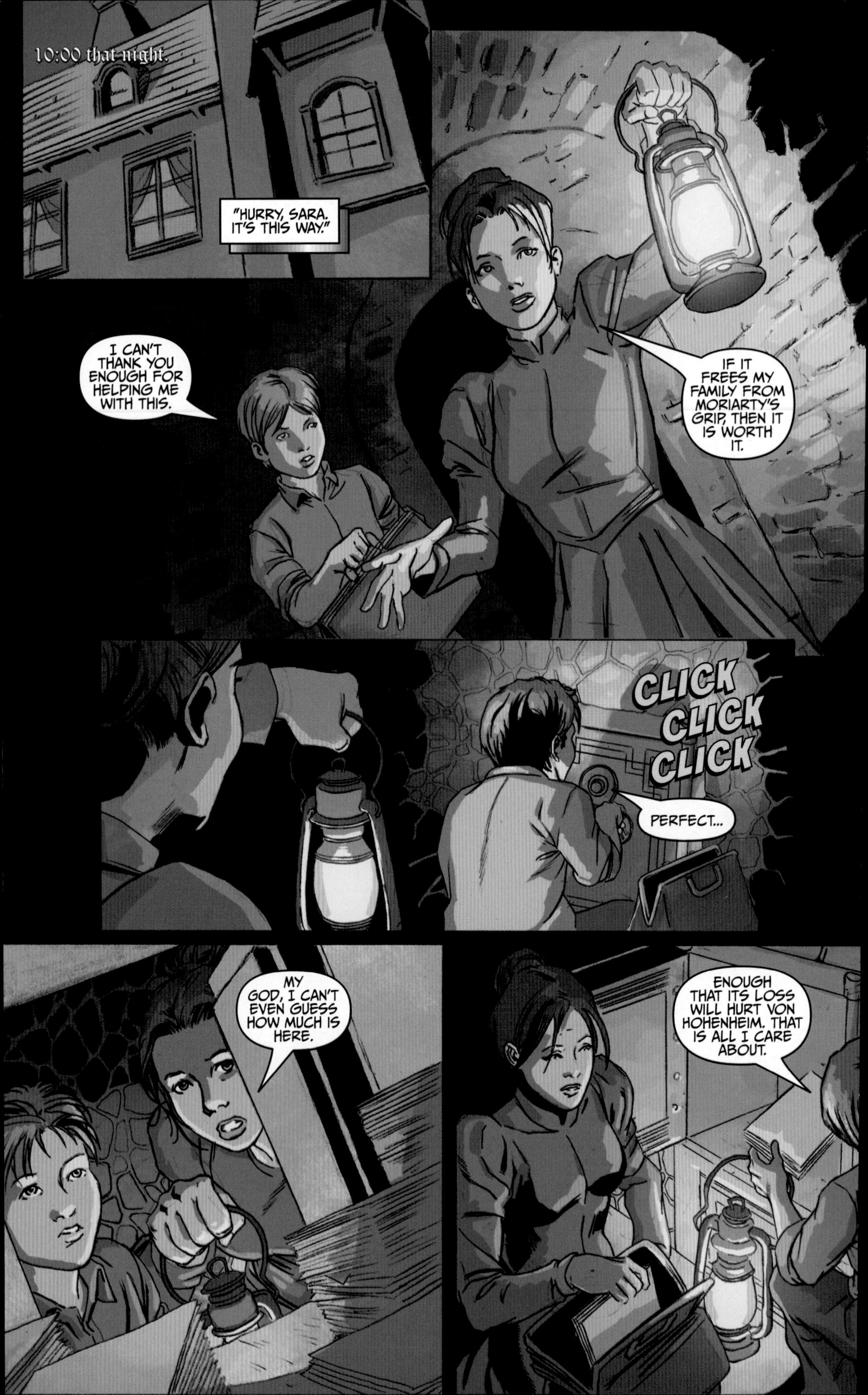
10:00 that night.
"HURRY, SARA. IT'S THIS WAY."
I CAN'T THANK YOU ENOUGH FOR HELPING ME WITH THIS.
IF IT FREES MY FAMILY FROM MORIARTY'S GRIP, THEN IT IS WORTH IT.
CLICK CLICK CLICK
PERFECT...
MY GOD, I CAN'T EVEN GUESS HOW MUCH IS HERE.
ENOUGH THAT ITS LOSS WILL HURT VON HOHENHEIM. THAT IS ALL I CARE ABOUT.

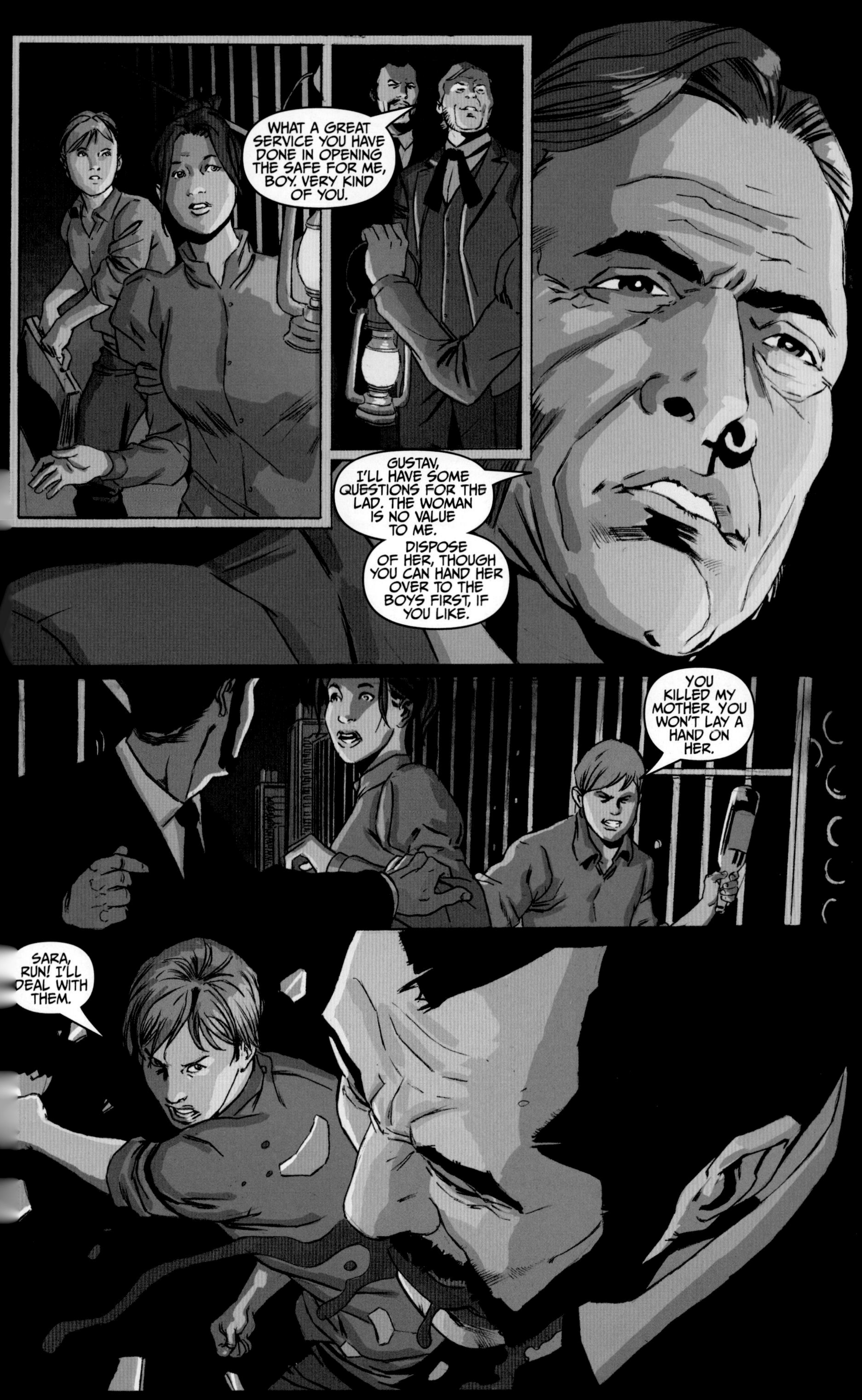
WHAT A GREAT SERVICE YOU HAVE DONE IN OPENING THE SAFE FOR ME, BOY. VERY KIND OF YOU.
GUSTAV, I'LL HAVE SOME QUESTIONS FOR THE LAD. THE WOMAN IS NO VALUE TO ME.
DISPOSE OF HER, THOUGH YOU CAN HAND HER OVER TO THE BOYS FIRST, IF YOU LIKE.
YOU KILLED MY MOTHER. YOU WON'T LAY A HAND ON HER.
SARA, RUN! I'LL DEAL WITH THEM.

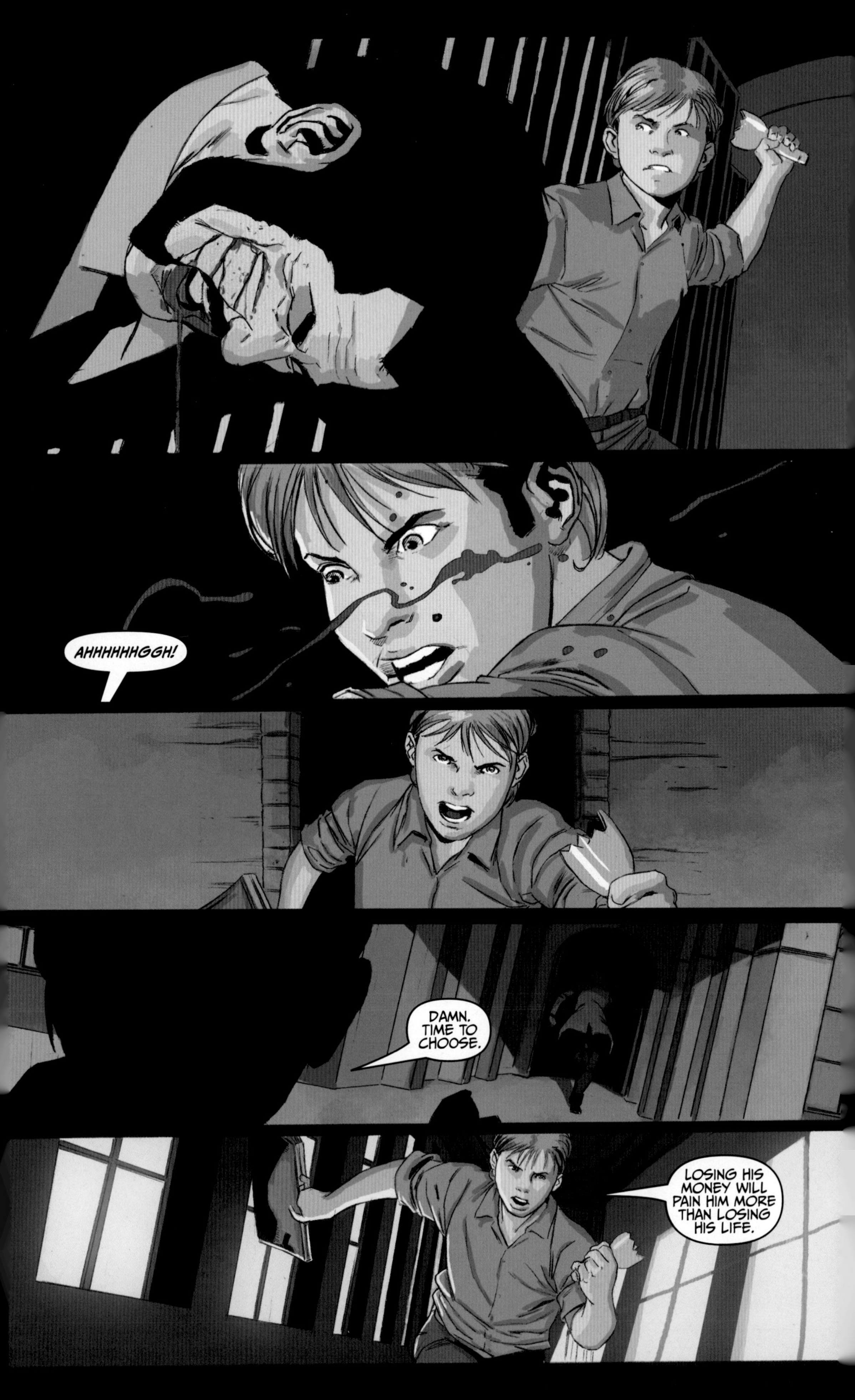
AHHHHHHGGH!
DAMN. TIME TO CHOOSE.
LOSING HIS MONEY WILL PAIN HIM MORE THAN LOSING HIS LIFE.

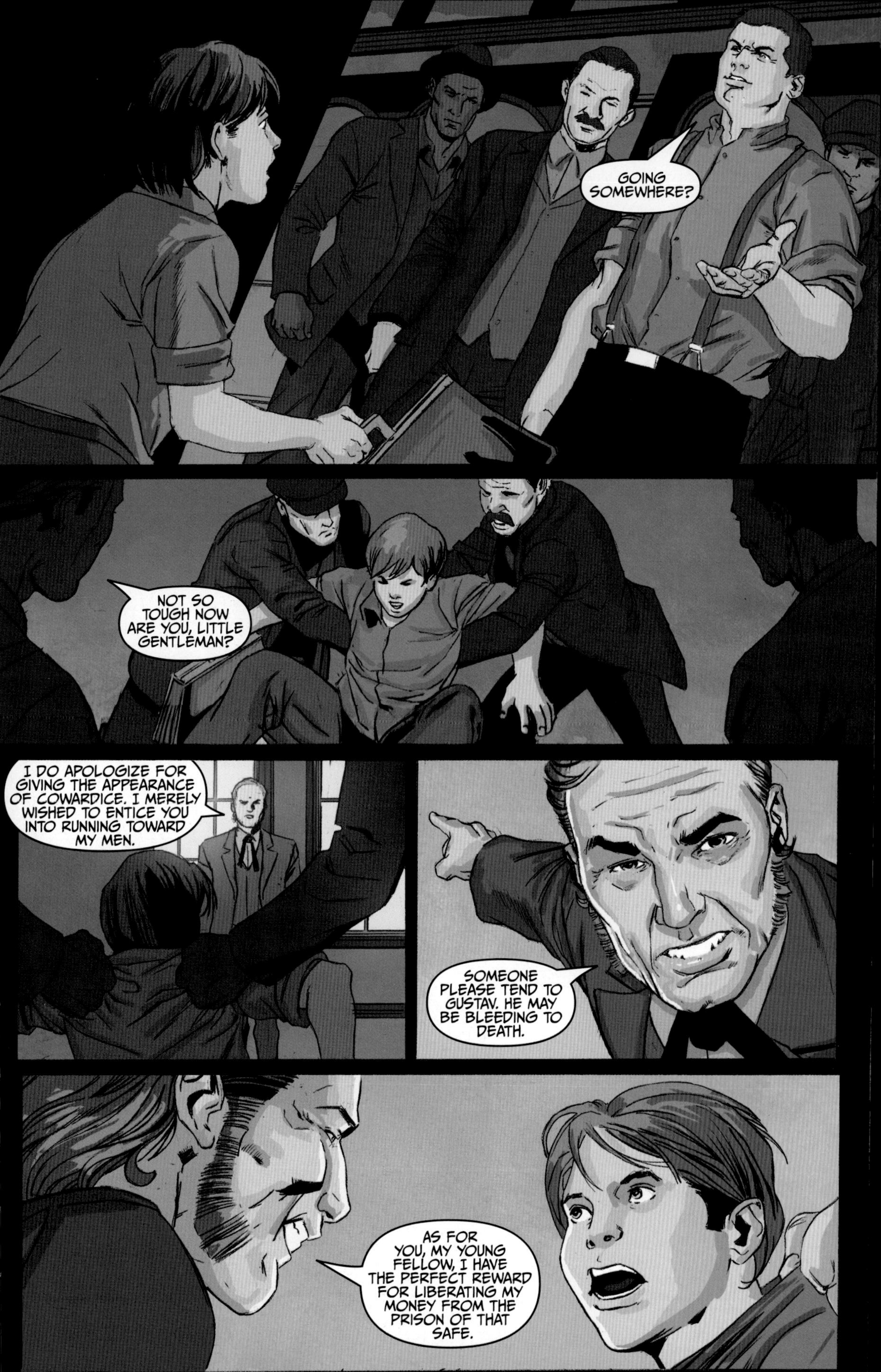
GOING SOMEWHERE?
NOT SO TOUGH NOW ARE YOU, LITTLE GENTLEMAN?
I DO APOLOGIZE FOR GIVING THE APPEARANCE OF COWARDICE. I MERELY WISHED TO ENTICE YOU INTO RUNNING TOWARD MY MEN.
SOMEONE PLEASE TEND TO GUSTAV. HE MAY BE BLEEDING TO DEATH.
AS FOR YOU, MY YOUNG FELLOW, I HAVE THE PERFECT REWARD FOR LIBERATING MY MONEY FROM THE PRISON OF THAT SAFE.

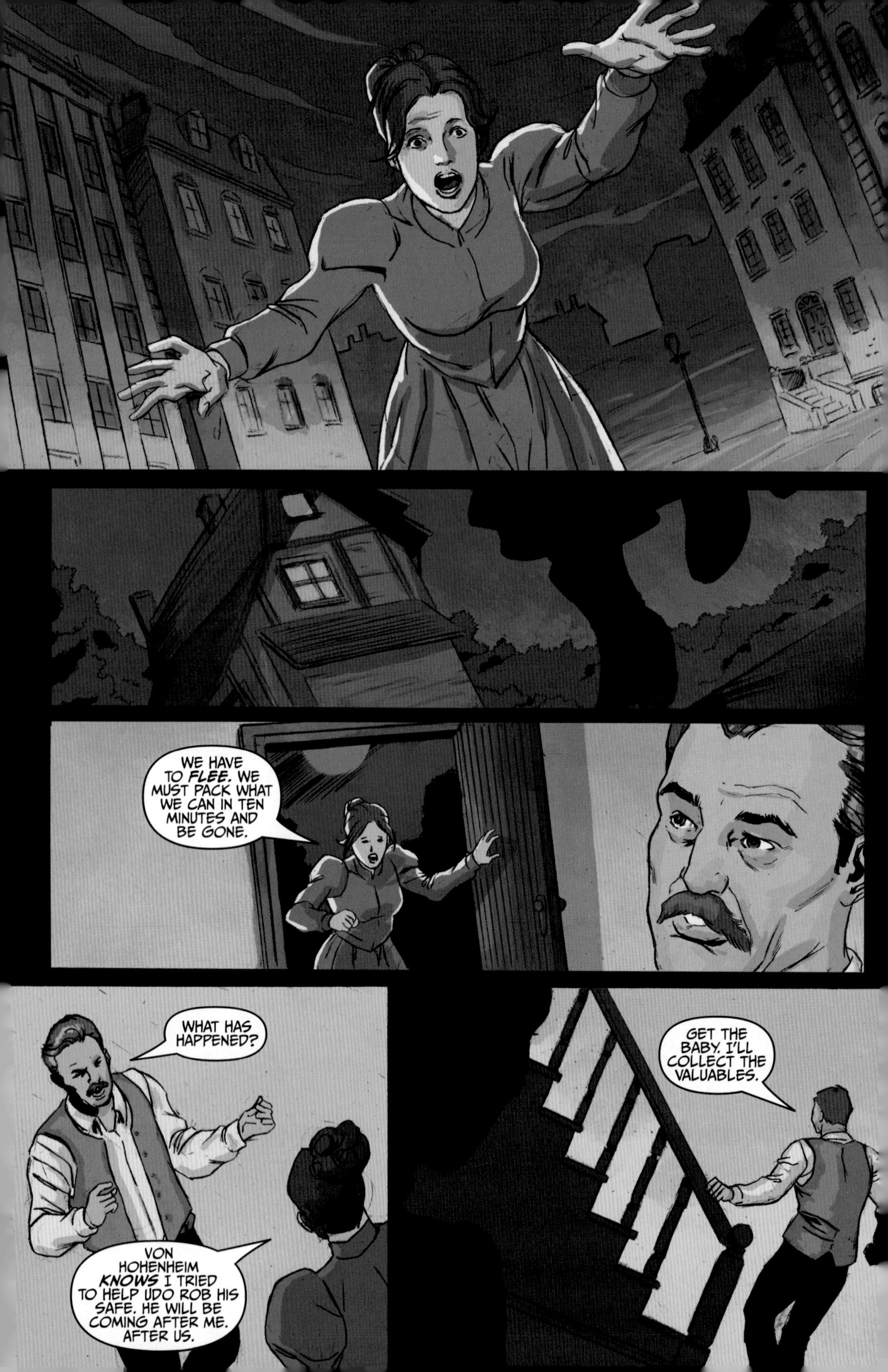
WE HAVE TO FLEE. WE MUST PACK WHAT WE CAN IN TEN MINUTES AND BE GONE.
WHAT HAS HAPPENED?
VON HOHENHEIM KNOWS I TRIED TO HELP UDO ROB HIS SAFE. HE WILL BE COMING AFTER ME. AFTER US.
GET THE BABY. I'LL COLLECT THE VALUABLES.

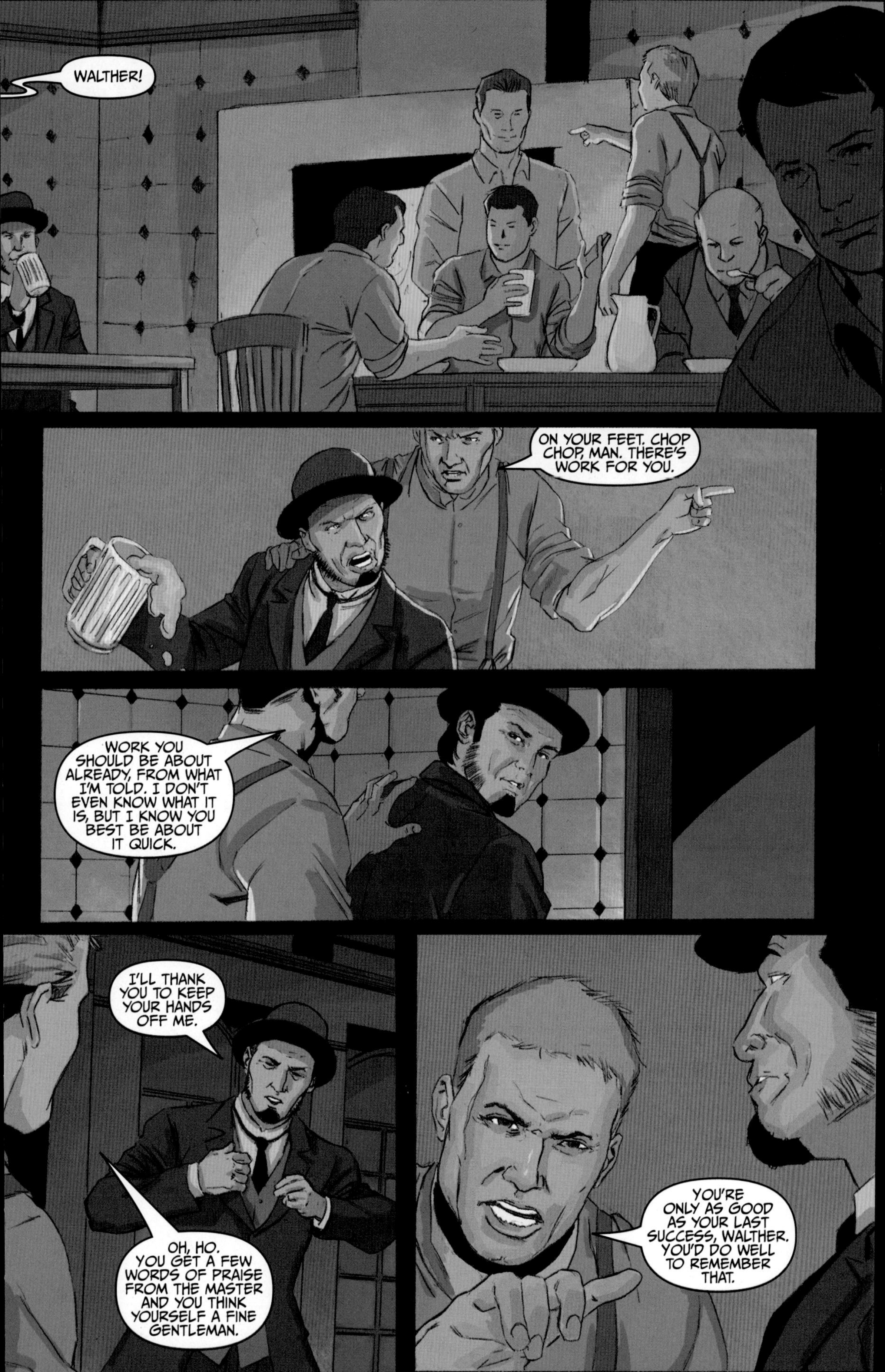
WALTHER!
ON YOUR FEET. CHOP CHOP, MAN. THERE'S WORK FOR YOU.
WORK YOU SHOULD BE ABOUT ALREADY, FROM WHAT I'M TOLD. I DON'T EVEN KNOW WHAT IT IS, BUT I KNOW YOU BEST BE ABOUT IT QUICK.
I'LL THANK YOU TO KEEP YOUR HANDS OFF ME.
OH, HO. YOU GET A FEW WORDS OF PRAISE FROM THE MASTER AND YOU THINK YOURSELF A FINE GENTLEMAN.
YOU'RE ONLY AS GOOD AS YOUR LAST SUCCESS, WALTHER. YOU'D DO WELL TO REMEMBER THAT.

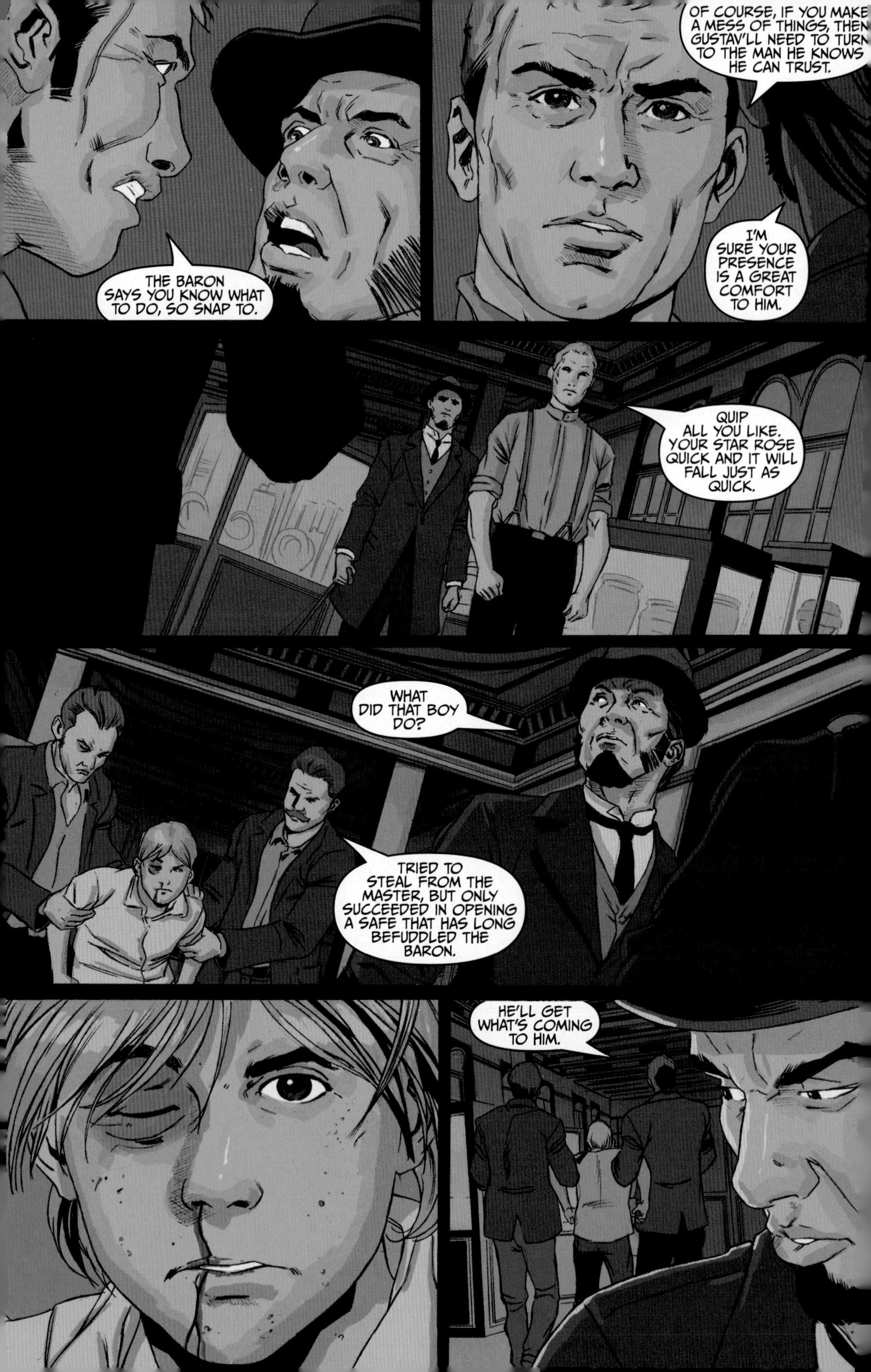
THE BARON SAYS YOU KNOW WHAT TO DO, SO SNAP TO.
OF COURSE, IF YOU MAKE A MESS OF THINGS, THEN GUSTAV'LL NEED TO TURN TO THE MAN HE KNOWS HE CAN TRUST.
I'M SURE YOUR PRESENCE IS A GREAT COMFORT TO HIM.
QUIP ALL YOU LIKE. YOUR STAR ROSE QUICK AND IT WILL FALL JUST AS QUICK.
WHAT DID THAT BOY DO?
TRIED TO STEAL FROM THE MASTER, BUT ONLY SUCCEEDED IN OPENING A SAFE THAT HAS LONG BEFUDDLED THE BARON.
HE'LL GET WHAT'S COMING TO HIM.

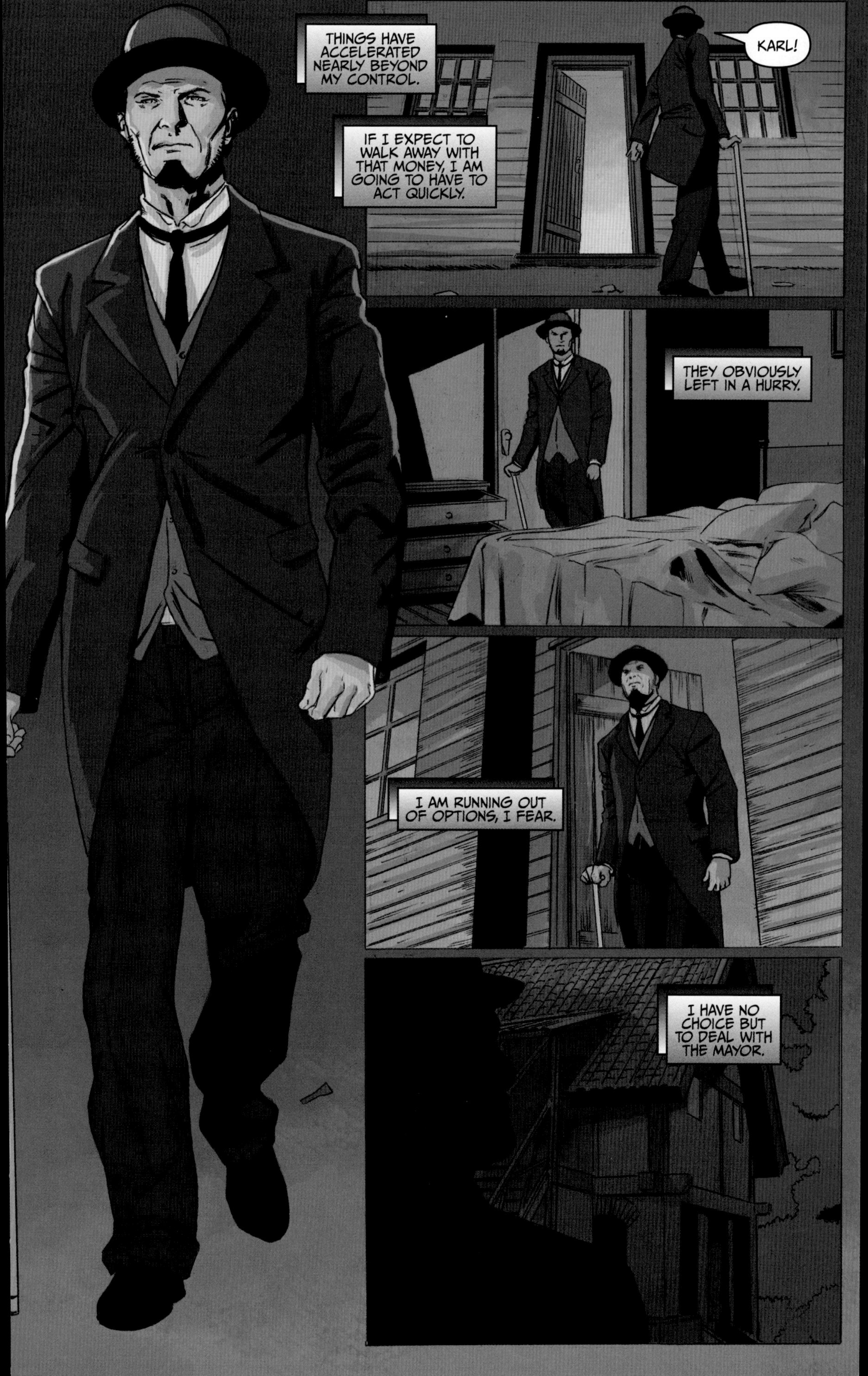
THINGS HAVE ACCELERATED NEARLY BEYOND MY CONTROL.
KARL!
IF I EXPECT TO WALK AWAY WITH THAT MONEY, I AM GOING TO HAVE TO ACT QUICKLY.
THEY OBVIOUSLY LEFT IN A HURRY.
I AM RUNNING OUT OF OPTIONS, I FEAR.
I HAVE NO CHOICE BUT TO DEAL WITH THE MAYOR.

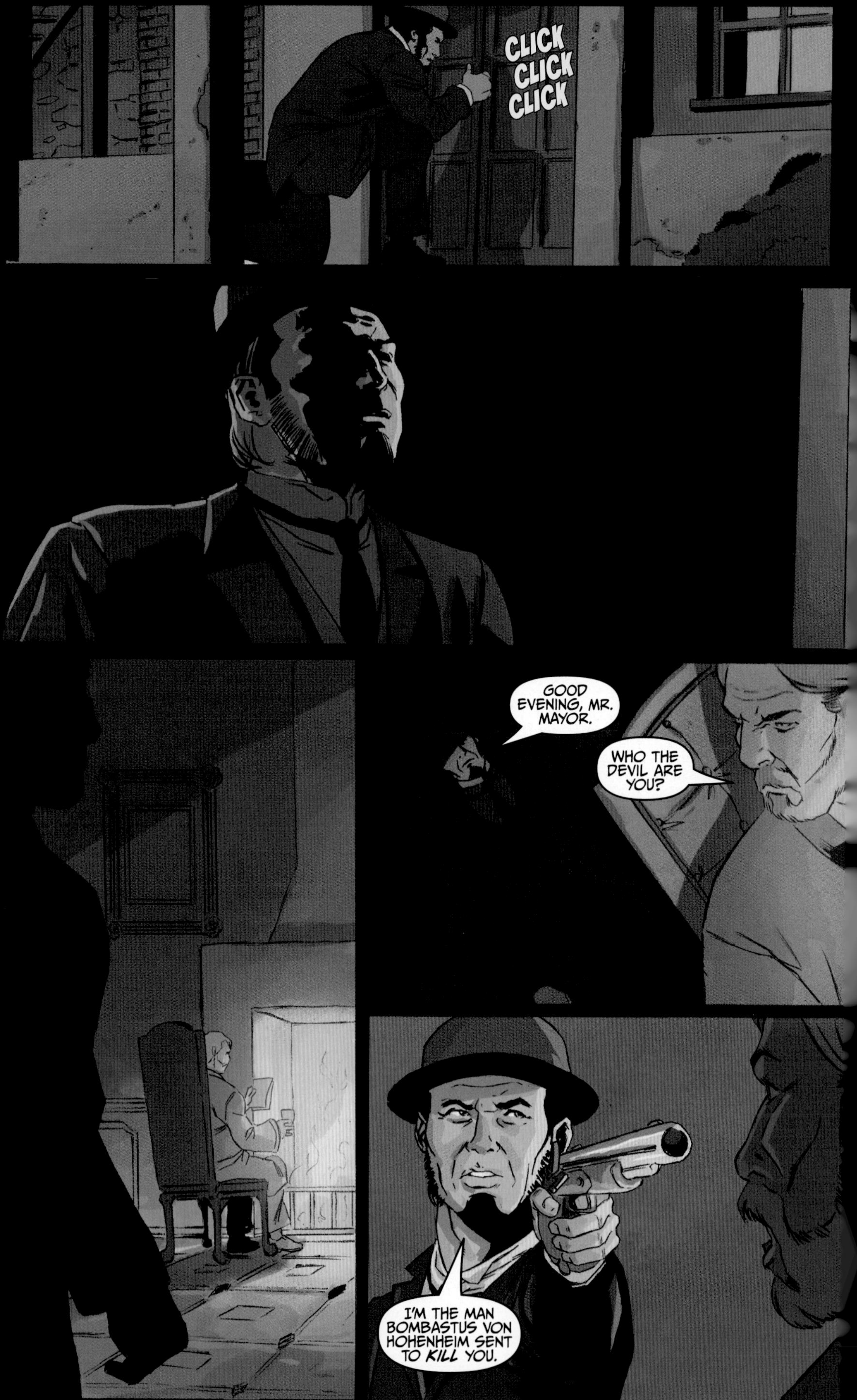

CLICK CLICK CLICK
GOOD EVENING, MR. MAYOR.
WHO THE DEVIL ARE YOU?
I'M THE MAN BOMBASTUS VON HOHENHEIM SENT TO KILL YOU.

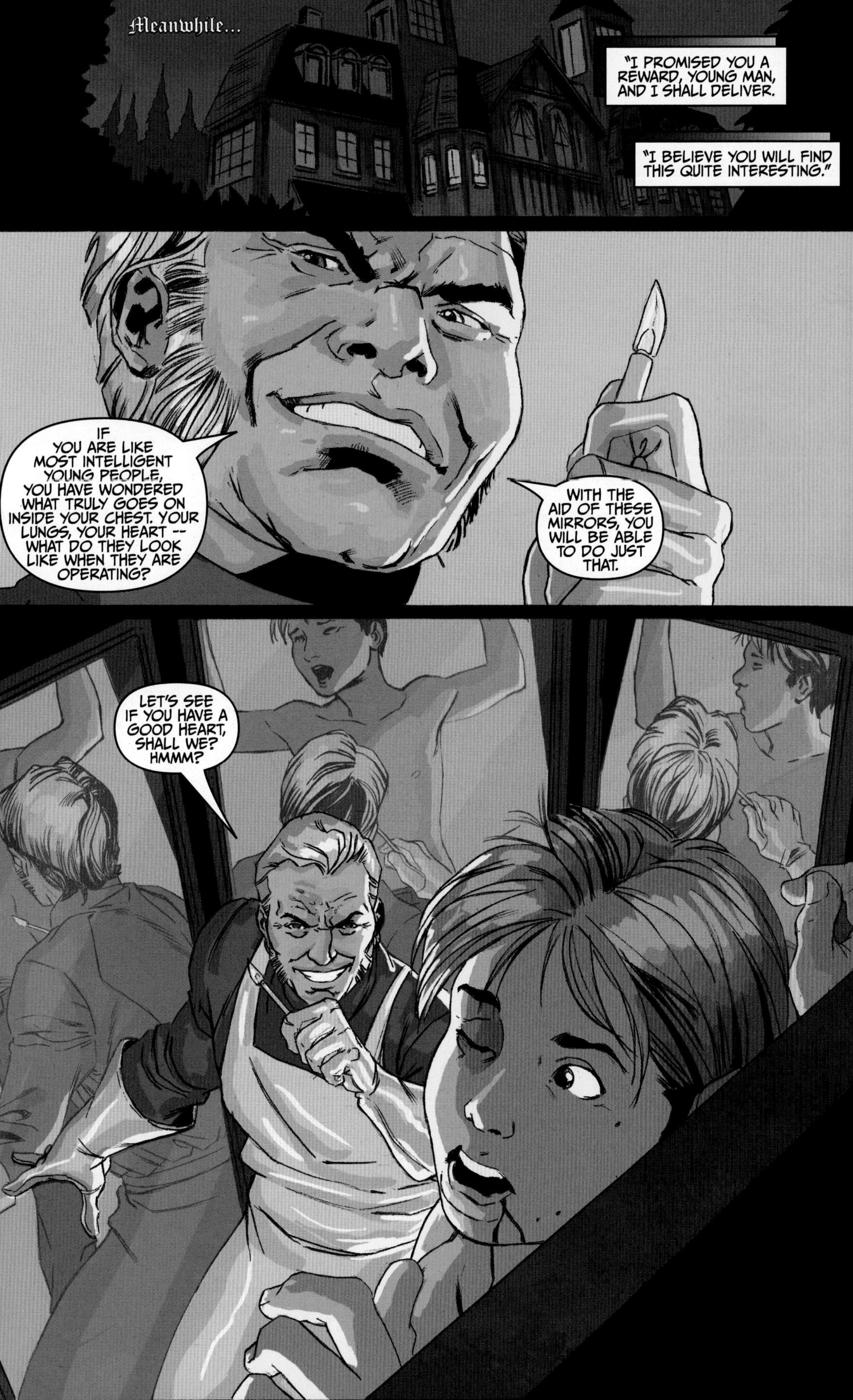
Meanwhile...
"I PROMISED YOU A REWARD, YOUNG MAN, AND I SHALL DELIVER.
"I BELIEVE YOU WILL FIND THIS QUITE INTERESTING."
IF YOU ARE LIKE MOST INTELLIGENT YOUNG PEOPLE, YOU HAVE WONDERED WHAT TRULY GOES ON INSIDE YOUR CHEST. YOUR LUNGS, YOUR HEART -- WHAT DO THEY LOOK LIKE WHEN THEY ARE OPERATING?
WITH THE AID OF THESE MIRRORS, YOU WILL BE ABLE TO DO JUST THAT.
LET'S SEE IF YOU HAVE A GOOD HEART, SHALL WE? HMMM?

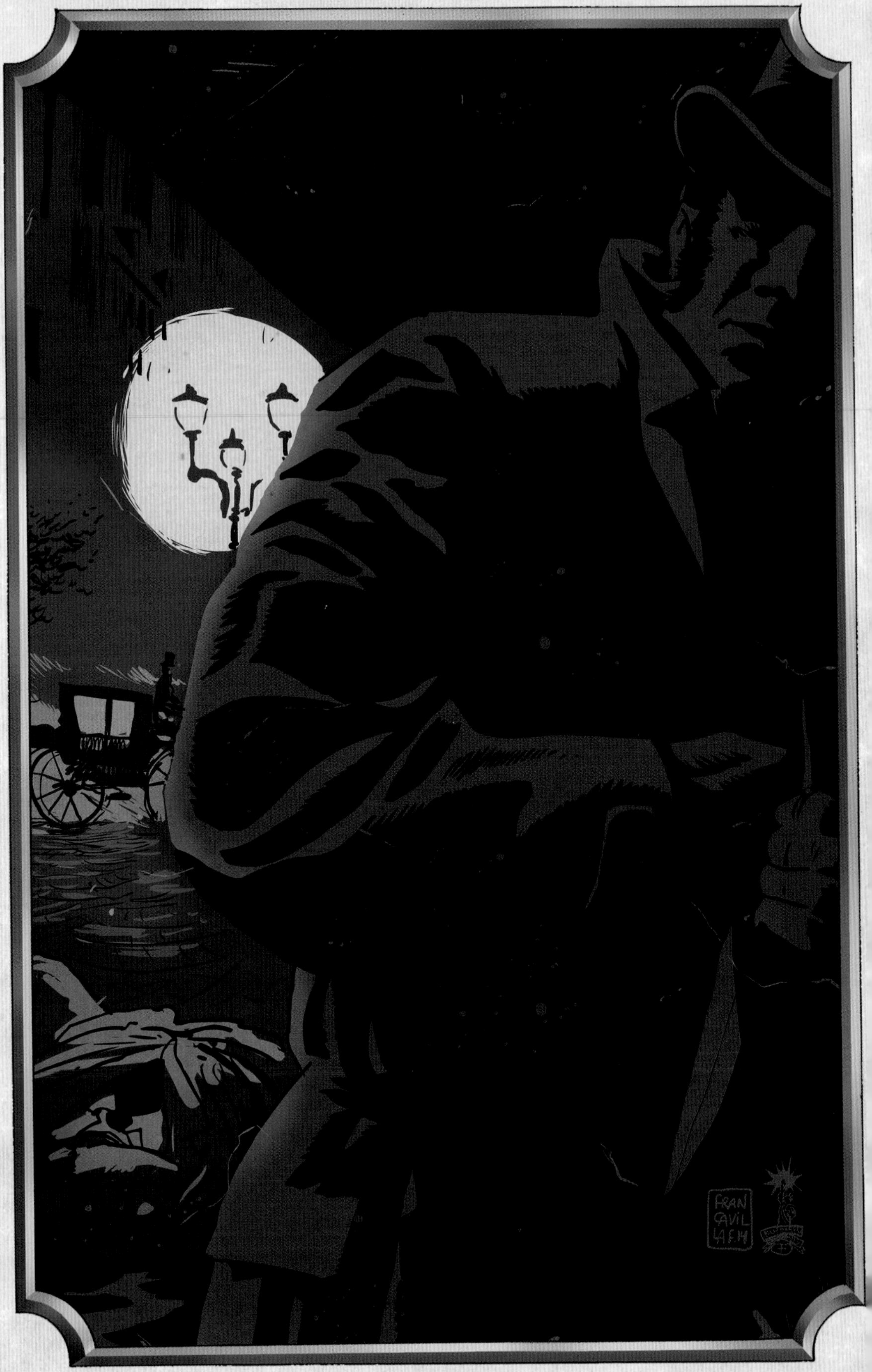
FRAN
CAVIL
LA F. 14

Issue five cover by
Francesco Francavilla

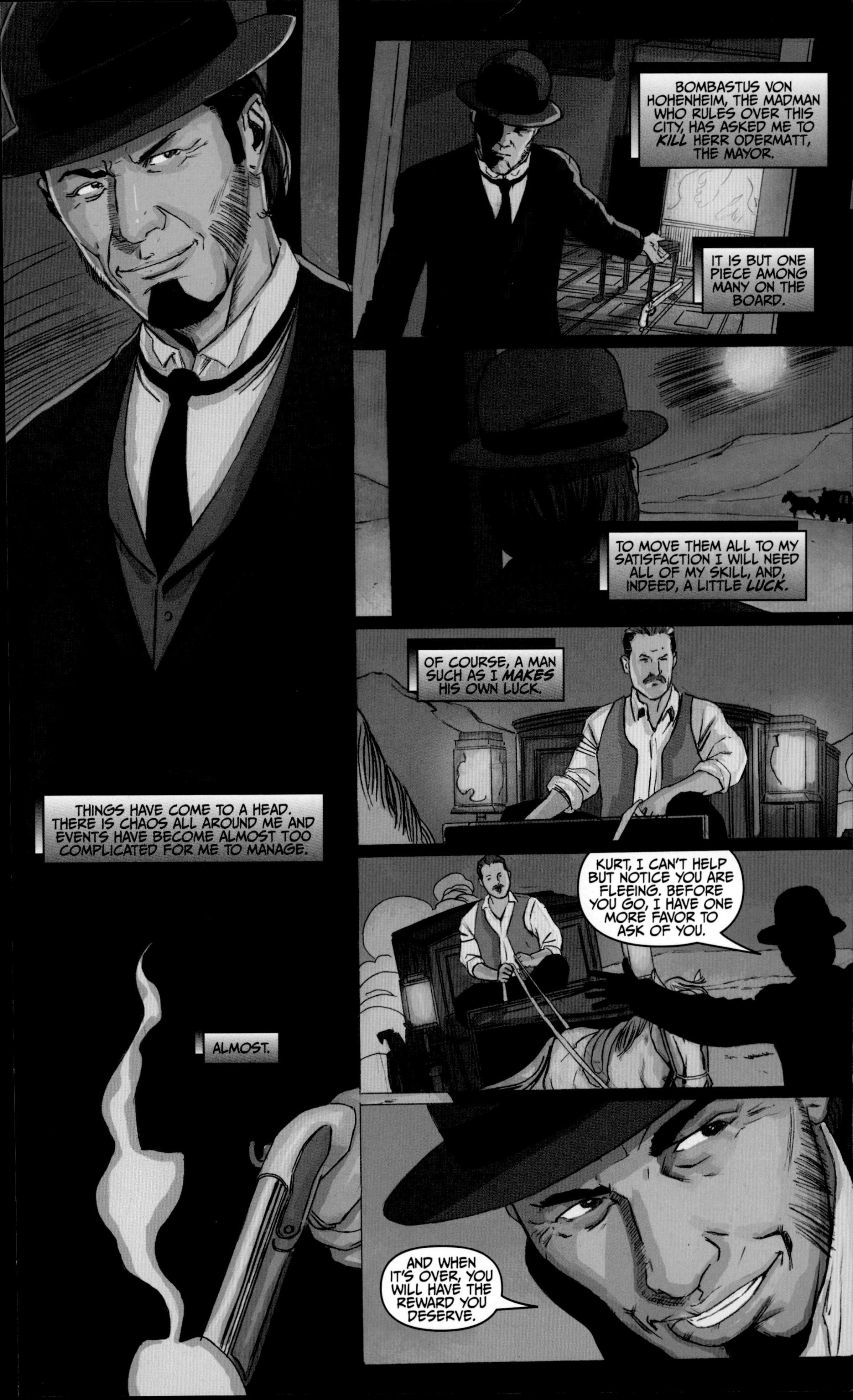
BOMBASTUS VON HOHENHEIM, THE MADMAN WHO RULES OVER THIS CITY, HAS ASKED ME TO *KILL* HERR ODERMATT, THE MAYOR.
IT IS BUT ONE PIECE AMONG MANY ON THE BOARD.
TO MOVE THEM ALL TO MY SATISFACTION I WILL NEED ALL OF MY SKILL, AND, INDEED, A LITTLE *LUCK*.
OF COURSE, A MAN SUCH AS I *MAKES* HIS OWN LUCK.
THINGS HAVE COME TO A HEAD. THERE IS CHAOS ALL AROUND ME AND EVENTS HAVE BECOME ALMOST TOO COMPLICATED FOR ME TO MANAGE.
KURT, I CAN'T HELP BUT NOTICE YOU ARE FLEEING. BEFORE YOU GO, I HAVE ONE MORE FAVOR TO ASK OF YOU.
ALMOST.
AND WHEN IT'S OVER, YOU WILL HAVE THE REWARD YOU DESERVE.

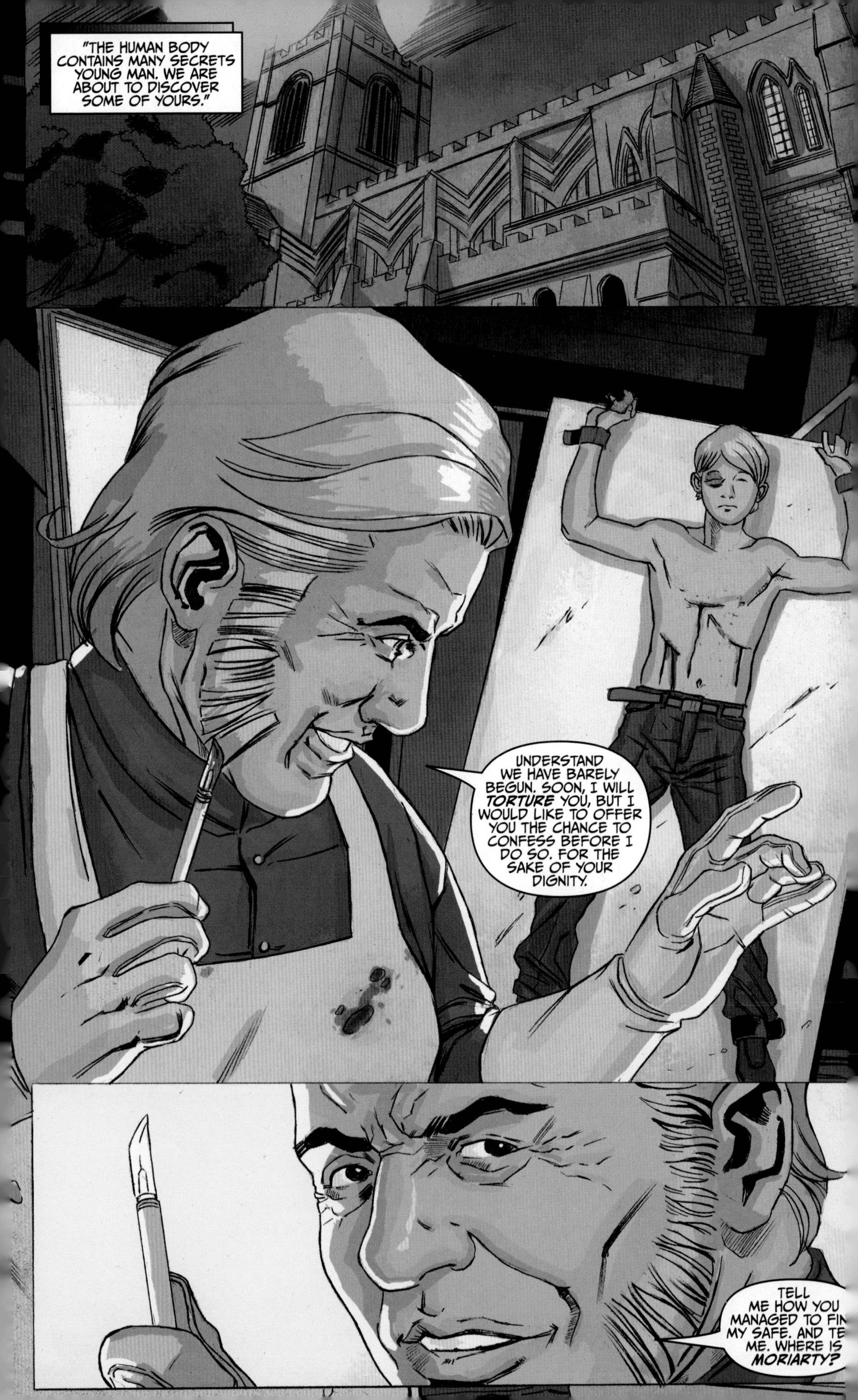
"THE HUMAN BODY CONTAINS MANY SECRETS YOUNG MAN. WE ARE ABOUT TO DISCOVER SOME OF YOURS."
UNDERSTAND WE HAVE BARELY BEGUN. SOON, I WILL *TORTURE* YOU, BUT I WOULD LIKE TO OFFER YOU THE CHANCE TO CONFESS BEFORE I DO SO. FOR THE SAKE OF YOUR DIGNITY.
TELL ME HOW YOU MANAGED TO FIN MY SAFE. AND TE ME. WHERE IS *MORIARTY?*

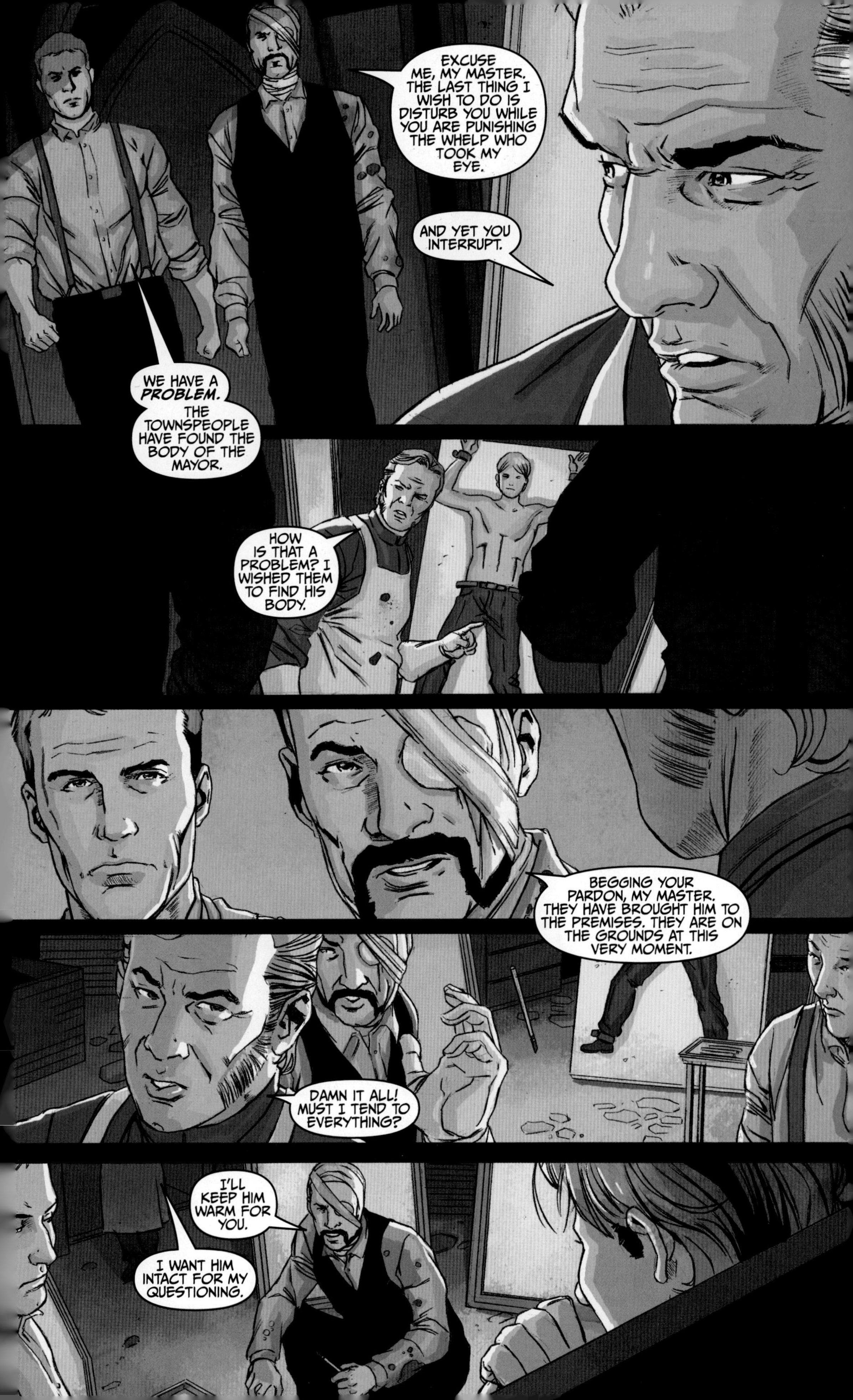
EXCUSE ME, MY MASTER. THE LAST THING I WISH TO DO IS DISTURB YOU WHILE YOU ARE PUNISHING THE WHELP WHO TOOK MY EYE.
AND YET YOU INTERRUPT.
WE HAVE A **PROBLEM.** THE TOWNSPEOPLE HAVE FOUND THE BODY OF THE MAYOR.
HOW IS THAT A PROBLEM? I WISHED THEM TO FIND HIS BODY.
BEGGING YOUR PARDON, MY MASTER. THEY HAVE BROUGHT HIM TO THE PREMISES. THEY ARE ON THE GROUNDS AT THIS VERY MOMENT.
DAMN IT ALL! MUST I TEND TO EVERYTHING?
I'LL KEEP HIM WARM FOR YOU.
I WANT HIM INTACT FOR MY QUESTIONING.

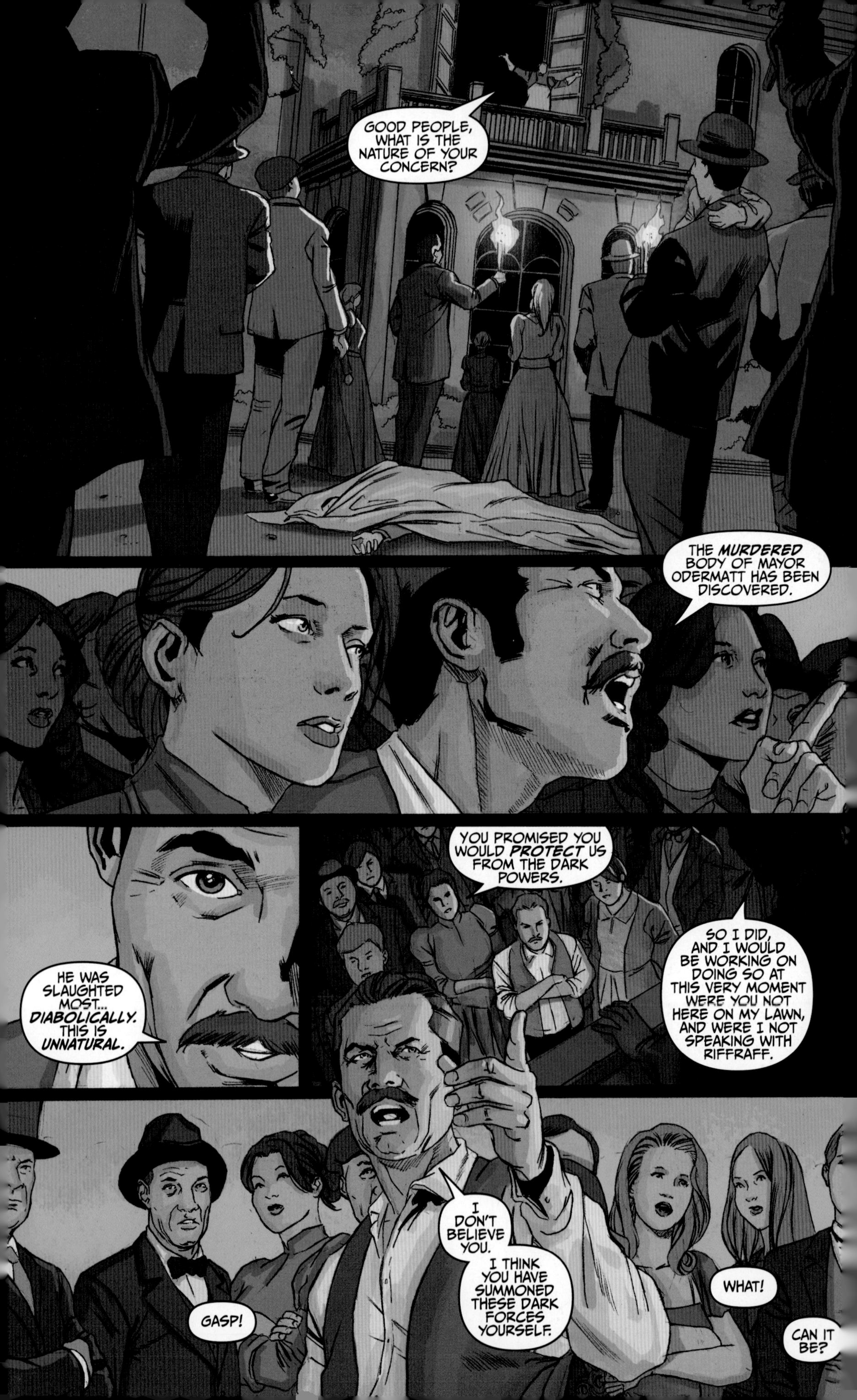
GOOD PEOPLE, WHAT IS THE NATURE OF YOUR CONCERN?
THE MURDERED BODY OF MAYOR ODERMATT HAS BEEN DISCOVERED.
HE WAS SLAUGHTERED MOST... DIABOLICALLY. THIS IS UNNATURAL.
YOU PROMISED YOU WOULD PROTECT US FROM THE DARK POWERS.
SO I DID, AND I WOULD BE WORKING ON DOING SO AT THIS VERY MOMENT WERE YOU NOT HERE ON MY LAWN, AND WERE I NOT SPEAKING WITH RIFFRAFF.
I DON'T BELIEVE YOU.
I THINK YOU HAVE SUMMONED THESE DARK FORCES YOURSELF.
GASP!
WHAT!
CAN IT BE?

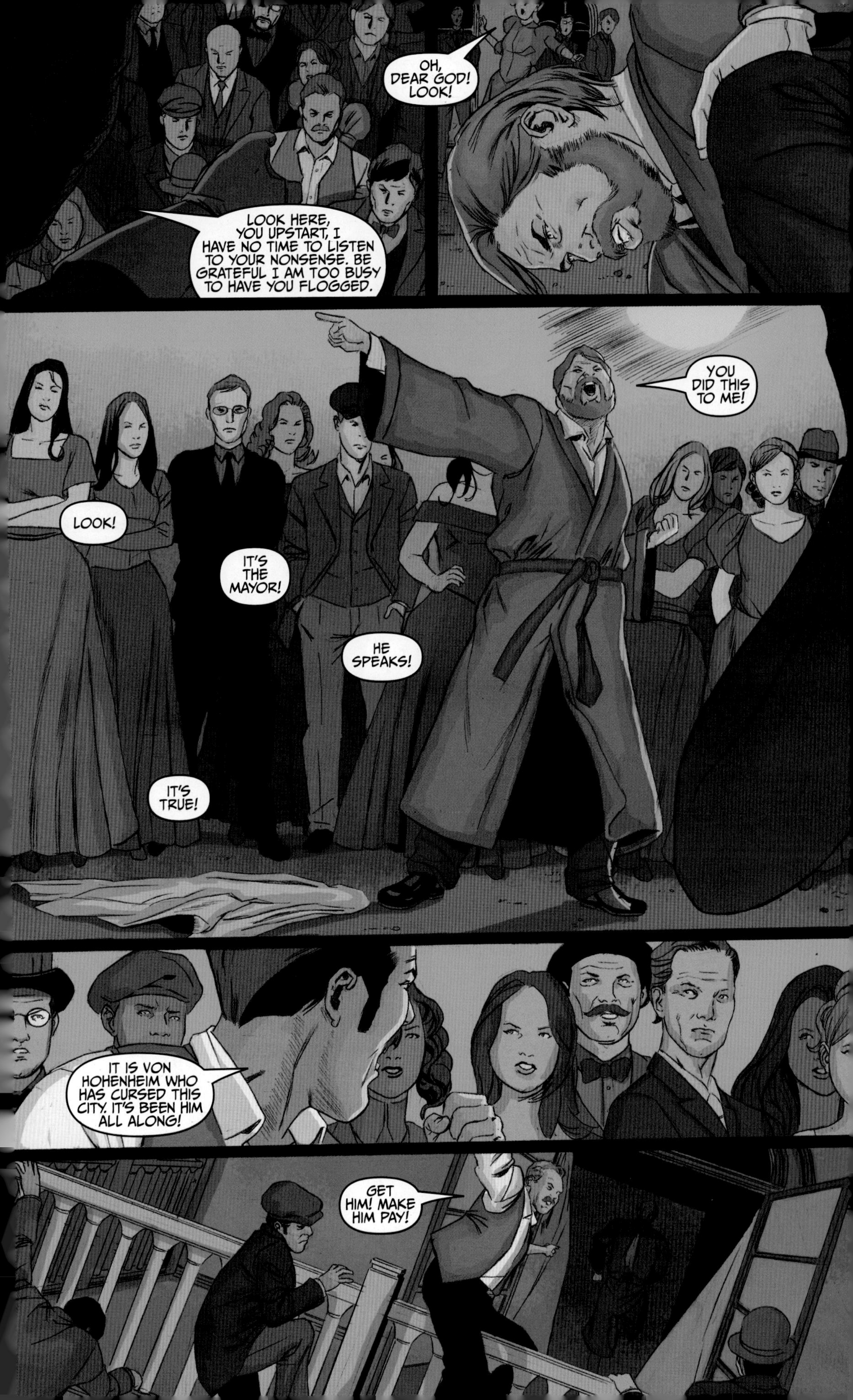
LOOK HERE, YOU UPSTART, I HAVE NO TIME TO LISTEN TO YOUR NONSENSE. BE GRATEFUL I AM TOO BUSY TO HAVE YOU FLOGGED.
OH, DEAR GOD! LOOK!
YOU DID THIS TO ME!
LOOK!
IT'S THE MAYOR!
HE SPEAKS!
IT'S TRUE!
IT IS VON HOHENHEIM WHO HAS CURSED THIS CITY. IT'S BEEN HIM ALL ALONG!
GET HIM! MAKE HIM PAY!

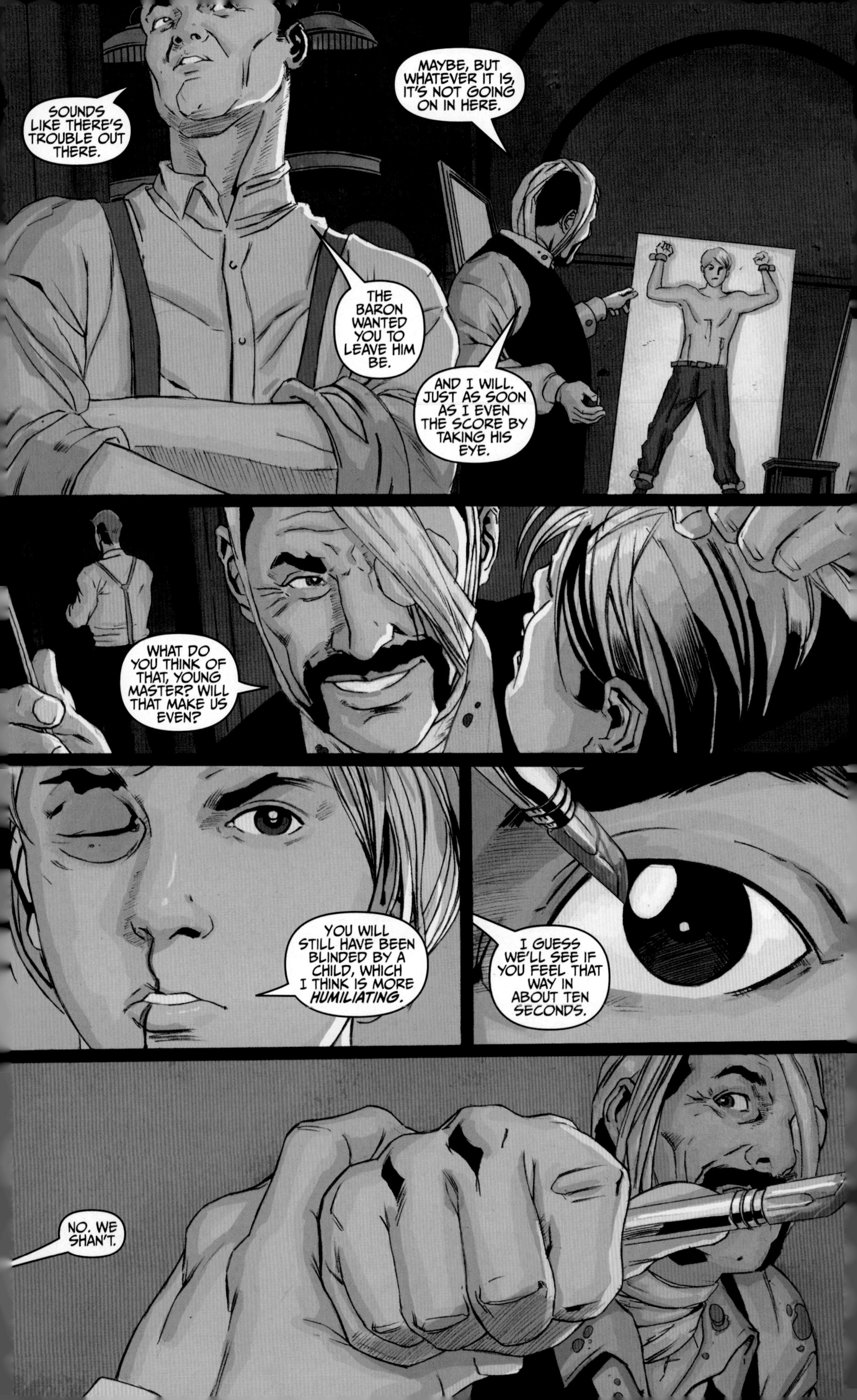
SOUNDS LIKE THERE'S TROUBLE OUT THERE.
MAYBE, BUT WHATEVER IT IS, IT'S NOT GOING ON IN HERE.
THE BARON WANTED YOU TO LEAVE HIM BE.
AND I WILL. JUST AS SOON AS I EVEN THE SCORE BY TAKING HIS EYE.
WHAT DO YOU THINK OF THAT, YOUNG MASTER? WILL THAT MAKE US EVEN?
YOU WILL STILL HAVE BEEN BLINDED BY A CHILD, WHICH I THINK IS MORE *HUMILIATING*.
I GUESS WE'LL SEE IF YOU FEEL THAT WAY IN ABOUT TEN SECONDS.
NO. WE SHAN'T.

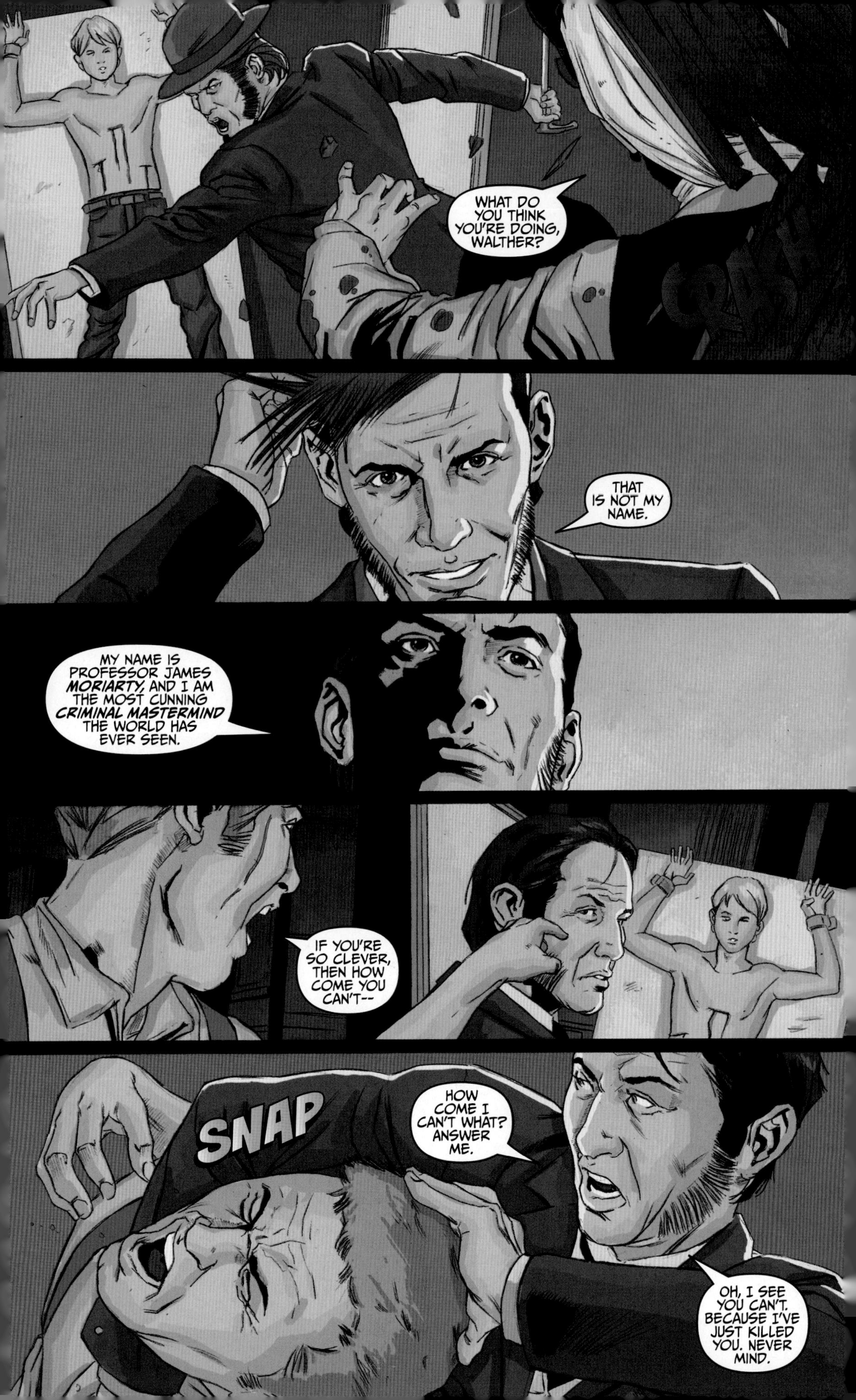
WHAT DO YOU THINK YOU'RE DOING, WALTHER?
THAT IS NOT MY NAME.
MY NAME IS PROFESSOR JAMES *MORIARTY*, AND I AM THE MOST CUNNING *CRIMINAL MASTERMIND* THE WORLD HAS EVER SEEN.
IF YOU'RE SO CLEVER, THEN HOW COME YOU CAN'T--
SNAP
HOW COME I CAN'T WHAT? ANSWER ME.
OH, I SEE YOU CAN'T. BECAUSE I'VE JUST KILLED YOU. NEVER MIND.

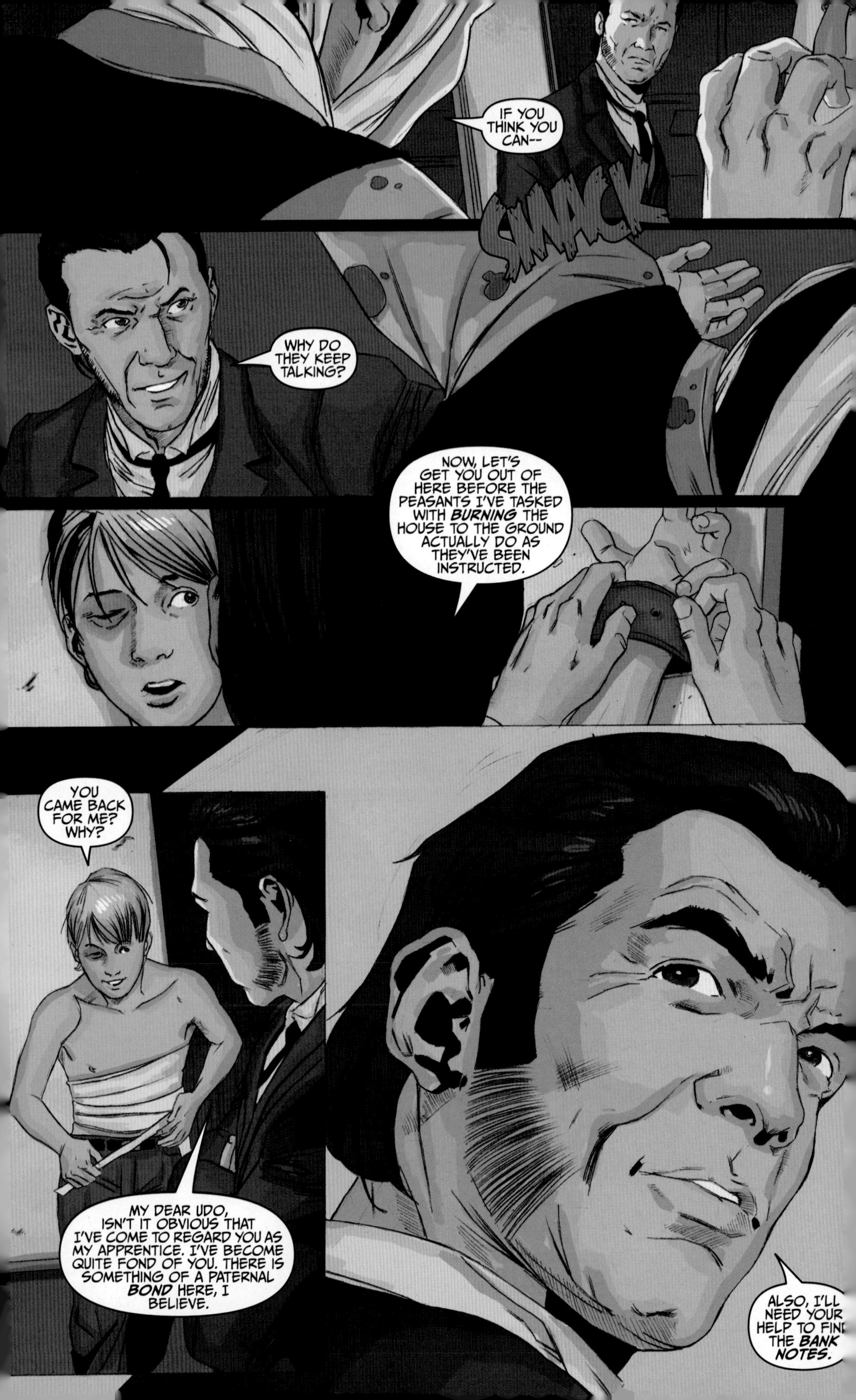
IF YOU THINK YOU CAN--
SMACK
WHY DO THEY KEEP TALKING?
NOW, LET'S GET YOU OUT OF HERE BEFORE THE PEASANTS I'VE TASKED WITH *BURNING* THE HOUSE TO THE GROUND ACTUALLY DO AS THEY'VE BEEN INSTRUCTED.
YOU CAME BACK FOR ME? WHY?
MY DEAR UDO, ISN'T IT OBVIOUS THAT I'VE COME TO REGARD YOU AS MY APPRENTICE. I'VE BECOME QUITE FOND OF YOU. THERE IS SOMETHING OF A PATERNAL *BOND* HERE, I BELIEVE.
ALSO, I'LL NEED YOUR HELP TO FIND THE *BANK NOTES.*

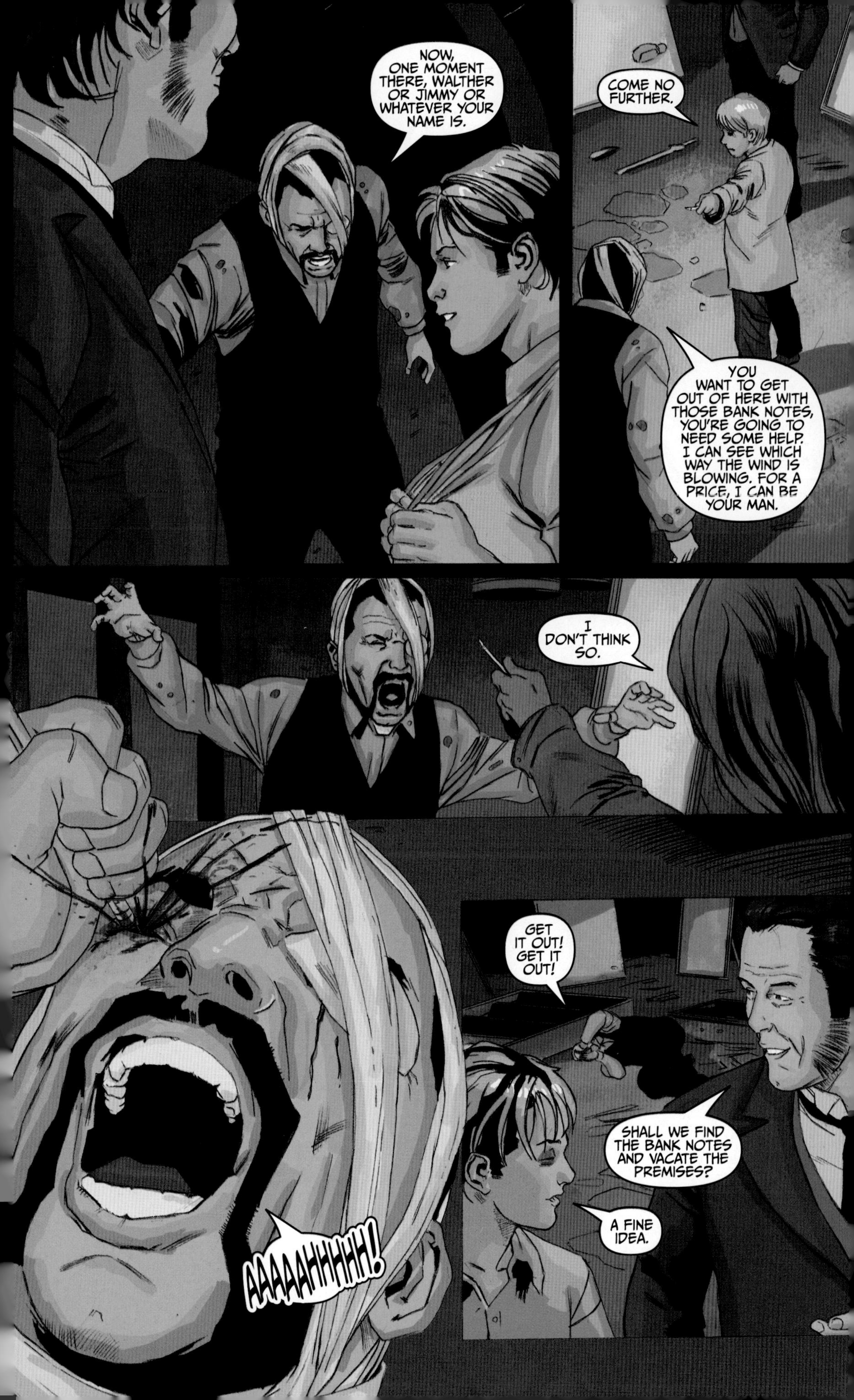
NOW, ONE MOMENT THERE, WALTHER OR JIMMY OR WHATEVER YOUR NAME IS.
COME NO FURTHER.
YOU WANT TO GET OUT OF HERE WITH THOSE BANK NOTES, YOU'RE GOING TO NEED SOME HELP. I CAN SEE WHICH WAY THE WIND IS BLOWING. FOR A PRICE, I CAN BE YOUR MAN.
I DON'T THINK SO.
AAAAAHHHHH!
GET IT OUT! GET IT OUT!
SHALL WE FIND THE BANK NOTES AND VACATE THE PREMISES?
A FINE IDEA.

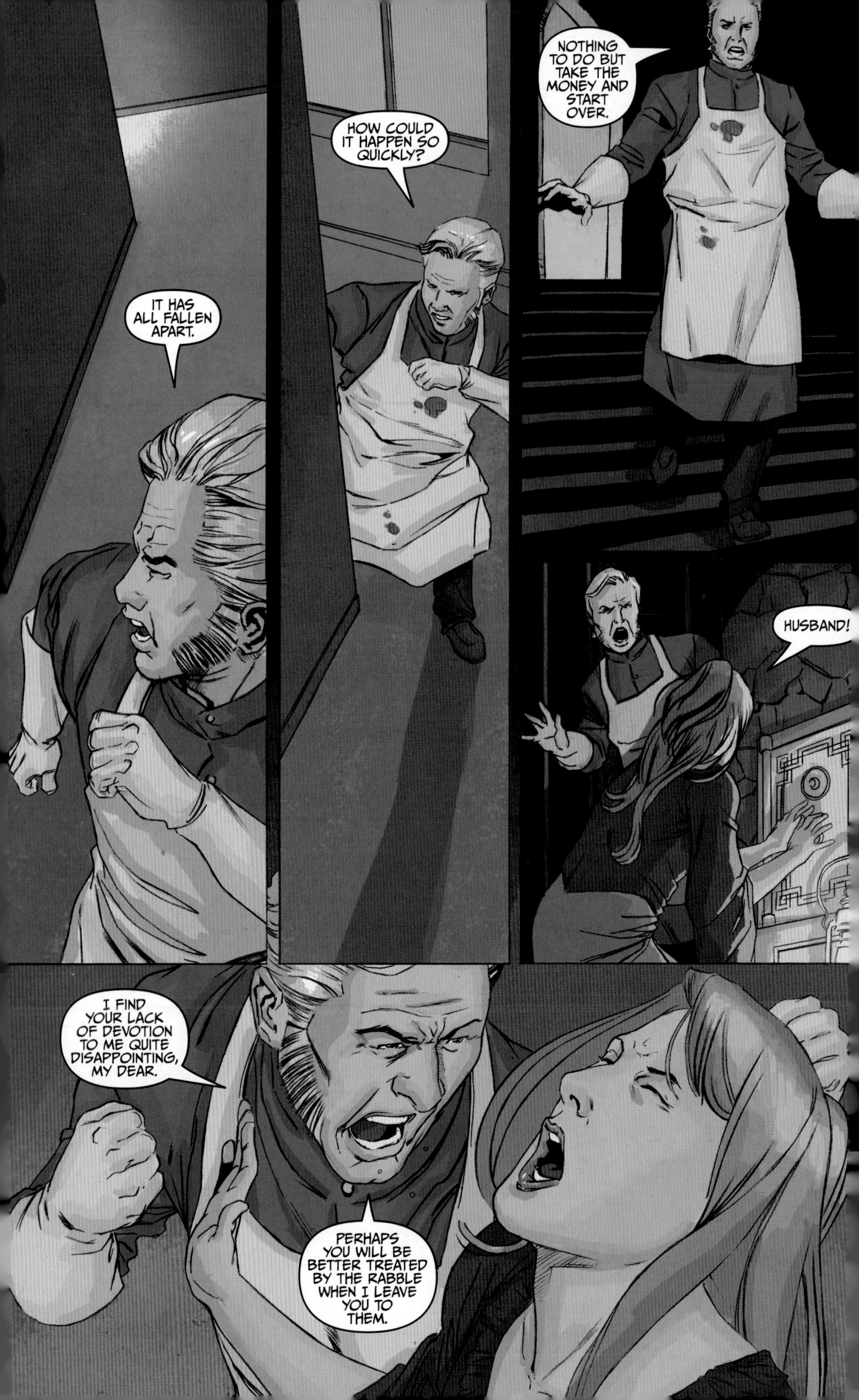
IT HAS ALL FALLEN APART.
HOW COULD IT HAPPEN SO QUICKLY?
NOTHING TO DO BUT TAKE THE MONEY AND START OVER.
HUSBAND!
I FIND YOUR LACK OF DEVOTION TO ME QUITE DISAPPOINTING, MY DEAR.
PERHAPS YOU WILL BE BETTER TREATED BY THE RABBLE WHEN I LEAVE YOU TO THEM.

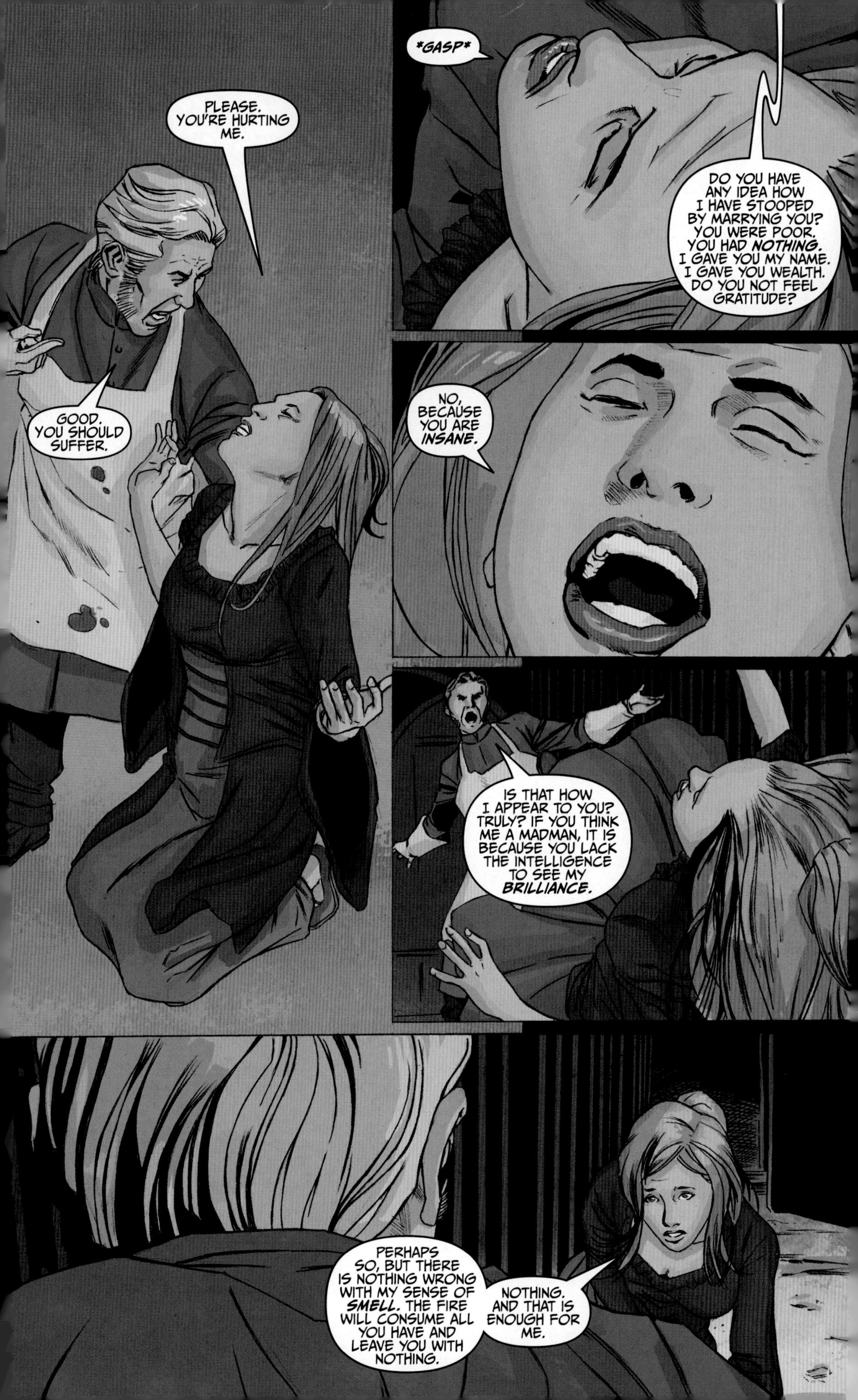
PLEASE. YOU'RE HURTING ME.
GOOD. YOU SHOULD SUFFER.
*GASP*
DO YOU HAVE ANY IDEA HOW I HAVE STOOPED BY MARRYING YOU? YOU WERE POOR. YOU HAD NOTHING. I GAVE YOU MY NAME. I GAVE YOU WEALTH. DO YOU NOT FEEL GRATITUDE?
NO, BECAUSE YOU ARE INSANE.
IS THAT HOW I APPEAR TO YOU? TRULY? IF YOU THINK ME A MADMAN, IT IS BECAUSE YOU LACK THE INTELLIGENCE TO SEE MY BRILLIANCE.
PERHAPS SO, BUT THERE IS NOTHING WRONG WITH MY SENSE OF SMELL. THE FIRE WILL CONSUME ALL YOU HAVE AND LEAVE YOU WITH NOTHING.
NOTHING. AND THAT IS ENOUGH FOR ME.

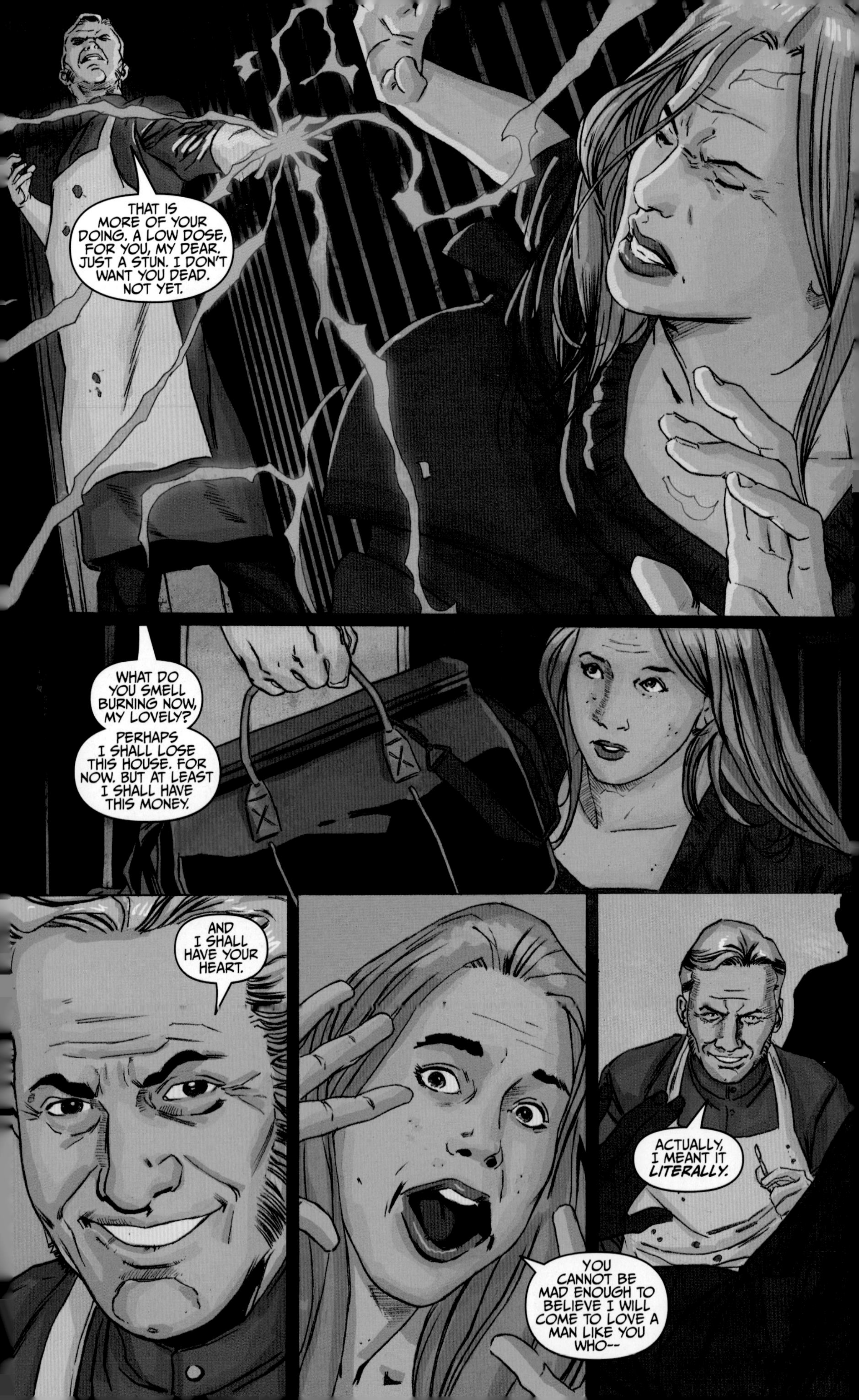
THAT IS MORE OF YOUR DOING. A LOW DOSE, FOR YOU, MY DEAR. JUST A STUN. I DON'T WANT YOU DEAD. NOT YET.
WHAT DO YOU SMELL BURNING NOW, MY LOVELY?
PERHAPS I SHALL LOSE THIS HOUSE. FOR NOW. BUT AT LEAST I SHALL HAVE THIS MONEY.
AND I SHALL HAVE YOUR HEART.
YOU CANNOT BE MAD ENOUGH TO BELIEVE I WILL COME TO LOVE A MAN LIKE YOU WHO--
ACTUALLY, I MEANT IT *LITERALLY.*

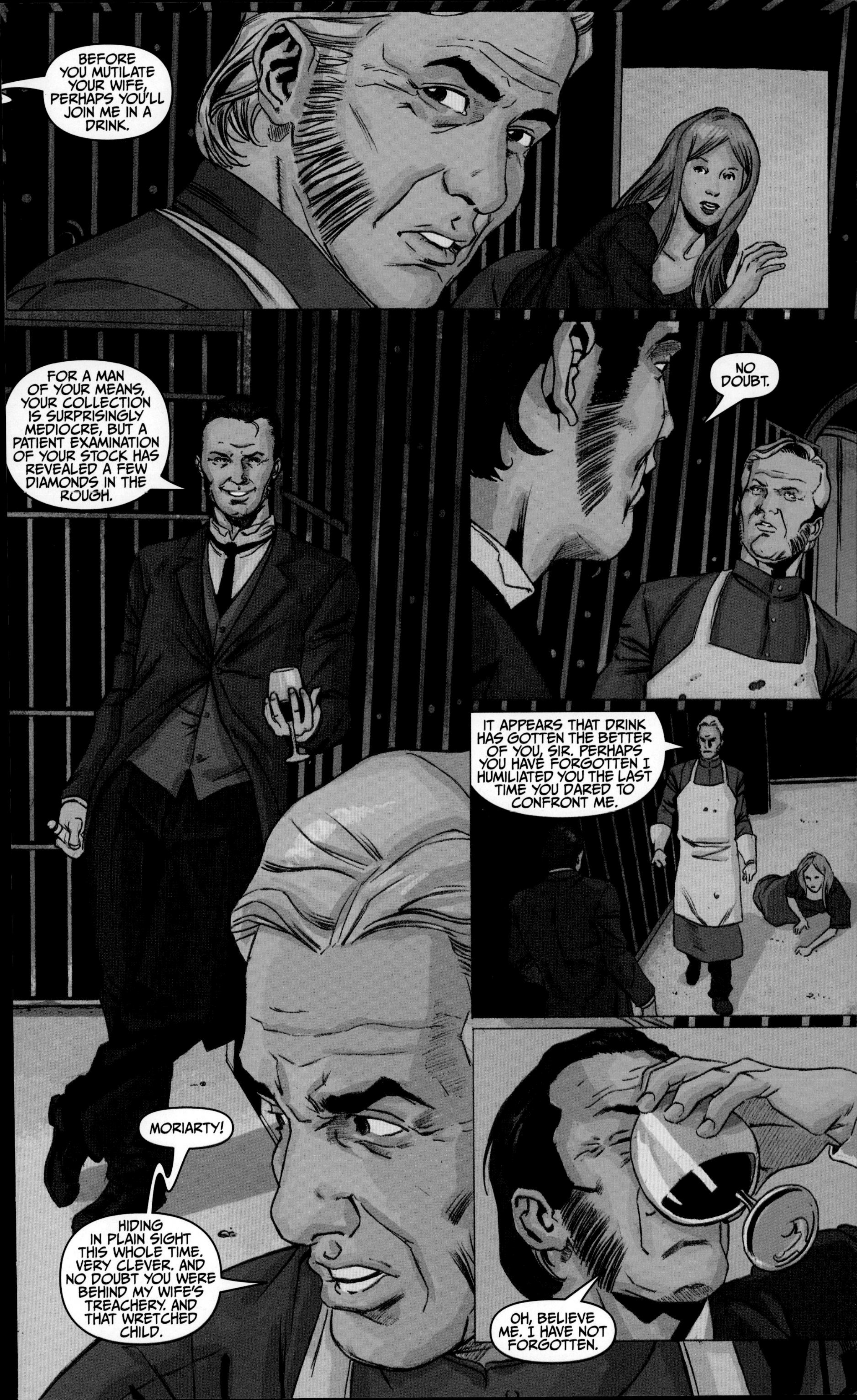
BEFORE YOU MUTILATE YOUR WIFE, PERHAPS YOU'LL JOIN ME IN A DRINK.
FOR A MAN OF YOUR MEANS, YOUR COLLECTION IS SURPRISINGLY MEDIOCRE, BUT A PATIENT EXAMINATION OF YOUR STOCK HAS REVEALED A FEW DIAMONDS IN THE ROUGH.
NO DOUBT.
IT APPEARS THAT DRINK HAS GOTTEN THE BETTER OF YOU, SIR. PERHAPS YOU HAVE FORGOTTEN I HUMILIATED YOU THE LAST TIME YOU DARED TO CONFRONT ME.
MORIARTY!
HIDING IN PLAIN SIGHT THIS WHOLE TIME. VERY CLEVER. AND NO DOUBT YOU WERE BEHIND MY WIFE'S TREACHERY. AND THAT WRETCHED CHILD.
OH, BELIEVE ME. I HAVE NOT FORGOTTEN.

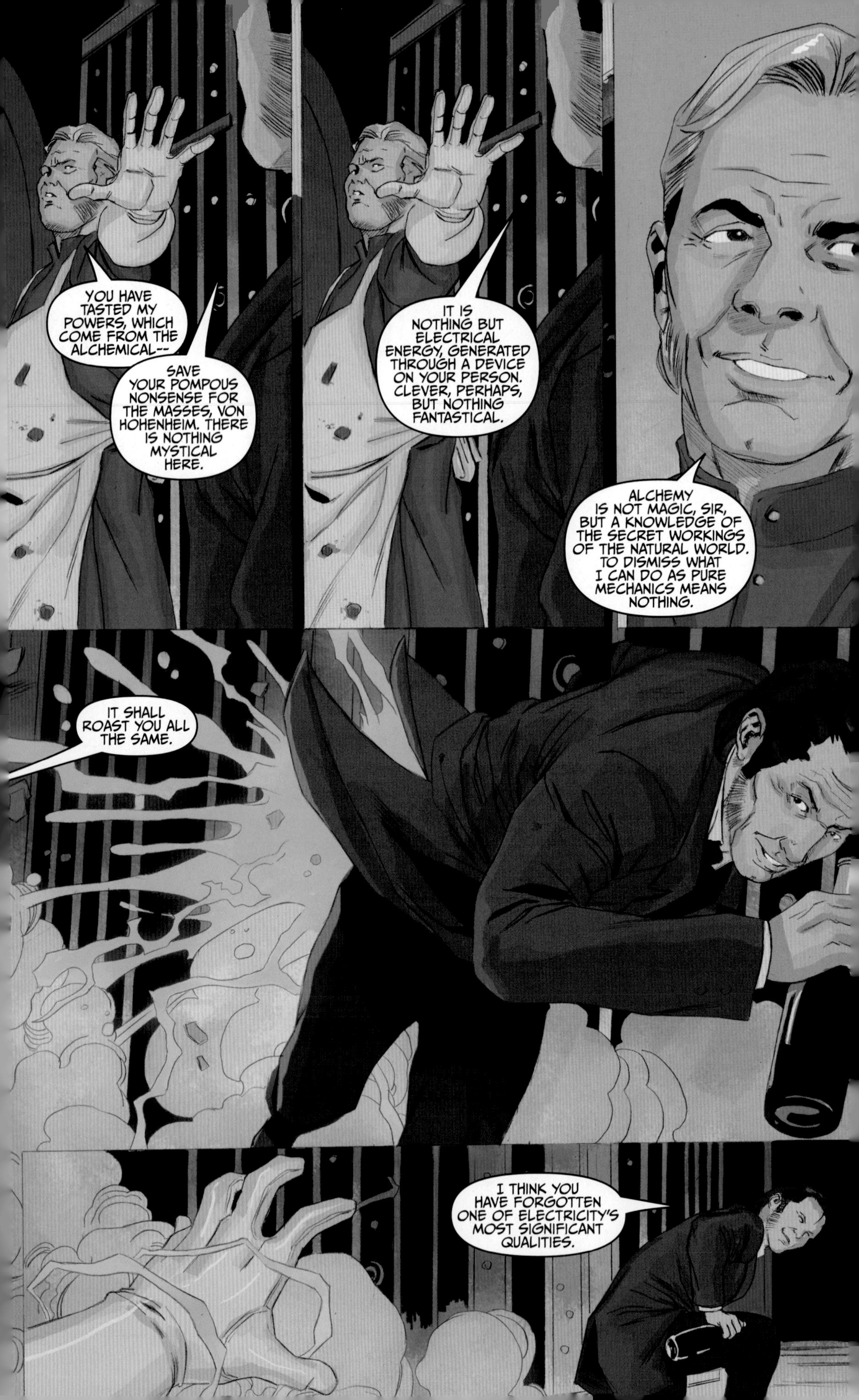
YOU HAVE TASTED MY POWERS, WHICH COME FROM THE ALCHEMICAL--
SAVE YOUR POMPOUS NONSENSE FOR THE MASSES, VON HOHENHEIM. THERE IS NOTHING MYSTICAL HERE.
IT IS NOTHING BUT ELECTRICAL ENERGY, GENERATED THROUGH A DEVICE ON YOUR PERSON. CLEVER, PERHAPS, BUT NOTHING FANTASTICAL.
ALCHEMY IS NOT MAGIC, SIR, BUT A KNOWLEDGE OF THE SECRET WORKINGS OF THE NATURAL WORLD. TO DISMISS WHAT I CAN DO AS PURE MECHANICS MEANS NOTHING.
IT SHALL ROAST YOU ALL THE SAME.
I THINK YOU HAVE FORGOTTEN ONE OF ELECTRICITY'S MOST SIGNIFICANT QUALITIES.

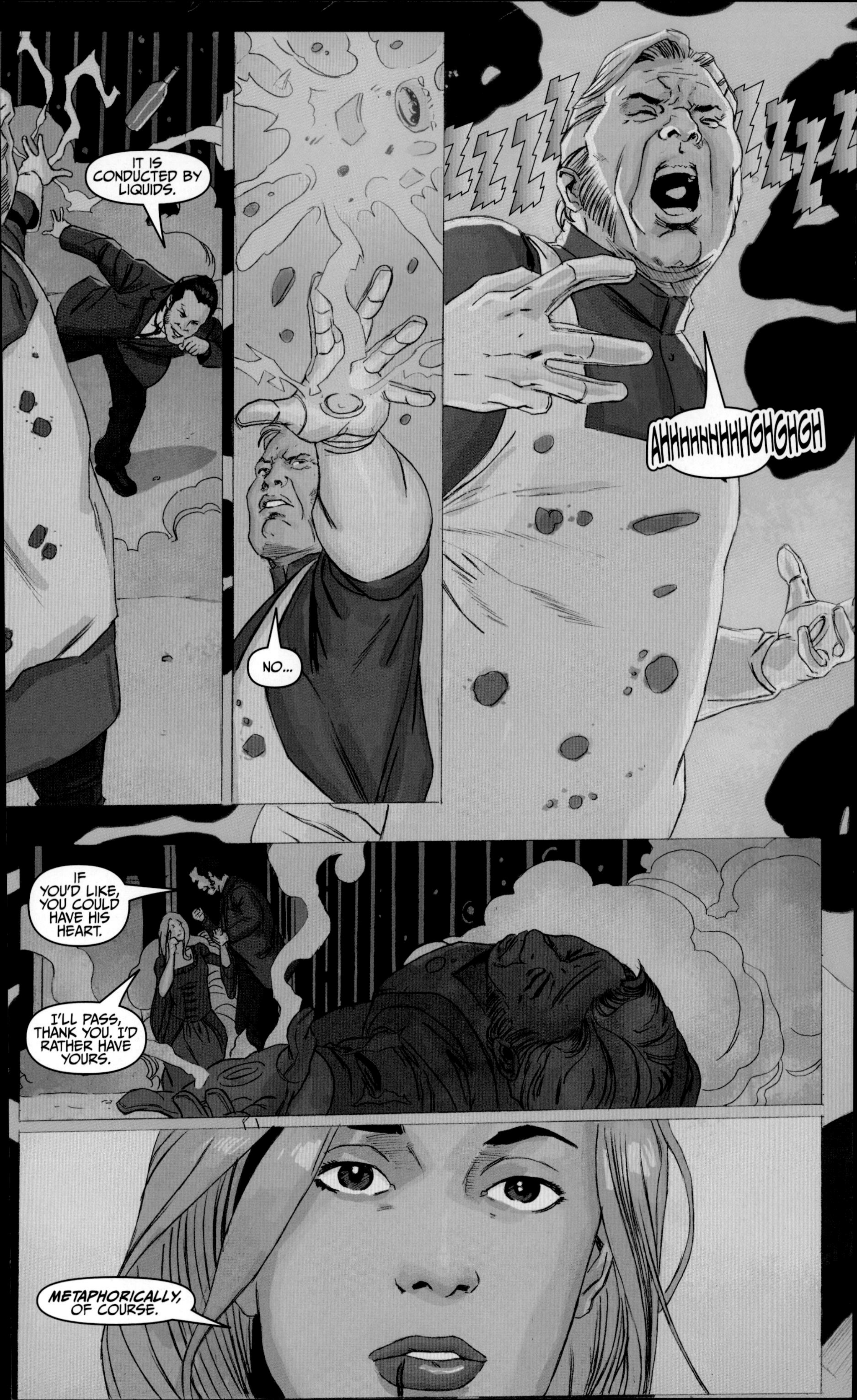
IT IS CONDUCTED BY LIQUIDS.
NO...
ZZZZZ
ZZZZ
AHHHHHHHHHGHGHGH
IF YOU'D LIKE, YOU COULD HAVE HIS HEART.
I'LL PASS, THANK YOU. I'D RATHER HAVE YOURS.
*METAPHORICALLY,* OF COURSE.

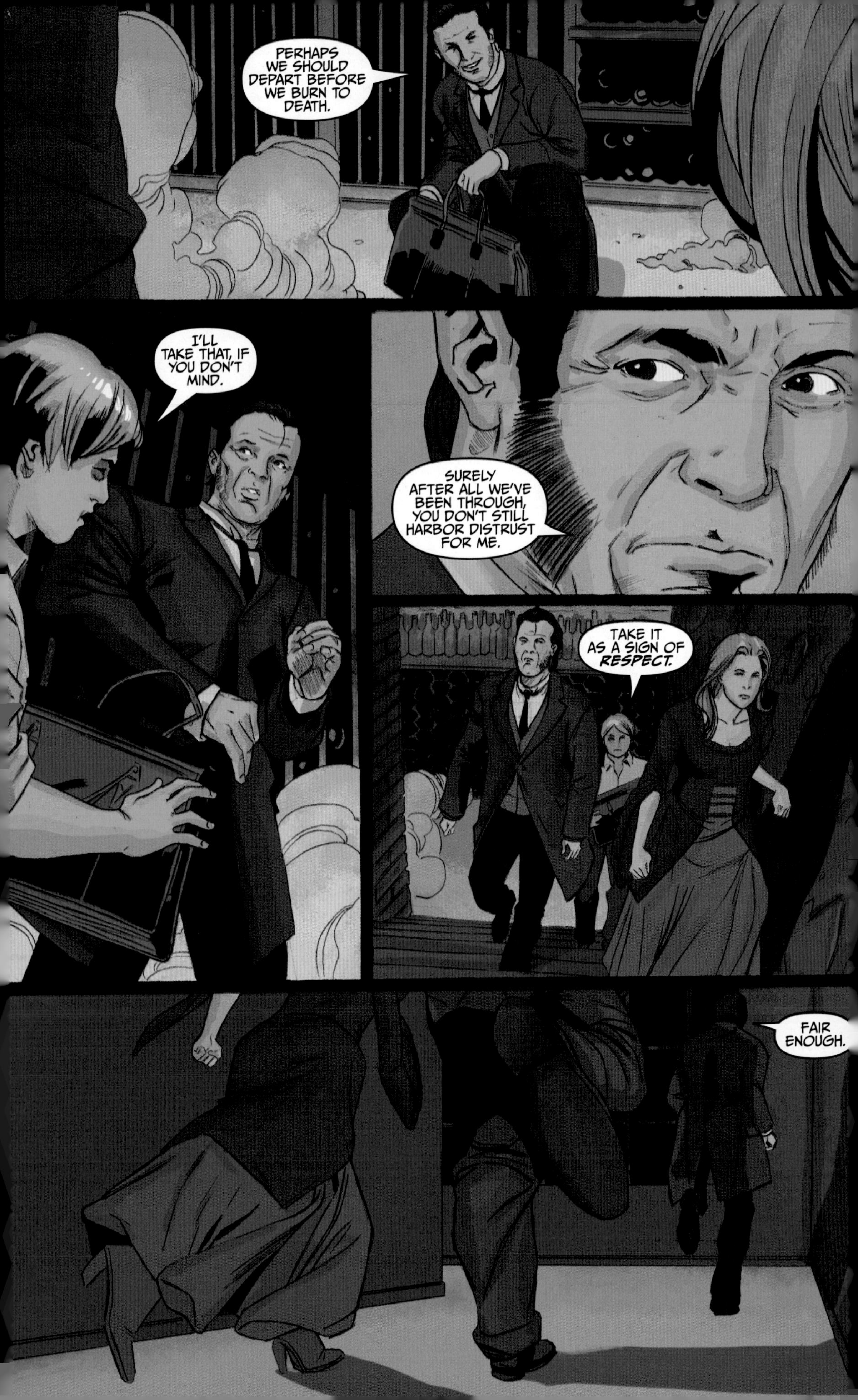
PERHAPS WE SHOULD DEPART BEFORE WE BURN TO DEATH.
I'LL TAKE THAT, IF YOU DON'T MIND.
SURELY AFTER ALL WE'VE BEEN THROUGH, YOU DON'T STILL HARBOR DISTRUST FOR ME.
TAKE IT AS A SIGN OF RESPECT.
FAIR ENOUGH.

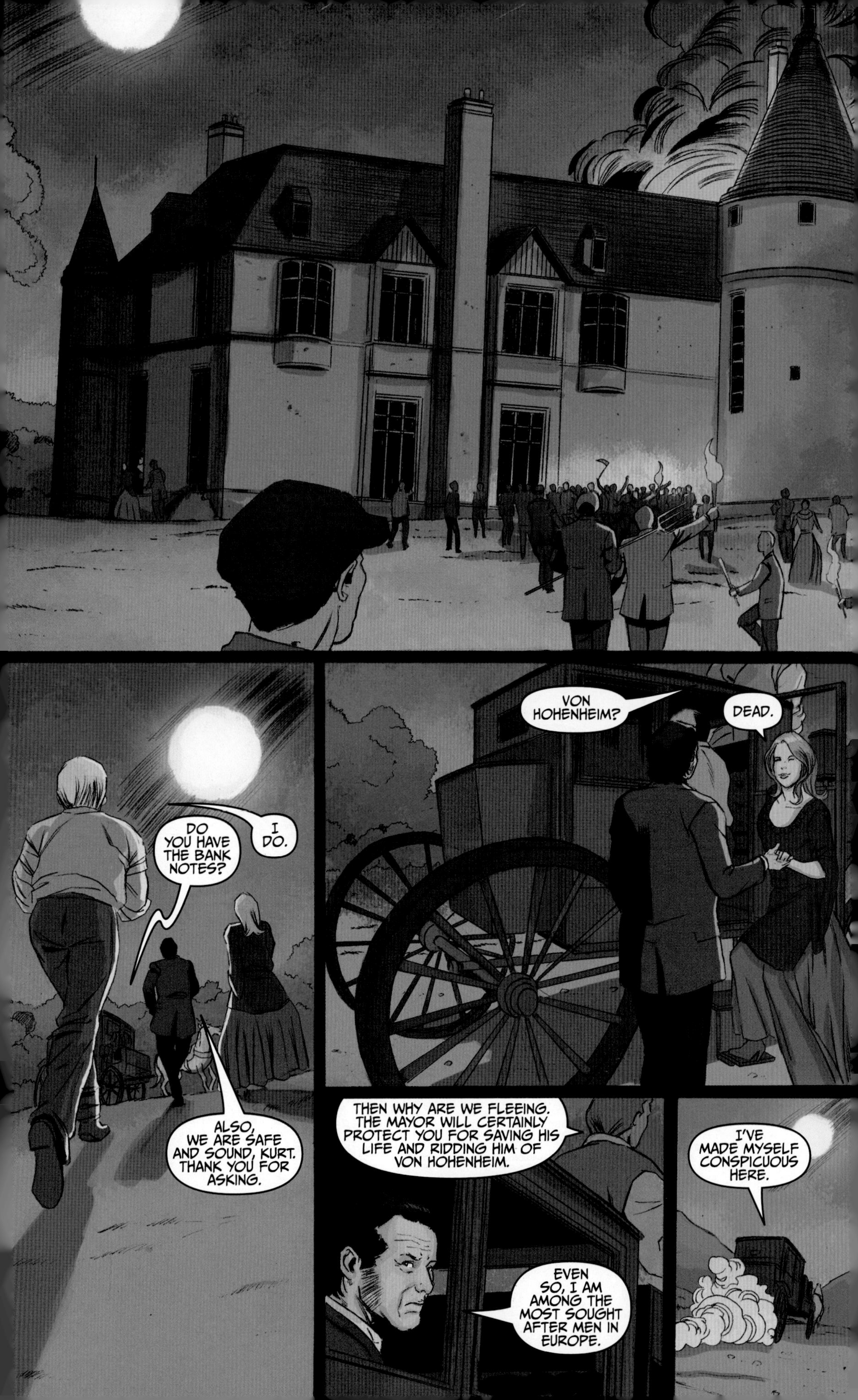
DO YOU HAVE THE BANK NOTES?
I DO.
ALSO, WE ARE SAFE AND SOUND, KURT. THANK YOU FOR ASKING.
VON HOHENHEIM?
DEAD.
THEN WHY ARE WE FLEEING. THE MAYOR WILL CERTAINLY PROTECT YOU FOR SAVING HIS LIFE AND RIDDING HIM OF VON HOHENHEIM.
EVEN SO, I AM AMONG THE MOST SOUGHT AFTER MEN IN EUROPE.
I'VE MADE MYSELF CONSPICUOUS HERE.

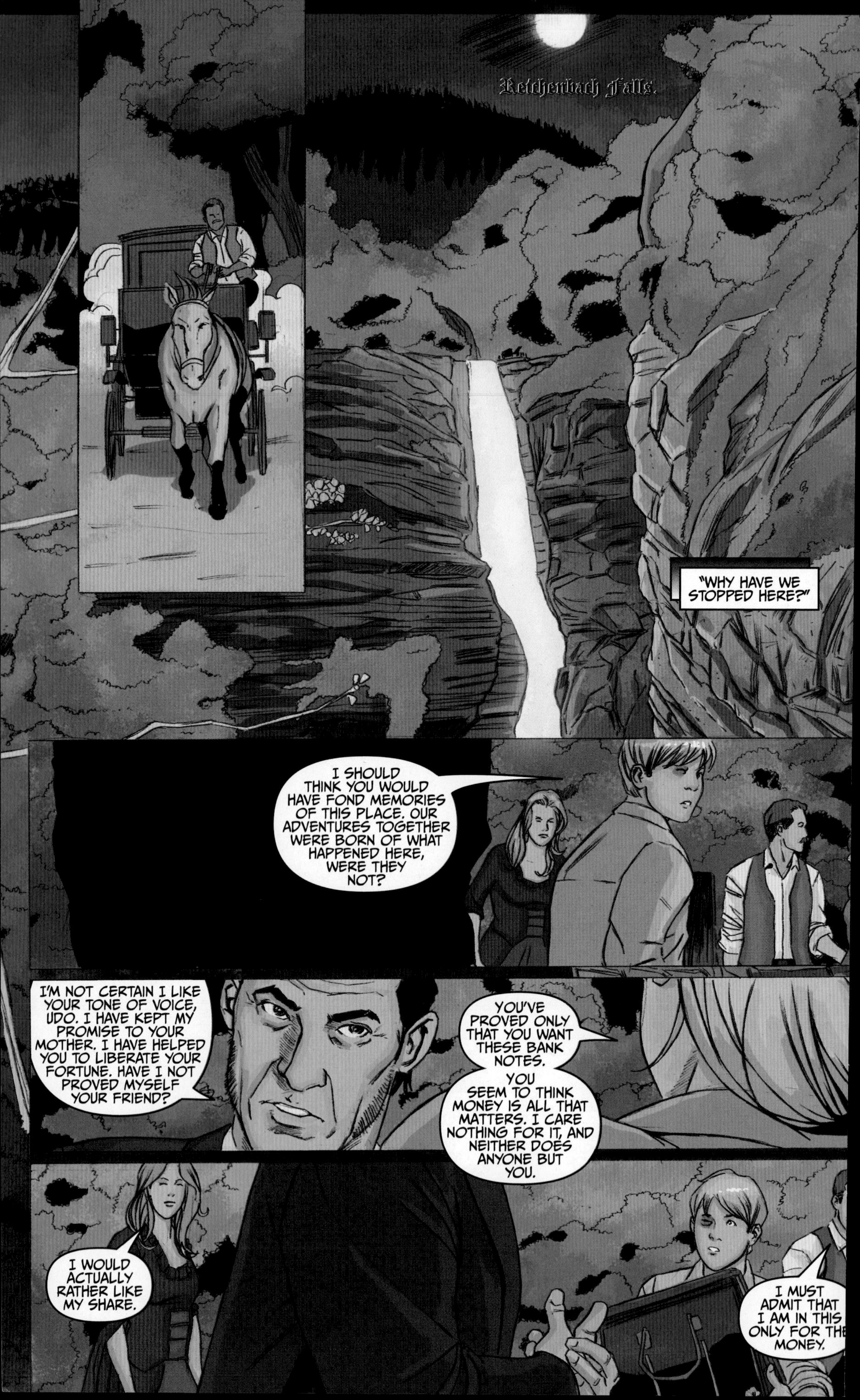
Reichenbach Falls.
"WHY HAVE WE STOPPED HERE?"
I SHOULD THINK YOU WOULD HAVE FOND MEMORIES OF THIS PLACE. OUR ADVENTURES TOGETHER WERE BORN OF WHAT HAPPENED HERE, WERE THEY NOT?
I'M NOT CERTAIN I LIKE YOUR TONE OF VOICE, UDO. I HAVE KEPT MY PROMISE TO YOUR MOTHER. I HAVE HELPED YOU TO LIBERATE YOUR FORTUNE. HAVE I NOT PROVED MYSELF YOUR FRIEND?
YOU'VE PROVED ONLY THAT YOU WANT THESE BANK NOTES.
YOU SEEM TO THINK MONEY IS ALL THAT MATTERS. I CARE NOTHING FOR IT, AND NEITHER DOES ANYONE BUT YOU.
I WOULD ACTUALLY RATHER LIKE MY SHARE.
I MUST ADMIT THAT I AM IN THIS ONLY FOR THE MONEY.

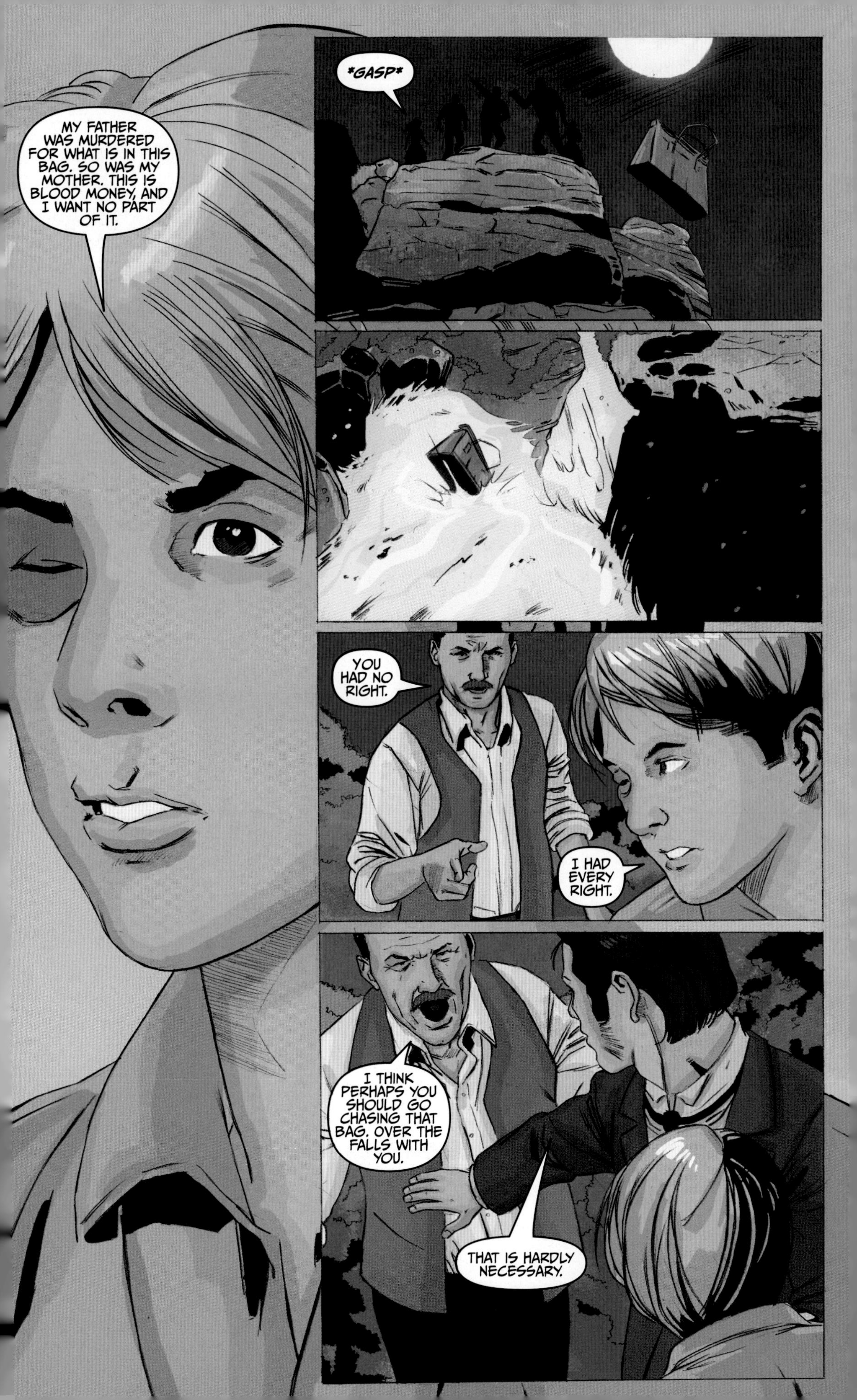
MY FATHER WAS MURDERED FOR WHAT IS IN THIS BAG. SO WAS MY MOTHER. THIS IS BLOOD MONEY, AND I WANT NO PART OF IT.
*GASP*
YOU HAD NO RIGHT.
I HAD EVERY RIGHT.
I THINK PERHAPS YOU SHOULD GO CHASING THAT BAG. OVER THE FALLS WITH YOU.
THAT IS HARDLY NECESSARY.

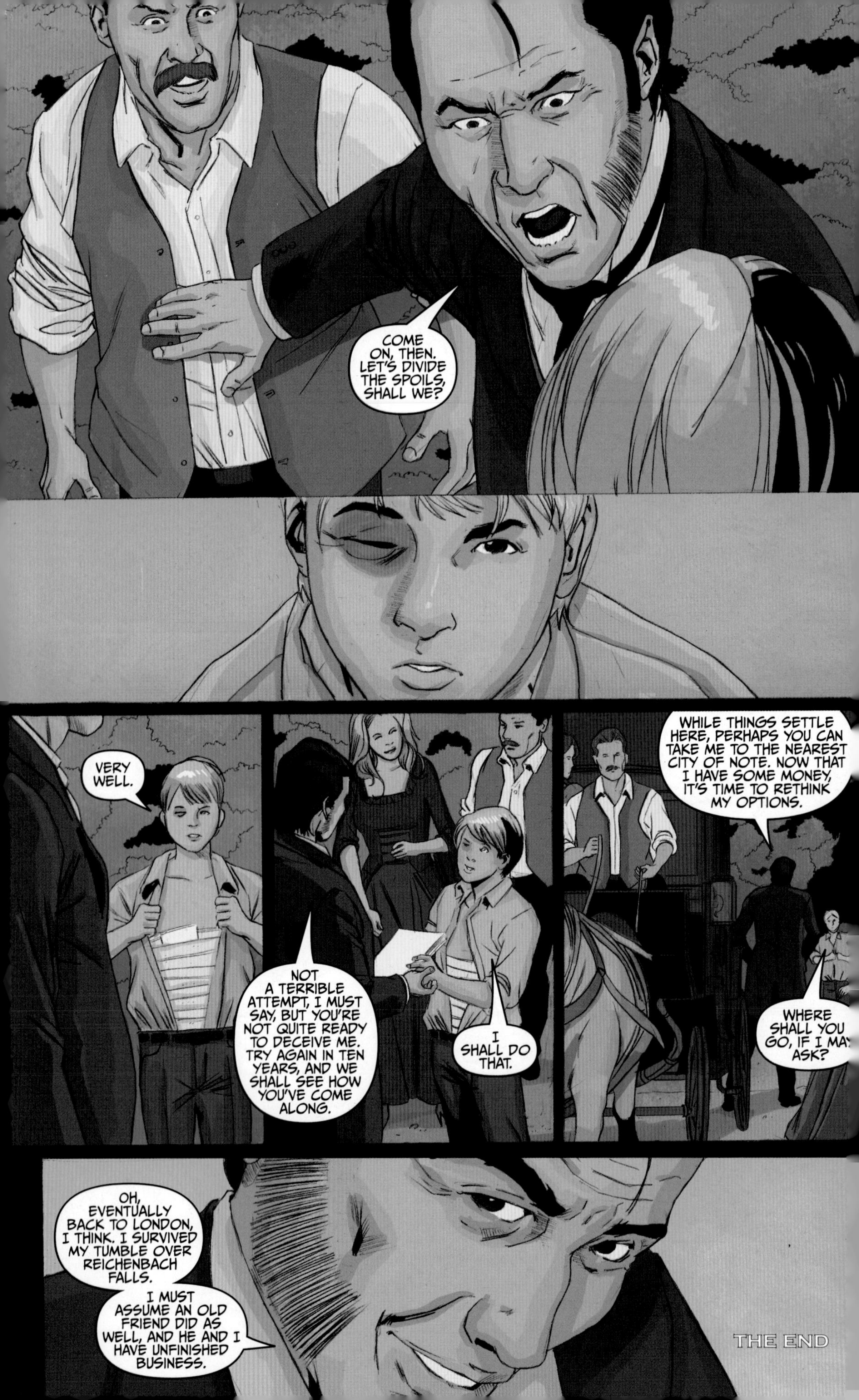
COME ON, THEN. LET'S DIVIDE THE SPOILS, SHALL WE?
VERY WELL.
NOT A TERRIBLE ATTEMPT, I MUST SAY, BUT YOU'RE NOT QUITE READY TO DECEIVE ME. TRY AGAIN IN TEN YEARS, AND WE SHALL SEE HOW YOU'VE COME ALONG.
I SHALL DO THAT.
WHILE THINGS SETTLE HERE, PERHAPS YOU CAN TAKE ME TO THE NEAREST CITY OF NOTE. NOW THAT I HAVE SOME MONEY, IT'S TIME TO RETHINK MY OPTIONS.
WHERE SHALL YOU GO, IF I MAY ASK?
OH, EVENTUALLY BACK TO LONDON, I THINK. I SURVIVED MY TUMBLE OVER REICHENBACH FALLS.
I MUST ASSUME AN OLD FRIEND DID AS WELL, AND HE AND I HAVE UNFINISHED BUSINESS.
THE END

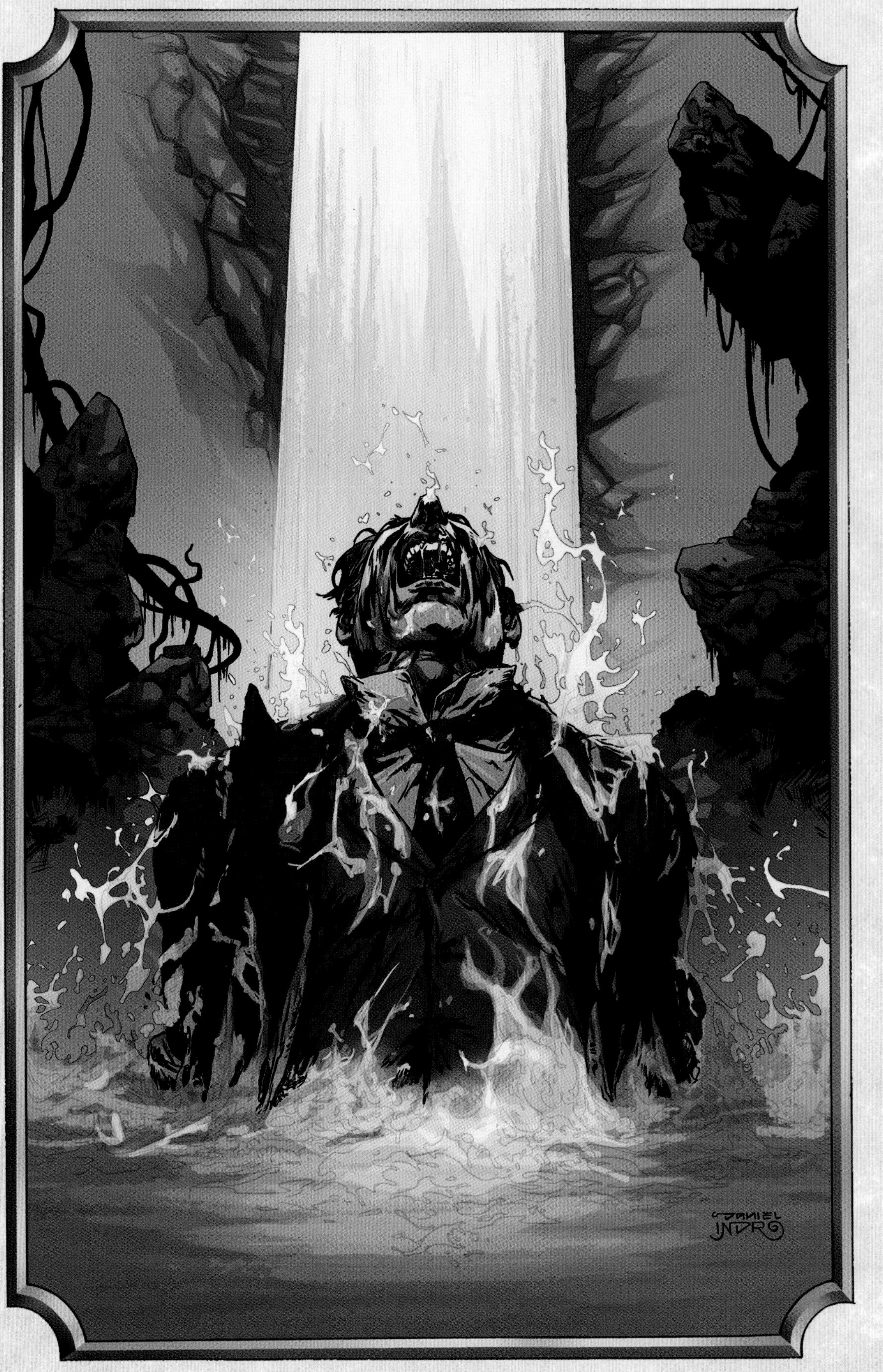
DANIEL INDRO

Issue one alternate cover by
Daniel Indro

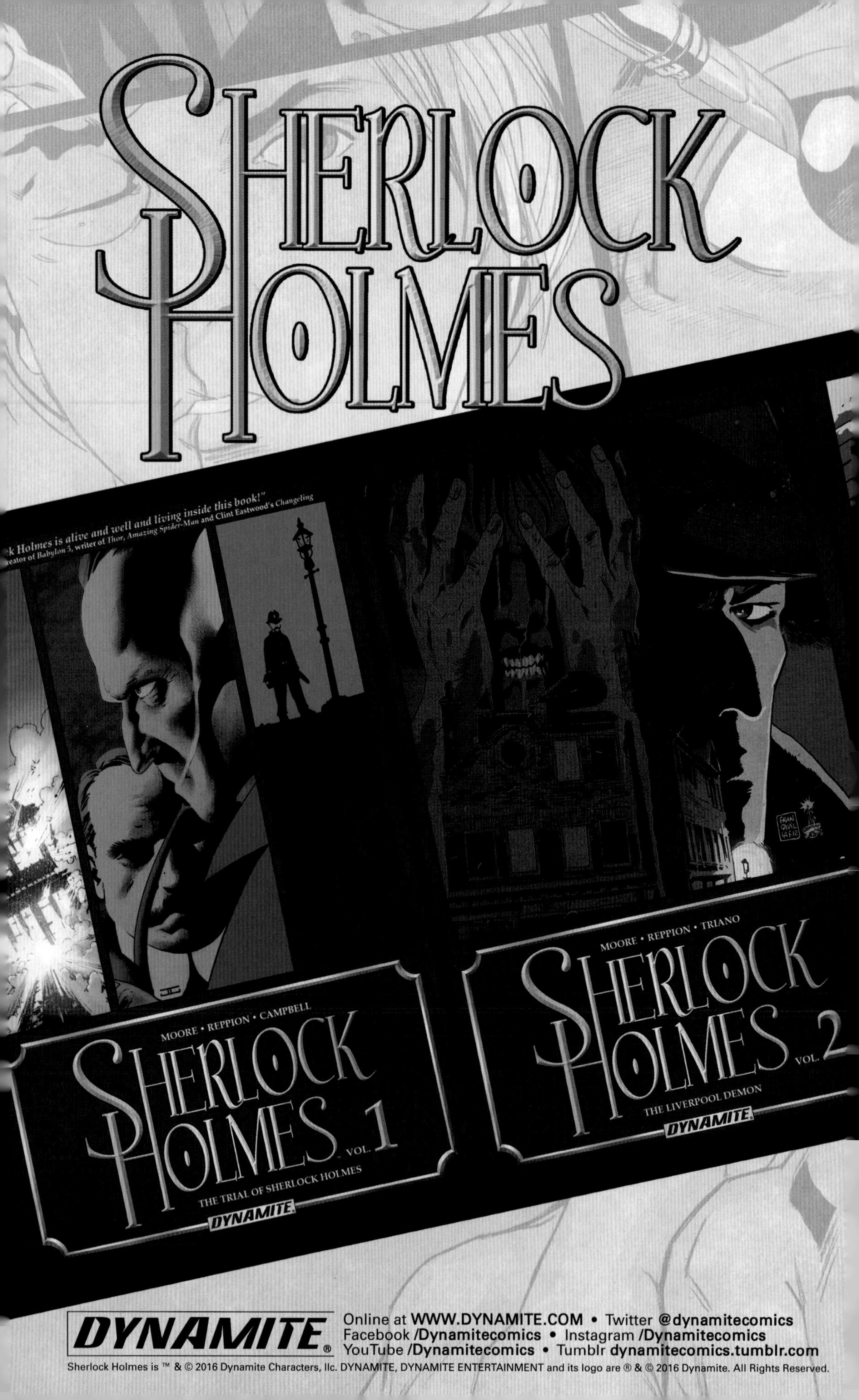
SHERLOCK HOLMES
k Holmes is alive and well and living inside this book!"
reator of Babylon 5, writer of Thor, Amazing Spider-Man and Clint Eastwood's Changeling
MOORE • REPPION • CAMPBELL
SHERLOCK HOLMES VOL. 1
THE TRIAL OF SHERLOCK HOLMES
DYNAMITE
MOORE • REPPION • TRIANO
SHERLOCK HOLMES VOL. 2
THE LIVERPOOL DEMON
DYNAMITE

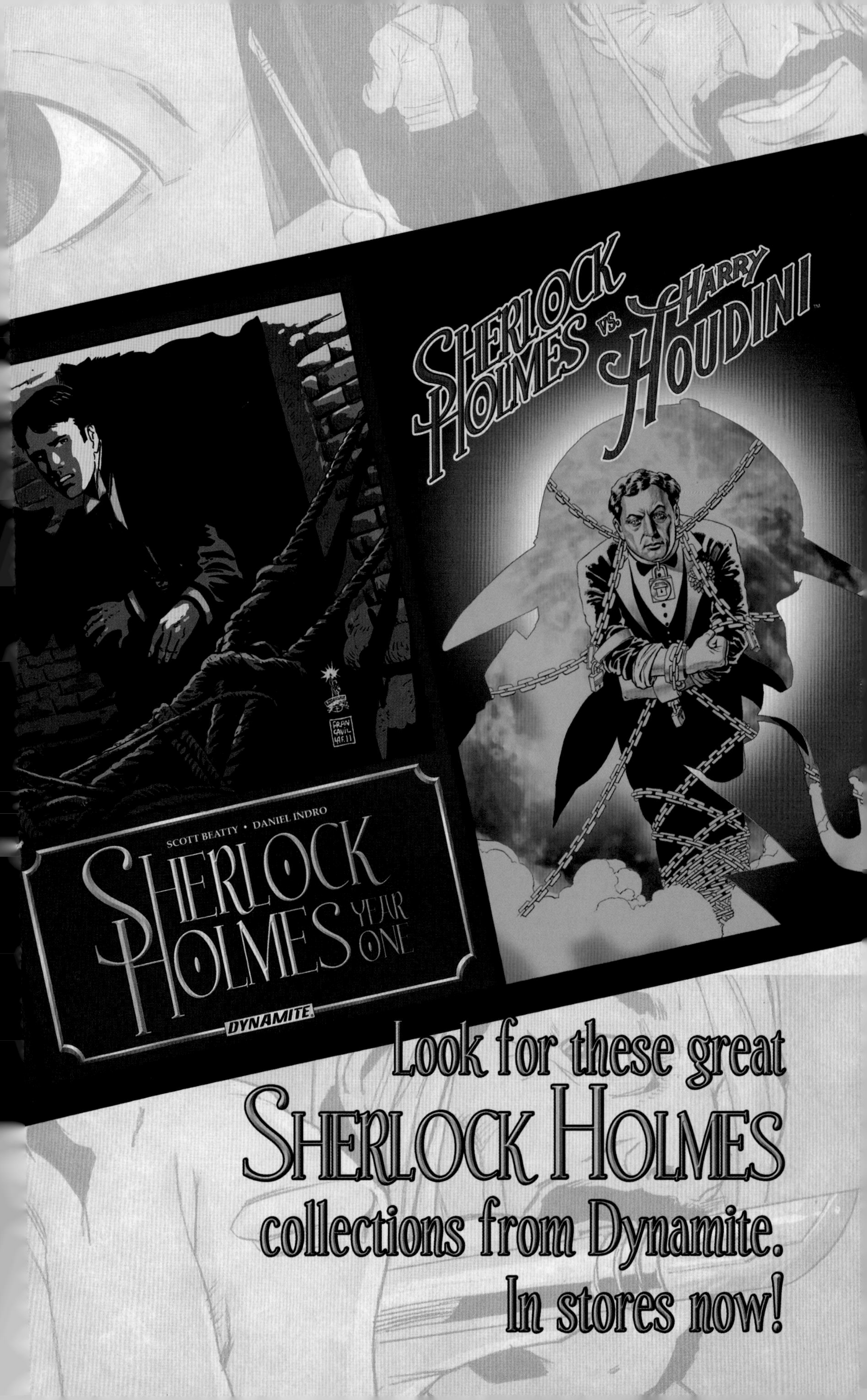
SHERLOCK HOLMES vs. HARRY HOUDINI
SCOTT BEATTY • DANIEL INDRO
SHERLOCK HOLMES YEAR ONE
DYNAMITE
Look for these great
SHERLOCK HOLMES
collections from Dynamite.
In stores now!

DYNAMITE ENTERTAINMENT PRESENTS

# SHERLOCK HOLMES™ VOL. 3

## MORIARTY LIVES

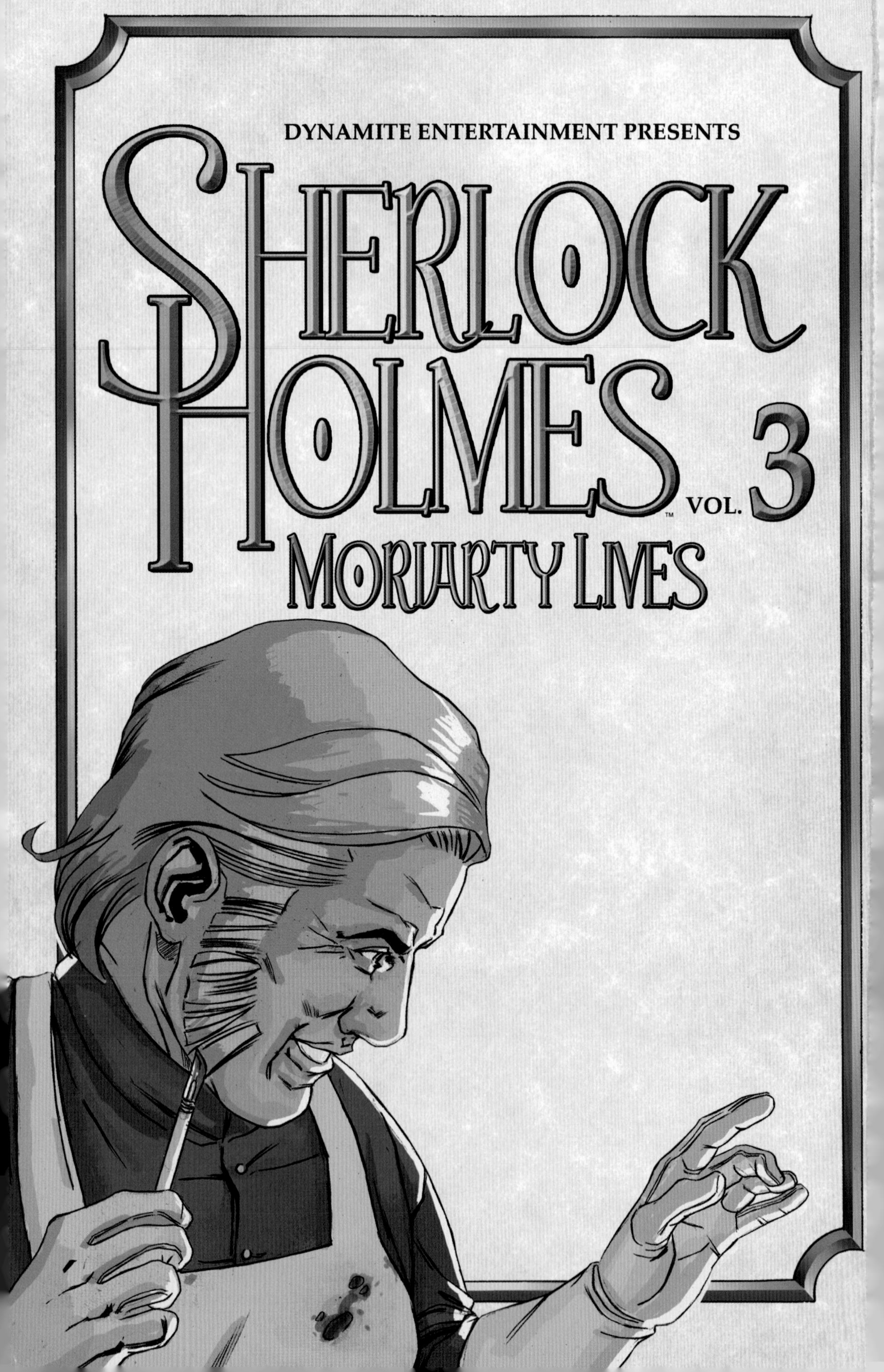